MEMORY:
A PHILOSOPHICAL STUDY

Memory:
A Philosophical Study

SVEN BERNECKER

OXFORD
UNIVERSITY PRESS

OXFORD

UNIVERSITY PRESS

Great Clarendon Street, Oxford OX2 6DP

Oxford University Press is a department of the University of Oxford.
It furthers the University's objective of excellence in research, scholarship,
and education by publishing worldwide in

Oxford New York

Auckland Cape Town Dar es Salaam Hong Kong Karachi
Kuala Lumpur Madrid Melbourne Mexico City Nairobi
New Delhi Shanghai Taipei Toronto

With offices in

Argentina Austria Brazil Chile Czech Republic France Greece
Guatemala Hungary Italy Japan Poland Portugal Singapore
South Korea Switzerland Thailand Turkey Ukraine Vietnam

Oxford is a registered trade mark of Oxford University Press
in the UK and in certain other countries

Published in the United States
by Oxford University Press Inc., New York

© Sven Bernecker 2010

First published 2010

British Library Cataloguing in Publication Data

Data available

Library of Congress Cataloging in Publication Data

Bernecker, Sven.
Memory : a philosophical study / Sven Bernecker.
p. cm.
Includes bibliographical references (p.) and index.
ISBN 978–0–19–957756–9 (hardback)
1. Memory (Philosophy) I. Title.
BD181.7.B47 2009
128'.3—dc22
2009032247

Typeset by Laserwords Private Limited, Chennai, India
Printed in Great Britain
on acid-free paper by the
MPG Books Group, Bodmin and King's Lynn

ISBN 978–0–19–957756–9

Acknowledgments

A first draft of this book was written while I was on sabbatical leave in 2005–6, supported by a Heisenberg Grant from the Deutsche Forschungsgemeinschaft. I am immensely grateful for this award.

Some of the ideas in this book have been tried out at a graduate seminar at the University of California at Irvine as well as in the course of a number of talks, which took place at the Humboldt University of Berlin, the Universities of Berne, Bristol, California at Riverside, Göttingen, Hertfordshire, Leipzig, Minnesota at Twin Cities, and Nottingham, the Federal University of Rio Grande do Sul at Porto Alegre, and at the following conferences: the Fourth European Congress for Analytic Philosophy at Lund University in 2002, the fifth meeting of the German Society of Analytic Philosophy at the University of Bielefeld in 2003, and a conference on first-person authority at the University of Duisburg in 2007. I am grateful to all the audiences on these occasions.

For useful conversations about the material in this book I thank Peter Graham, Frank Hofmann, Brendan Larvor, David Makinson, Philip Nickel, Kristopher Rhodes, Steven M. Smith, and Thomas Spitzley. I especially thank Peter Baumann, Aaron Bogart, Chris Daly, Dorothea Debus, and Fred Dretske who gave me valuable comments on draft chapters of the book. I also benefited from the comments of two anonymous referees engaged by Oxford University Press to read the manuscript, and from the encouragement and patience of my editor, Peter Momtchiloff. Thanks also to my copy editor, Sylvie Jaffrey, and to the helpful staff at Oxford University Press including Jacqueline Baker and Tessa Eaton.

While in grateful mood, I should also thank my father, Dietrich Bernecker, and Robert Cramer and Kate Pool for invaluable practical advice. Finally I would like to thank my wife, Narghes, and my children, Lilly and Paul, for putting up with me spending an excessive portion of my days writing the book, and for their help and encouragement, especially when things got difficult and motivation was needed to complete the project.

Sections 3.1 to 3.5 are based on 'Remembering Without Knowing', *Australasian Journal of Philosophy* 85 (2007). Chapter 7 is based on

'Memory and Externalism', *Philosophy and Phenomenological Research* 64 (2004). Sections 8.3 and 8.6 draw on work published in 'Self-Knowledge and the Bounds of Authenticity', *Erkenntnis* 71 (2009). I am grateful to the editors concerned for their permission to make use of this material. Some of the ideas contained in Chapters 1, 4, and 5 were originally put forward in substantially different and less satisfactory ways in parts of my *The Metaphysics of Memory*.

This book is dedicated to my parents and to the memory of Narghes's grandparents.

Contents

Introduction

Remembering is a fundamental cognitive process, subserving virtually all other important cognitive functions such as reasoning, perception, problem solving, and speech. Since without memory one couldn't think, some philosophers go as far as to claim that memory is the mark of being human. Norman Malcolm (1963: 212), for example, declares: 'A being without factual memory would have no mental powers to speak of, and he would not really be a man even if he had the human form'. Similarly, Tyler Burge (2003: 305, 328) states that because memory 'is at the root of representation' it is 'a necessary condition for being a person, or other agent with a psychology'.

If one needs to be convinced of the significance of memory for our mental life, one only needs to ponder the fate of someone deprived of memory. A first-hand account of what it is like to have memory deficit is given by the clinical psychologist Malcolm Meltzer who encountered memory problems as result of anoxia following a heart attack. When Meltzer came out of a six-week coma, he was moderately amnesic. He knew who he was, knew his job, and recognized his family, although not all his friends. His house was familiar but he could not remember where things were kept. He had to relearn his age, how many children he had, how to play the stereo, how to set the alarm clock, etc. Other problems Meltzer encountered concerned general cognitive processing: 'Organization of thinking was hampered . . . I had trouble keeping the facts in mind, which made it difficult to organize them . . . Comparing things along a number of variables is difficult to do when you cannot retain the variables or retain the comparison after you have made it' (1983: 4). As a result of his memory deficit, interpersonal relationships were hampered: 'Having conversations could become a trial. Often in talking with people I was acquainted with, I had trouble remembering their names or whether they were married or what our relationship had been in the past. I worried about asking where someone's wife is and finding out that I had been at her funeral two years ago' (ibid. 6). More severely amnesic patients than Meltzer cannot achieve even the insight necessary for them to realize that they suffer from memory deficit. They forget that they don't remember.

Paradoxically, not being able to forget is almost as obstructive and debilitating as not being able to remember. A well-studied case of near perfect memory is Jill Price who, when given a date from the last 30 years, can instantly summon up the day of the week and can report what she did and how she felt (Parker, Cahill, and McGaugh 2006). Her memory is non-stop, uncontrollable, and remarkable accurate. Though it might seem like a blessing, Price's extraordinary memory not only fails to provide her with an advantage on IQ tests but also comes with significant cognitive cost. Time that would otherwise be spent on other cognitive tasks (such as acquiring new knowledge) is devoted to retrieval. That is why Price tends to regard her superior memory as a curse.

At any given moment, anything at all that someone said to me, or some hurtful or ridiculous thing that I said to someone that I desperately wish I could take back, may pop into my mind and yank me back to that difficult day and exactly how I was feeling about myself. The emotional intensity of my memories, combined with the random nature in which they're always flashing through my mind, has, on and off through the course of my life, nearly driven me mad.

(Price and Davis 2008: 38)

Since Price recalls every bad decision, every insult and excruciating embarrassment her memory is 'eating her up' and 'paralyzes' her. She remarks, 'I run my entire life through my head every day and it drives me crazy!' (Parker, Cahill, and McGaugh 2006: 48).

Since memory is a central component of the mind it is not surprising that thought about memory is as old as philosophy itself. But although discussion about memory has a long history, memory is a neglected topic in contemporary philosophy. When contemporary philosophers deal with the issue of memory at all, they confine themselves to discussing specific issues, such as the role of memory in epistemic justification, memory and personal identity, memory and the experience of time, collective memory, the hypothesis of extended memory, non-conceptual memory contents, and the ethics of memory. The basic question 'What is memory?' is usually left out of consideration. It is this basic question that will be addressed here, if only regarding propositional (or factual) memory. The analysis of what memory is will focus on metaphysical and epistemological aspects. The overarching aim is to explain what it is that qualifies a person's mental state as a (propositional) memory rather than some other kind of mental state.

Prima facie, the identifying criterion of memory states is that they store objects with semantic properties (content, reference, truth-conditions, truth-values, etc.). Yet a little thought reveals that storage of objects with semantic properties is not a unique feature of memories. Dispositional or ongoing beliefs also involve the storage of semantic objects (cf. Field 1978: 80–4; Lycan 1988: 36–7, 56–7). When someone learns a particular fact, he acquires an occurrent belief that may be stored in memory and recalled when necessary.[1] A dispositional or ongoing belief is the state of having such a semantic object stored. And when the semantic object is retrieved from memory for active deployment in reasoning or planning, the subject once again has an occurrent belief. Though beliefs are memories, memories aren't necessarily beliefs. Thus, it should be possible to identify the features that memories have and other kinds of mental states such as beliefs lack.

The book consists of eight chapters and a short conclusion. Chapters 1 to 3 set the stage by offering a tentative analysis of memory, by explaining the relation between memory and personal identity, and by distinguishing memory from both knowledge and belief. Chapters 4 and 5 elaborate and defend a naturalist version of the causal theory of memory. Chapters 6 and 7 develop and motivate an externalist account of memory content. Chapter 8 proposes an account of memorial authenticity and Chapter 9 summarizes the discussion. In the remainder of this introduction I will briefly sketch what lies ahead.

It is common among philosophers to distinguish between practical memory, propositional memory and experiential memory. Practical memory is remembering how to do something. Propositional memory is remembering that p, where 'p' stands for a veridical proposition. Experiential memory is remembering from the first-person perspective an event one has personally experienced. Chapter 1 shows that this tripartite classification of kinds of memory is defective and replaces it by a classification in terms of the grammatical objects of the verb 'to remember'. According to the proposed taxonomy, there are four main kinds of remembering. One can remember persons and things, properties, events, and facts and propositions. This study concentrates on propositional memory. And to cut the topic to a manageable size,

---

[1] Here and throughout the book gender-unspecific reference is made with 'he' and its cognates, which may then be read as 'she or he', 'her and him', etc.

this study is primarily concerned with propositional memory that is conscious, explicit, veridical, and non-inferential.

Propositional memory comes in different flavors. When I remember that p, 'p' can stand for a past mental state of mine (e.g. that I believed that Brutus stabbed Caesar) or for any other state of affair (e.g. that Brutus stabbed Caesar). Propositional memory of one's own mental states I call *introversive memory*. Propositional memory of other things than one's own mental states I label *extroversive memory*. The content of introversive memory is necessarily in the first-person mode while the content of extroversive memory may be in the third-person mode (e.g. that Caesar is the author of *Commentarii de Bello Gallico*) or the first-person mode (e.g. that Caesar is the author of the book I had to translate in high school).

Chapter 1 sets forth a tentative analysis of propositional memory: S remembers at t_2 that p, where 'p' stands for an extroversive proposition in the first-person mode only if (1) S represents at t_2 that p, (2) S represented at t_1 that p^*, (3) p is true at t_2, (4) p is identical with, or sufficiently similar to, p^*, and (5) S's representation at t_2 that p is suitably causally connected to S's representation at t_1 that p^*. These five conditions may be labeled, respectively, the *present representation condition* (1), the *past representation condition* (2), the *truth-condition* (3), the *content condition* (4), and the *connection condition* (5). This is not the final analysis but only a first approximation. The final analysis is stated in Chapter 9.

Three terminological notes: First, the value of the index in the subscript to 't' determines whether the time referred to is in the past or the present: the relatively biggest number indicates the present. So here 't_2' is the present and 't_1' is the past. When there is more than one past time involved, 't_1' indicates the distant past, 't_2' the close past, and 't_3' the present. Second, the term 'representation' in the above analysis of memory is meant to indicate that propositional memory can take the form of a number of different kinds of cognitive attitudes towards a proposition. Contrary to received wisdom in epistemology, I argue (in Ch. 3) that propositional memory requires neither the past nor the present cognitive attitude to be a (justified) belief or knowledge. Third, not any kind of cognitive attitude that stands in a memory-relation to another cognitive attitude qualifies as a memory state. For instance, an occurrent fear that p does not count as a memory—not even if it was previously formed and is now being retrieved from memory.

Since to remember is to retain some previously acquired representation, the analysis of memory must include some provision for one's having had the representation in question in the past and for one's still possessing the representation. This is the motivation for the past and the present representation condition. The truth-condition demands that one can only remember what is the case. The content condition ensures that the memory content is the same as, or sufficiently similar to, a content one has previously represented. By allowing that the contents of the past and the present representation are not the same but only sufficiently similar the content condition contradicts the *identity theory of memory*, that is, the thesis that for a propositional representation token at t_2 to stand in a memory-relation to a propositional representation token at t_1, the contents of both tokens must be type-identical. Finally, the connection condition is meant to exclude relearning from the ranks of remembering and establish that the remembered representation is a retained representation. The idea is that a claim to remember something implies not merely that the subject represented it in the past, but that his current representation is in some way due to, that it comes about because of, his past representation.

Whether memory presupposes personal identity depends crucially on whether the memory content involves an indexical reference to the rememberer. According to the proposed analysis of extroversive memory, when the memory content is in the first-person mode the bearer of the present representation must be the same person as the bearer of the past representation. Chapter 2 argues, however, that the dependence of memory on personal identity is of a contingent rather than a logical kind.

The suggested analysis of propositional memory takes issue with the widely held *epistemic theory of memory*, that is, the view that to remember something is to know it, where this knowledge was previously acquired and preserved. According to the epistemic theory of memory, S remembers at t_2 that p only if (1) S knows at t_2 that p, (2) S knew at t_1 that p and (3) S's knowing at t_2 that p is suitably connected to S's knowing at t_1 that p. Chapter 3 criticizes the epistemic theory of memory. Unlike knowledge, memory implies neither belief nor justification. Not only is it possible to remember something one didn't justifiably believe in the past or doesn't believe in the present but also one might acquire between t_1 and t_2 some misleading but reasonable evidence that destroys the status as justified belief of the once-genuine justified belief that one still remembers. Memory doesn't imply knowledge, for sometimes memory, though hitting the mark of truth, succeeds in an epistemically defective way.

Though memory doesn't imply justification and knowledge, memory beliefs can, of course, be justified and qualify as knowledge. And so the question arises whether memory is merely a preservative source of justification and knowledge or whether it may also function as a generative source. Chapter 3 argues for what I call *moderate generativism*. Moderate generativism has it that, though memory is a generative source of justification, it cannot bring about new elements of justification. The only way for memory to function as a generative source of justification is by removing defeaters and thereby unleashing the justificatory potential that was already present at the time the belief was initially entertained. All of the elements required for a memory belief to be justified must already have been present when the belief was encoded. If the original belief had no justificatory potential because, say, it was gettierized, then memory cannot turn it into a justified belief. Memory generates justification only by lifting justificatory elements that were previously rebutted or undermined by defeating evidence.

Chapters 4 and 5 examine the connection condition of memory. The connection condition states that, to remember a proposition, not only must it have been represented before, but the present representation must be suitably connected to the past representation. The memory content must not only correspond to, but must stand in an appropriate relationship to, the past representation. Without the connection condition remembering would be indistinguishable from relearning.

The accounts of the memory connection proposed in the literature fall into three categories: the evidential retention theory, the simple retention theory, and the causal theory. The basic idea of the causal theory of memory is that for S to remember at t_2 that p his representation at t_2 that p must be suitably causally connected to his representation at t_1 that p^*. Chapter 4 develops three arguments in favor of the causal theory of memory. First, unlike the evidential retention theory, the causal theory is not committed to the view that memory implies knowledge. Second, unlike the simple retention condition, the causal condition is neither too stringent nor too liberal. Third, the causal theory of memory provides a better explanation of the truth of the commonsensical counterfactual 'If S had not represented at t_1 that p^*, he wouldn't represent at t_2 that p' than either the simple retention theory or the evidential retention theory.

Chapter 5 investigates the nature of memory causation. It is shown that the causal process connecting a past representation and its subsequent recall involves intermediary memory traces (or engrams). Between any two diachronic mental events that are causally related there must be a series of intermediary events, each of which causes the next, and each of which is temporally contiguous to the next. Memory traces account both for the propagation of mental contents through time and for the production of states of recall. Insofar as traces bring about states of recall they are intracerebral occurrences; insofar as they transmit mental content they are mental states. Depending on whether traces transmit conceptual or non-conceptual content they are dispositional beliefs or subdoxastic states. Since the theory of memory causation cannot manage without the stipulation of memory traces and since traces are intracerebral occurrences, the question whether someone remembers something or whether he is mistaken in believing that he remembers something is, in part, an empirical question; it is partly a question about the person's brain.

The causal relation constitutive of remembering can be characterized by the conjunction of three conditions: the *trace condition*: S's representation at t_1 that p and S's representation at t_2 that p^* are connected by a persisting memory trace (or a contiguous series of memory traces); the *causal strength condition*: the memory trace is an independently sufficient condition (which is not preempted by another independently sufficient condition) of the representation at t_2 that p or is at least a necessary condition of such an independently sufficient condition; the *counterfactual condition*: if S had not represented at t_1 that p^*, then he would not represent at t_2 that p. The trace condition simply expresses commitment to the theory of memory traces. Since we frequently remember only after being given the appropriate prompt (or retrieval cue) there is the question of how to distinguish remembering something upon being prompted from merely repeating back the prompt itself. The causal strength condition specifies the causal contribution of memory traces vis-à-vis prompts for the production of states of recall. And the counterfactual condition demands that the causal chain connecting the present and past representation supports a counterfactual correlation. This condition is needed to eliminate cases of suggestibility from the ranks of memory.

As was explained above, the content condition says that for someone's representation to qualify as a memory its propositional content must be identical with, or sufficiently similar to the propositional content of a representation that he had in the past. This condition gives rise to two questions. First, what does it mean for diachronic content tokens to be of the same type? Second, in what respect and to what extent may diachronic content tokens differ from one another and one of them still count as sufficiently similar to the other so as to be memory-related to it? Chapters 6 and 7 tackle the first question, Chapter 8 the second one.

Chapter 6 proposes a content externalist account of the identity of diachronic content tokens and Chapter 7 defends this account against objections. Content externalism is the thesis that the individuation conditions of mental content depend, in part, on external (or relational) properties of the subject's physical or social environment rather than on internal properties of the subject's mind and brain. The contents of an individual's thoughts supervene on systematic relations that the individual bears to aspects of his environment. Consequently, diachronic content tokens are type-identical if they supervene on the same states of affairs in the subject's environment. Chapter 6 explains and motivates content externalism, sets it apart from environmentalism, defends it against internalist challenges, and applies it to memory contents.

Given the dependence of memory contents on the environment and given that a person can move from one environment to another (perhaps without even noticing the move), the question arises whether the content of an occurrent memory state is determined by the environment the person inhabited at the time he originally formed the representation (pastist externalism), by the environment he inhabits at the time recollection takes place (presentist externalism), or by the present environment *and* the environment(s) he will inhabit in the future, after recollection has taken place (futurist externalism). Do memory contents (and the concepts contained in them) supervene on past, present, or future environmental conditions? The view argued for in Chapter 6 is that the content of a memory state is fixed by the environment the subject was in at the time he had the original representation. Once some content is stored in memory it is not affected by any subsequent environmental change.

Pastist externalism in conjunction with other premises has the consequence that an environmental change can bring about a conceptual shift which, in turn, can rob us of the ability to remember insofar as we lose the ability to entertain anew some of our past thought contents. This conclusion strikes some as implausible, for the ability to remember is commonly taken to depend in the first instance on our mental condition—on factors inside the head—rather than on the physical and social environment we live in. Chapter 7 explains and defends the context-dependency of memory that follows from content externalism. Doubts concerning the externalist thesis that environmental changes can bring about memory failure don't have to be taken seriously, because there are neither psychological nor philosophical arguments to substantiate them.

In what respect and to what extent may diachronic content tokens differ from one another while still being memory-related? Chapter 8 argues that diachronic propositional attitude tokens are sufficiently similar for the token at t_2 to be memory-related to the token at t_1 only if the content of the token at t_2 is entailed by the content of the token at t_1. To illustrate the *entailment thesis* consider this example. Suppose at t_1 you came to believe that Caesar was assassinated by Brutus. At t_2, all you can remember is that Caesar died of unnatural causes; you have forgotten the circumstances of his death. Notwithstanding the fact that *Caesar was assassinated by Brutus* and *Caesar died of unnatural causes* are different propositions, this may be a genuine instance of remembering, for the former proposition is entailed by the latter one.

Granted that a memory content must only be similar to, not identical with, the content of the relevant past representation, one can remember a proposition one has not entertained before. The content of a memory state may be entertained for the first time at the time of recollection. This view contradicts the intuition that to remember something one must have thought of it before and that this is what distinguishes remembering from learning afresh. I agree with the platonic position according to which remembering (anamnesis) and learning afresh are compatible. Yet there are only few instances where learning afresh and remembering coincide. Learning afresh and remembering concur only when the memory content is entailed by something one has thought of previously (content condition) and when the memory state is suitably causally connected to the previous thought (connection condition).

Introversive memory involves a twofold classification. Remembering at t_2 that one represented (at t_1) that p involves remembering that the representation at t_1 was about p^* (where p^* is either identical with, or sufficiently similar to p) *and* remembering the kind of attitude one took at t_1 towards p^*. Just as memory doesn't require type-identity of diachronic content tokens it doesn't require type-identity of diachronic attitude tokens. The attitude that one represents at t_2 oneself having taken at t_1 towards p^* may be the same as, or sufficiently similar to the attitude that one took at t_1 towards p^*. This raises the question of what are the criteria for the identity and similarity of diachronic attitude tokens. Chapter 8 argues that diachronic attitude tokens are the same if their functional roles are the same and they are similar if they share the direction of fit and polarity. Finally, chapter 9 summarizes the analysis of introversive and extroversive memory, respectively, and spells out its wider ramifications.

1

The Concept of Memory

'Memory' is a single term, but it refers to a multitude of human capacities. There are many different kinds of memory but there is no generally agreed-upon classification of the kinds of memory. There is no periodic table of types of memory. Not only do philosophers, psychologists, and neurologists use different taxonomies, but also there are competing taxonomies within philosophy. Moreover, different philosophers take different kinds of memory to be the most significant, or for which analysis is most profitable.

Section 1.1 gives an overview of taxonomies of memory and argues that the standard taxonomy in philosophy is highly problematic. Section 1.2 sets forth a grammatical categorization system of the multifarious forms of memory. Section 1.3 discusses some more distinctions among kinds of memory. Section 1.4 explains and justifies methodological externalism about memory and sections 1.5 and 1.6 present preliminary analyses of extroversive and introversive memory.

1.1 THE STANDARD CLASSIFICATION OF MEMORY

There are at least four ways by which psychologists distinguish between kinds of memories: the length of time the information is stored, the degree of awareness the subject has of the stored information, the kind of prompt that triggers the retrieval of the information, and the kind of information that is stored. Let's briefly discuss each of these axes of taxonomy.

When memories are divided up in terms of the length of time the information is stored, we get the distinction between short-term memory and long-term memory. Short-term memory stores information for mere seconds (milliseconds in some cases). Once in the short-term memory, information can meet one of two fates: it can be transferred to the long-term memory, or it can be forgotten. Long-term memory, as the name suggests, is the memory system that is responsible for storing information for such long periods of time that its limits are unknown.

Memories are not only distinguished by the storage duration but also by the degree of awareness the subject has of the stored information. Psychologists classify memories as unconscious, dispositional, partially conscious, or conscious. A memory is unconscious if no direct awareness is even in principle possible. Any awareness regarding memory at this level is gained indirectly, by external observation or inferential reasoning. Dispositional memories are memories of which one is currently not aware but, were one given the appropriate retrieval cue, one would be able to recall them. A tip-of-the-tongue phenomenon is an instance of a partially conscious memory.

Memories can also be classified by the kind of prompt that triggers the retrieval of the information. Psychologists distinguish between memories arising from explicit demands and memories arising from spontaneous triggers. Free recall occurs when the subject recalls information without any external information to help him. In the case of cued or prompted recall, subjects are given some explicit information (which is not the same as the stored information) to help them recall. The cues that trigger the recall can be either internal or external. In recognition, the subject is presented with a cue that bears a resemblance to the past experience or learned information and is asked whether he remembers it.

Distinguishing kinds of memory by their content is, of course, the most common approach. The way psychologists interpret 'content' for making distinctions between kinds of memory is different from the way philosophers interpret 'content'. The most basic distinction in psychology is that between memories that the subject can express (declarative memory) and memories that one can only demonstrate but not express (non-declarative memory).[1] The main difference within non-declarative memory is between associative and non-associative learning. Non-associative learning encompasses elementary forms of behavioral plasticity such as habituation and sensitization. In associative learning an unconditioned stimulus and a conditioned stimulus become linked so that a response normally triggered by the unconditioned stimulus is triggered by the conditioned stimulus. The most famous example of

---

[1] The declarative/non-declarative distinction more or less corresponds to the distinctions philosophers make between propositional and experiential memory, on the one hand, and practical memory, on the other.

associative learning is Pavlov's dog who learned to associate the presence of food with the ringing of a bell.

Following a suggestion by Endel Tulving (1972), psychologists break down declarative memory into two subtypes: semantic and episodic memory. Semantic memory is the store of general knowledge about the world, concepts, rules, and language. The characteristic feature of semantic memory is that it can be used without reference to the events that account for its formation in the first place. Episodic memory, on the other hand, is accompanied by the experience of remembering, or mentally traveling back in time and re-experiencing the events. Thus, whereas semantic memory involves retrieval of the information acquired during a given learning episode, episodic memory involves, in addition, remembering something about the specific learning episode itself, namely the context in which the information was acquired. Larry Squire and Eric Kandel (1999: 106.) characterize the semantic/episodic distinction thus: semantic memory is

> declarative memory for facts—for factual knowledge about objects, places, and odors . . . for organized world knowledge. In recalling this type of information, an animal or human subject need not remember any particular past event. . . . Episodic memory, unlike semantic memory, stores spatial and temporal land-marks that identify the particular time and place when an event occurred. . . . Both episodic and semantic memory are declarative. Information is retrieved consciously and subjects are aware that they are accessing stored information.

When philosophers distinguish kinds of memory by their content they usually come up with a tripartite classification: experiential (or personal), propositional (or factual), and practical (or procedural) memory.[2] *Experiential memory* has two characteristics. First, one can experientially remember only what one has personally experienced. Experiential memory is restricted to cases in which the claim to remember something incorporates the claim to have experienced it for oneself. Second, experiential memory represents the remembered content from

---

[2] Burge (2003: 289–93) is an exception. He distinguishes between experiential memory, substantive content memory, and purely preservative memory. Experiential memory consists in representations of a particular thing, event, property instance, experience, state, or act and requires previous direct perception or experience of the particular thing. Substantive content memory consists in purely general, non-*de re* presentations, or in *de re* propositional representations that don't go back to a direct perception or experience of the particular. Purely preservative memory consists in the retention of representational content for future use. Unlike the experiential memory and substantive content memory, purely preservative memory does not introduce new subject matter into current thinking.

the first-person perspective—from 'within'—and involves qualitative experiences (qualia) and imagery. Experiential memory consists in the evocation of parts of the original experience in imagination, allowing to relive or re-experience the original situation and going over what it was like. Like imagination and fantasy, experiential memory is an 'iconic' state—roughly one that can be conceived as a sort of theatrical presentation to oneself.[3] C. B. Martin and Max Deutscher (1966: 162–3) write:

If someone is asked whether he remembers what he did last Friday at lunchtime, he may be able to say that he went down the street. Yet he may feel scarcely in a position to say that he remembers actually going down the street. What he needs in order to be able to say that he does [experientially] remember going down the street is at least more detailed remembering that . . . certain things happened when he went down the street. . . . [T]his addition of detail must be due to the original perception.

To experientially remember something one must not only remember what happened but also remember what it was like. John Locke (1979: 150) seems to have experiential memory in mind when he defines memory as the power of the mind 'to revive perceptions, which it has once had, with this additional perception annexed to them, that it has had them before'.[4] This passage makes it clear that it is not enough to re-experience a perception; the perception must be experienced as something that has been experienced before. As Tulving (1985: 3) emphasizes in Hermann Ebbinghaus's words: Remembering is 'calling back into consciousness a seemingly lost state that is then "immediately recognized as something formerly experienced" ' (1913: 1).[5]

---

[3] The phrase 'iconic mental state' is borrowed from Wollheim. An iconic mental state, in representing an event, has a tendency to produce 'a residual condition', the condition that the subject found himself in when he experienced the event (1984: 72–3, 81, 98). Wollheim describes this fact about iconic mental states by appealing to an analogy with theater. The three theatrical roles of director, actor, and audience have their analogues in iconic mental states. The 'residual condition' is compared to the feelings, desires, and so on, brought about in the audience as it watches the action on stage.

[4] I acknowledge that Locke's famous phrase 'sameness of consciousness' may refer to some richer phenomenon than experiential memory. Cf. Hughes (1975).

[5] Since experientially remembering a perception consists in re-experiencing a past perception Broad (1925: 222) calls it 'perceptual memory'. Malcolm holds that perceptual memories are distinct from experiential memories, or 'personal memories' as he calls them. He defines personal memory thus: 'A person, B, personally remembers something, X, if and only if B previously perceived or experienced X *and* B's memory of X is based wholly or partly on his previous perception or experience of X' (1963: 215). And he defines perceptual memory thus: 'B perceptually remembers X if and only if B personally remembers X *and* B can form a mental

Instances of *propositional memory* are substituends of the schema 'S remembers that p', where 'p' stands for a true proposition. Like practical and experiential memory, propositional memory is truth-entailing. As Norman Malcolm (ibid. 191) aptly says, 'a totally delusive memory is no more a memory than a fictitious occurrence is something that happened, or no more than a painted fire is a fire'. One can remember true propositions about the past (e.g. that Caesar was assassinated in 44 BC), the present (e.g. that one's partner is currently in the library returning books), the future (e.g. that one's partner's birthday is next Tuesday), as well as timeless truths (e.g. $2 + 2 = 4$). Though the object of propositional memory need not deal with the past, one's learning of what one propositionally remembers must precede the remembering. One cannot remember that p if one has only just learned that p.

Unlike experiential memory, propositional memory is not limited to things with which one has had direct or personal acquaintance. One need not have witnessed the event to remember, say, that Brutus stabbed Caesar. Consequently propositional memory doesn't require qualitative experiences and imagery. And provided the individual is the final authority on the existence and nature of his mental images and qualia, self-ascriptions of experiential memory have an epistemic authority that self-ascriptions of propositional memory lack.

Malcolm (ibid. 214) has an argument to the effect that experiential memory implies propositional memory. The argument can be parsed in five steps: (1) S experientially remembers some person, place, thing, event, situation X only if S can form an image of X; (2) if S forms an image of X he can correctly describe the image; (3) if S can correctly describe the image of X, he can correctly describe facts learned in the past; (4) if S can correctly describe facts learned in the past, he can remember that p, where 'p' is a true sentence which describes these facts; (5) 'It appears, therefore, that [experiential] memory does logically require factual memory'. The problem with this argument is premiss (4) which Malcolm formulates as follows: 'When a person has imagery he must be able to give an account of what it is *of*, if it is *of* anything.' Malcolm seems to overlook that a person can misinterpret his imagery to the extent that he might think that the imagery is of X when in fact it is of nothing.[6]

---

image of X' (ibid. 219). Thus Malcolm's notion of perceptual memory is synonymous with the standard notion of personal (or experiential) memory.

[6] In response to objections raised by Saunders (1965*b*), Malcolm (1977: 16n9) later gave up the idea that experiential memory implies propositional memory. Stanley and Williamson

Experiential and propositional memory have in common that they seek to represent the world and that their contents can in principle be articulated. Neither of the features apply to *practical memory*, which is remembering how to do something, where this refers to previously acquired and retained skills. Examples of practical memory are remembering how to swim and remembering how to ride a bicycle. It is customary to distinguish between occurrent and dispositional practical memory. To attribute to someone the occurrent sense of 'remembering how to swim', he need not be able to visualize or describe the activity of swimming—all he needs to do is to actually swim. In the dispositional sense of 'remembering how', someone may be said to remember how to swim but may not presently be swimming because, say, he is asleep or because he has a leg in plaster. So dispositionally remembering how to do something doesn't imply currently being able to do it.

The distinction between propositional memory and experiential memory is not sharp. Consider my remembering that last summer I spent a few days in Rome. Is it a piece of experiential memory or does it belong to the class of propositional memory? To answer this question, proponents of the tripartite taxonomy will presumably enquire whether the content of the memory consists merely of a proposition or whether it also includes imagery and qualia. But the problem with this strategy is that the frequency and intensity of mental imagery varies greatly from one person to another. Since Francis Galton's studies conducted in the 1880s, it has been known that there is a wide range of imaging in our species. Some people report that their mental lives are replete with imagery as vivid and detailed as the actual scenes they recall. (There are even some, eidetikers, who can apparently summon up such images at will and can 'project' them onto surfaces, or combine them to make a combined image.) For others, imagery is uniformly vague, dim, and fleeting. And, for a final group, there seems to be no imagery at all. Galton found that people belonging to the last group don't even comprehend requests to summon up images. For them, talk of mental imagery is empty, to the extent that Galton (1883: 58) compared them to the color-blind who are unable to comprehend color terms.[7]

(2001) have recently argued that knowledge-how is just another form of knowledge-that. It would be interesting to see whether analogous arguments suggest that remembering-how is just another form of remembering-that.

[7] Galton found a correlation between people who report dim or no imagery at all, and those who deal in professional work with considerable abstraction and generality. This result

The reason the boundary between propositional memory and experiential memory is not sharp is that these kinds of memory are governed
by different criteria. The criterion for identifying propositional memory
is a grammatical one: the memory content must have the form of a
tensed that-complement clause. The criterion for identifying experiential memory is, on the one hand, a phenomenological one—they present
themselves to the mind as images and qualitative experiences—and,
on the other, a metaphysical one—they refer to events that one has
personally experienced. Some experiential memories are expressed by
a combination of 'remember' with a gerund (e.g. I remember having
spent a few days in Rome), others by a that-clause (e.g. I remember
that I spent a few days in Rome), and again others by some other
construction. Since experiential memory cannot be defined by the kind
of complement phrase used to express it, there is no clear correlation
between the grammatical form of a memory report and the kind of
memory expressed. Don Locke, a principal in devising the tripartite
classification scheme, concedes this point when he writes:

[R]emembering Hamlet's soliloquy might be classified as personal memory
(remembering the speech) or as practical memory (remembering how to
recite it) or as factual memory (remembering that the words as 'To be
or not to be . . .' etc.). And although the three forms are each associated
with a particular grammatical construction—remembering *that* such-and-
such, remembering *how* to do such-and-such, remembering *such-and-such
itself*—grammar provides only a rough guide to which form of memory is
involved.

(1971: 48; see also Burge 2003: 289, 328–9n2; Wollheim 1984: 101)

Now some proponents of the tripartite classification scheme employ
Bertrand Russell's distinction between knowledge by acquaintance and
knowledge by description to differentiate between experiential and
propositional memory (Broad 1925: 222; Locke 1971: 70; Malcolm
1963: 207; Pollock 1974: 184). Something is known by acquaintance
when there is direct experience of it; it is known by description if it can
only be described as a thing with such-and-such properties. Experiential
memory is said to be memory by acquaintance and its intentional
objects are not facts or propositions but people, places, things, events,
and situations. Propositional memory, on the other hand, is thought to
be analogous to knowledge by description.

was confirmed by Betts (1909). For a survey of recent literature on the range of imaging see
Schwitzgebel (2002).

Using the distinction between knowledge by acquaintance and knowledge by description to explicate the distinction between experiential and propositional memory doesn't work for three reasons. First, many autobiographical data are remembered by description and many memories of impersonal propositions are due to us having been acquainted with the things they are about. Second, in one respect propositional memory is analogous to knowledge by acquaintance. Russell himself thought that in entertaining a proposition, one is acquainted with that proposition. So appealing to Russell's notion of acquaintance doesn't have the consequence that the advocates of the standard taxonomy of kinds of memory aim for. Third, construing the experiential/propositional distinction along the lines of the acquaintance/description distinction yields the counterintuitive consequence that, strictly speaking, I cannot experientially remember *that p*. Malcolm, a proponent of the tripartite taxonomy of kinds of memory, bites the bullet. He claims that one cannot experientially remember that the city hall burned down 'since it would be senseless to speak of having been contemporaneous with the *fact that* the city hall burned down' (1963: 216).[8] Likewise John Pollock (1974: 184) holds that experiential memory always has the form 'I remember its being the case that p' rather than 'I remember that p'. This position, I reckon, is too implausible to be acceptable.

An advocate of the distinction between memory by acquaintance and memory by description might respond to the third objection as follows: Even though we cannot experientially remember that p solely by getting acquainted with a relevant experience, we *can* remember that p by having a relevant experience as an intermediate step. We are fooled into thinking that we can remember that p experientially because there is an indirect connection between our memory that p and our acquaintance with the relevant experience. Now I don't want to deny that there are ways to salvage the distinction between memory by acquaintance and memory by description. My point is rather that employing the acquaintance/description distinction doesn't really help to make the distinction between experiential and propositional memory sharp and intuitively compelling.

---

[8] After discussing factual memory and experiential memory Malcolm acknowledges that there is a another 'derivative sense' in which one might be said to personally factually remember something. 'A person who personally remembers the burning of the city hall could be said, in this derivative sense, to personally remember that it burned. The object of personal factual memory, as we might call it, would be restricted to a narrower range than are the objects of non-personal factual memory' (ibid.).

Yet another attempt to draw a sharp and intuitively compelling distinction between experiential and propositional memory is to align this distinction with the psychologist's distinction between semantic and episodic memory. Tyler Burge (2003: 329n3) and John Sutton (2004), among others, maintain that 'propositional memory' is more or less synonymous for 'semantic memory' and that 'experiential memory' corresponds to 'episodic memory'. Sutton (2006: 122) writes: ' "Propositional memory" is "semantic memory" or memory for facts, the vast network of conceptual information underlying our general knowledge of the world: this is naturally expressed as "remembering that", for example, that Descartes died in Sweden'. However, we saw that what distinguishes experiential from propositional memory is that the former, but not the latter, is limited to items with which one has had direct acquaintance. The distinction between semantic and episodic memory, however, does not turn on direct acquaintance with the remembered thing but instead on the contextual wealth of the stored information.[9]

In the end there is no way of drawing a sharp and intuitively compelling boundary between experiential and propositional memory. Though this doesn't amount to a knock-down argument against the tripartite classification scheme it does point to a structural weakness of this way of distinguishing kinds of memory. It would therefore be desirable to establish an alternative taxonomy of kinds of memory.

1.2 A GRAMMATICAL TAXONOMY

In lieu of the philosopher's tripartite classification scheme, I propose a classification in terms of the grammatical objects of the verb 'to remember' and of its (near) synonyms, such as 'to recall', 'to memorize', 'to reminisce', and 'to recollect'. Given this approach, there are four main kinds of remembering. One can remember persons and things (e.g. S remembers the Colosseum), properties (e.g. S remembers the elliptical shape of the Colosseum), events (e.g. S remembers visiting

---

[9] Another philosopher who seems to misconstrue the semantic/episodic distinction is Fernandez who uses 'semantic memory' as a synonym for 'veridical memory' and 'episodic memory' as a synonym for 'ostensible memory': 'S semantically remembers that p if, had she not believed that p some time in the past, S would not remember that p now . . . S episodically remembers that p if S would now remember that even if she had never believed that p before' (2006: 42).

the Colosseum), and facts or propositions (e.g. S remembers that the Colosseum was completed in AD 80). Consequently, I will speak of *object*, *property*, *event*, and *propositional memory*. Object, property, and event memory may collectively be labeled *non-propositional memory*.

I will take the term 'propositional memory' to refer to *any* substituend of the schema 'S remembers that p', irrespective of whether 'p' refers to something one has personally experienced, and irrespective of whether the memory content consists merely of the proposition p or whether, in addition, it includes images and qualia.

Frequently 'to remember' is used with wh-clauses, that is, clauses beginning with 'who', 'whom', 'what', 'where', 'when', and 'why'. Examples of wh-clause constructions with 'to remember' are 'I remember why Brutus stabbed Caesar', 'I remember what happened to Caesar on the Ides of March of 44 BC', and 'I remember whom Brutus stabbed'. The combinations of 'to remember' with wh-clauses do not refer to a distinct kind of memory; they are nothing but incomplete attributions of propositional memory. To say 'I remember whom Brutus stabbed' is just another way of saying 'I remember that Brutus stabbed so-and-so'; and to say 'I remember what Brutus did' is tantamount to saying 'I remember that Brutus did such-and-such'. 'S remembers-wh' is truth-conditionally equivalent to 'there is a proposition p such that S remembers p, and p answers the indirect question of the wh-clause'.[10]

Sometimes we say that we remember someone or something as having a certain property. For example, I can remember Caesar's *Commentarii de Bello Gallico* as having bored me. Yet to say 'I remember Caesar's *Commentarii* as having bored me' is just another way of saying 'I remember that Caesar's *Commentarii* bored me'. Likewise 'remembering to' constructions, as in 'I remember to return Caesar's *Commentarii* to the library on its due date', are disguised 'remembering that' constructions. For remembering to return Caesar's *Commentarii* to the library on its due date is to return the book because one remembers that it is due. (I prescind from specialized usages of the verb 'to remember', such as 'Remember me to your partner' or 'I will remember so-and-so in my will'.)

What propositional memory one is capable of attaining is dependent on what concepts one possesses. One cannot remember that Brutus

---

[10] Given that memory doesn't imply knowledge (cf. Ch. 3), reductionism about memory-wh doesn't imply reductionism about knowledge-wh. My reductionist position regarding memory-wh is compatible both with reductionism about knowledge-wh (Higginbotham 1996) and with anti-reductionism about knowledge-wh (Schaffer 2006).

stabbed Caesar unless one can have the thought that Brutus stabbed Caesar, and one cannot have that thought unless one possesses the concept *to stab*.[11] Object, property, and event memory, on the other hand, don't require the possession of concepts. A young child may remember Caesar's laurel wreath (property memory) long before he acquires the concept *laurel wreath*.

Remembering Caesar's laurel wreath without possessing the concept of a laurel wreath presumably amounts to visualizing the laurel wreath in one's mind and recognizing Caesar on the basis of 'seeing' his laurel wreath. Yet given the grammatical taxonomy of memory proposed here, phenomenological aspects are irrelevant for determining what kind of memory a mental episode belongs to. What qualifies a state of remembering as a token of propositional memory is the fact that the natural expression of its content involves a 'that' clause; whether the memory state is accompanied by imagery and qualitative experiences is of no importance for determining what kind of memory it is. And given that the presence or absence of images and qualia doesn't affect the classification of memory, combinations of 'remember' with a gerund (e.g. I remember reading Caesar's *Commentarii*) can be translated into 'remembering that' constructions (e.g. I remember that I read Caesar's *Commentarii*).

It goes without saying that by proposing a grammatical criterion for the classification of kinds of memory I do not wish to deny that non-language-users (or at least those with a central nervous system) can remember things, and that human remembering is only a special case of the general multi-systemed phenomenon of remembering. A dog may indicate in his behavior that he remembers where his food is kept.

Beyond remembering an object, property, event, or fact we can remember how to do something. When the verb 'to remember' is

---

[11] The claim that one cannot remember that p unless one has the concepts involved in p has been challenged by Bach (1997). According to Bach, that-clauses do not univocally denote propositions. This claim arises from the observation that sometimes a 'that p' clause attached to a propositional attitude verb cannot be replaced *salva veritate* by a definite description of the form 'the proposition that p'. For example, it may be unacceptable to interpret 'S remembers that Brutus stabbed Caesar' as meaning 'S remembers the proposition that Brutus stabbed Caesar'. The acceptability can be restored by substituting a different noun phrase—for example, 'the fact'—for the noun phrase 'the proposition'. Granted that facts are truth-makers of propositions, it may be argued that one can remember the fact that Brutus stabbed Caesar without possessing the concepts *Brutus*, *Caesar*, and *to stab*. But if this is so, it follows that 'remembering that' does not imply the deployment of concepts. In this study I will prescind from Bach's observation.

combined with 'how to' clauses, as in 'I remember how to swim', it expresses practical memory. Yet in this study I will prescind from practical memory. Instead the focus will be squarely on propositional memory.

A non-propositional representation can be remembered in propositional format and a propositional representation can be remembered in non-propositional format. Jennifer Lackey (2005: 650) describes a case that might be interpreted as involving a propositional memory of a past non-propositional representation. S drives to work along a highway and pays attention only to the other cars on the road and the radio program. Later someone asks S if there is construction on another highway that S passes on his way to work. S is able to call to mind passing the highway and correctly remembers seeing construction work being done on the highway in question. To cut the topic of this study to a manageable size, I will concentrate on propositional memories that are memory-related to past episodes of propositional awareness; the only exception is section 3.3.

The propositions that are the object of memory can be of two different kinds. When I remember that p, 'p' can refer to a past mental state of mine (e.g. that I believed that Brutus stabbed Caesar) or to any other fact (e.g. that Brutus stabbed Caesar). When I remember that Brutus stabbed Caesar, the content of the memory state *reproduces* the content of a past mental state of mine. Yet when I remember that I believed that Brutus stabbed Caesar, the memory content represents not only the content of the past mental state but also the psychological attitude I had toward that content. This memory content has the form of a *meta-representation*—it represents the past mental state *as a representation*. Metarepresentational memory makes available two kinds of information—information about the world and information about one's past mental states. The latter information is a 'metarepresentational comment' (Perner 1991: 163) on one's take on the former information.

I will refer to propositional memory of one's own mental states as *introversive propositional memory* or *introversive memory*, for short. The class of introversive memories contains second-order propositional memories that are expressed as 'I remember that I remembered that p'. Propositional memory of other things than one's own mental states I will label *extroversive propositional memory* or *extroversive memory*, for short. Extroversive memory is a kind of delayed perception while introversive memory is a kind of delayed self-knowledge.

When recalling thoughts, beliefs, inferences, and memories, I have a choice between merely reproducing the past content or representing the past mental state as such. I can entertain and express the past belief that Brutus stabbed Caesar by thinking or saying 'Brutus stabbed Caesar'—no mentioning of the past psychological attitude of believing—or by thinking or saying 'I believed that Brutus stabbed Caesar'. Yet there are other types of propositional attitudes where I don't have the choice whether I remember them inwardly or outwardly. A case in point is doubt. Suppose I remember having doubted that Brutus stabbed Caesar. I cannot entertain or express this memory by thinking or saying 'Brutus stabbed Caesar, not?' I must mention the past psychological attitude of doubting. The same is true of the propositional attitude of regretting. Moreover, conative states can be recalled only by means of introversive memory, for I cannot remember the content of my conative states without remembering their attitudes.

Although the distinction between extroversive and introversive memory is grounded on a difference in the way we express what we remember, there are instances where memory reports are not reliable indicators of which camp a given state belongs to. Occasionally extroversive memories are phrased as introversive memories. When someone asks you 'What did you think about such-and-such?' you may respond 'I thought that p' even though your response is an expression of extroversive memory. Instead of referring to the attitudinal component of a past mental state of yours, the phrase 'I thought' simply takes up the formulation of the question you are answering. Just as there are instances where extroversive memories are phrased as introversive memories, there might be instances where introversive memories are phrased as extroversive memories. Moreover, memory reports are sometimes not reliable indicators of whether a given state is a propositional or a non-propositional memory. For example, when someone asks me, 'Which year was Caesar assassinated?' and I immediately answer '44 BC'. In this case we can safely say that my memory claim can be expressed by: I remember that Caesar was assassinated in 44 BC.

1.3 FURTHER DISTINCTIONS

Apart from the distinction between propositional, experiential, and practical memory, philosophers usually distinguish between kinds of memory according to a number of other criteria. The distinctions I have in mind are the ones between veridical and ostensible memory, between memory contents in the first-person mode and the third-person mode, between inferential and non-inferential memory, between conceptual and non-conceptual memory contents, between *de re* and *de dicto* memory attributions, between occurrent and dispositional memory, between conscious, subconscious, and unconscious memories, as well as between explicit and implicit memory. In this section I attempt further to explicate my taxonomy of kinds of memory by relating it to these distinctions.

Veridical/Ostensible

According to the veridical (or factive) sense of 'to remember', the statement 'S remembers that p' implies that p is the case. (It is important not to confuse 'factive memory' in the sense of veridical memory with 'fact memory' or 'factual memory' in the sense of propositional memory.) You cannot remember that Brutus stabbed Caesar if he didn't do it. Yet it may seem to you as if you remember that Brutus stabbed Caesar and you can remember it seeming to you that Brutus stabbed Caesar. Like propositional memory, non-propositional memory is governed by an existence condition: you cannot remember Caesar's laurel wreath without Caesar having had a laurel wreath.[12] Given the ostensible usage of 'to remember', on the other hand, it is possible to remember something when that thing is nothing but a figment of one's imagination. There are a number of stock expressions that indicate ostensible memory: 'as I recall it, p', 'according to my best recollection, p', 'I seem to remember that p', and so on. I will assume the veridical (or factive) sense of 'to remember'. There will be more on the veridicality constraint on pages 36–9 and in section 8.1.

First-Person Mode/Third-Person Mode

Memory contents often involve an indexical reference to the rememberer. I remember what *I* had for breakfast or I remember what is *my* favorite book by Caesar. A memory content in the first-person mode is false when the bearer of the content is not the same person as the one referred to in the memory content. However, the truth-condition of memory contents in the third-person mode is consistent with the bearer

---

[12] The cases of object memory I have in mind here are those where the object is expressed by a singular term. Problems arise when the grammatical object of memory is a quantifier. Does remembering no one imply that no one was there? The answer is probably 'no'.

of the memory state being a different person from the bearer of the original belief. Suppose that the person currently occupying my body is different from the person who occupied it this morning. Due to the change of personal identity, I would say something false if I claimed to remember what *I* had for breakfast (first-person mode). But I would still speak the truth if I claimed to remember that *someone or other* had cereal for breakfast (third-person mode). Unlike memory contents in the first-person mode, those in the third-person mode don't presuppose the diachronic identity of the rememberer. I will be concerned with both modes of extroversive memory contents. There will be more on the relation between personal identity and memory on pages 41–2 and in Chapter 2.

Inferential/Non-Inferential

Frequently memories are admixed with inferential reasoning involving background knowledge or fresh evidence. Inferential memory is memory based on inferential reasoning. Inferential reasoning is (conscious or subconscious) reasoning that is based on additional premises that are evidence for its conclusion, that entail its conclusion, or that make its conclusion plausible. (Note that it doesn't matter whether the additional premises have been known all along or whether the subject has become aware of them only since the original representation that is being recalled.) In this study I will focus, for the most part, on non-inferential memory.

In an example that Malcolm (1963: 223) gives of inferential memory, S observes a certain blue bird. Later S learns that such birds are blue jays (*cyanocitta cristata*). Still later S claims to remember that he saw a blue jay. However, S does not really remember that he saw a blue jay. When S claims to remember that he saw a blue jay he is using the verb 'to remember' elliptically. What he says amounts to something like this: 'I remember that I saw a certain blue bird, and I now know that it was a blue jay.' (For a more sophisticated analysis of inferential memory see sect. 3.5.) So S knows that he saw a blue jay, via inference from the claim that such a blue bird as he saw is a blue jay.

A terminological note. What I call 'non-inferential memory' and 'inferential memory' is often labeled 'pure memory' and 'impure memory'. I find these labels unfortunate since 'impure memory' makes it seem as if it is second-rate memory. Yet most of our memories are in this sense 'impure'.

Conceptual/Non-Conceptual

The paradigm case of states with conceptual content are propositional attitudes. Specifications of the content of a propositional attitude state must not employ concepts that are not possessed by the subject. Some philosophers stipulate that there is a kind of content which is not a reflection of the concepts possessed by the subject. Consider Michael Martin's (1992) example of non-conceptual content of perception and memory. S plays a game with dice, one of which is 8-sided and one of which is 12-sided. At the time S lacks the concept of a dodecahedron and of a octahedral. He treats all dice with more than six sides as the same. Later on, after having acquired the concept of a dodecahedron, S recalls his experience playing the game and is able to come to believe, on the basis of memory alone, that one of the dice was a dodecahedron. From this Martin draws two inferences. First, if S can infer a belief involving the concept *dodecahedron* from remembering his past perceptual experience, then *dodecahedron* must have been part of the content of his past perceptual experience. Since, by hypothesis, S didn't possess this concept in the past, it must mean that the content of his perceptual experience was non-conceptual. Second, '[i]f [S's] memory experience is faithful to [his] past perception, its content, as reflected in this belief, matches that of [his] past perception' (1992: 755). In other words, given that the content of S's perceptual experience was non-conceptual and that S faithfully remembers his perceptual experience, it follows that the content of his memory state is also non-conceptual.

Given my focus on propositional memory, I will be concerned with conceptual memory content. Even when I examine non-propositional memory I will concentrate on states with conceptual content.

De Re/De Dicto

The difference between *de re* and *de dicto* memory attributions is that the former but not the latter allows for the substitution *salva veritate* of co-referential expressions. On the *de re* reading of memory attributions, the statements 'S remembers so-and-so', 'S remembers so-and-so φing' and 'S remembers that so-and-so φed' don't say anything about how S describes so-and-so and φ; 'so-and-so' and 'φ' are referentially transparent. If S remembers, say, Tully exposing Catiline's conspiracy to seize control of the Roman Republic he thereby also remembers Cicero exposing Catiline's conspiracy, regardless of whether S knows that 'Tully' and 'Cicero' are coextensive. Yet on the *de dicto* reading of memory attributions, S may remember that Tully exposed Catiline's conspiracy without thereby remembering that Cicero exposed Catiline's conspiracy. The substitution of co-referring terms or phrases in *de dicto* memory attributions could potentially alter their truth value. Since propositional memory attributions are usually taken to be referentially opaque and since I focus on propositional memory, I will adopt the *de dicto* reading of memory attributions. Unless stated otherwise, propositional memory attributions are assumed to be sensitive to the choice of words and don't automatically allow for the substitution of co-referential terms and phrases *salva veritate*.[13]

Occurrent/Dispositional

When saying of a person that he remembers something, we ascribe either a dispositional state or a kind of episode or event. According to the dispositional usage, we can say of someone that he remembers that p even while he is sound asleep. A dispositional claim is a claim, not about anything that is actually occurring at the time, but rather that some particular thing is prone to occur, under certain circumstances. Occurrent memories come and go, depending on the presence of appropriate retrieval cues; dispositional memories endure. In this study I will concentrate, for the most part, on the use of 'to remember' which refers to occurrent cases of memory.

Conscious/Subconscious/Unconscious

The distinction between occurrent and dispositional memory roughly coincides with the distinction between conscious memory, on the one hand, and subconscious and unconscious memory, on the other. Occurrent memories are those that we are conscious of having now—even though we may not be conscious of our occurrent memories as memories. Dispositional memories, however, need not be currently entertained for their ascription to be true. Dispositional memories as such are opaque

---

[13] It has been suggested that there is an everyday linguistic device that allows us to tell apart beliefs *de re* from beliefs *de dicto*. The *de re* style of believing is said to be captured by 'S believes *of* Tully that he exposed Catiline's conspiracy' and the *de dicto* style by 'S believes *that* Tully exposed Catiline's conspiracy'. Even if this should work for the verb 'to believe', it doesn't carry over to 'to remember'. 'Remembering that' is used to express either memory *de re* or memory *de dicto*.

to the mind. What we are conscious of are not dispositional memories but the memory episodes they give rise to.

A memory is subconscious at a given time if it is not being entertained by the agent at that time, but, given the appropriate retrieval cues, he would entertain it. An unconscious memory is one that is in principle beyond the reach of conscious awareness because it is repressed. Sigmund Freud suggested that certain types of events, extremely painful or horrible or traumatic ones, are repressed because they cannot be tolerated by the subject. Repressed information, though inaccessible to introspection, may, according to Freud, manifest itself as inadverted slips of tongue or pen, in which the speaker or writer makes an error that is said to reflect his underlying feelings rather than the intended meaning. Repressed information is also said to disrupt ongoing behavior in the form of neurotic symptoms and find expressions in dreams.[14] Provided the existence of unconscious memories can be verified at all, it takes psychoanalysis rather than introspection or reflection to do so. Given my focus on occurrent memories, I concentrate on conscious memory. And insofar as I examine dispositional memory it is the subconscious rather than the unconscious variety that will be dealt with.

Explicit/Implicit

Suppose you remember that Caesar was assassinated in 44 BC. It seems natural to say that as a consequence of what you remember you also remember that he was assassinated after 45 BC, and also that he was assassinated after 46 BC, and so on. Granted that there is something to this way of speaking, it could be maintained that in virtue of remembering that p you remember an infinite number of

---

[14] Although the concept of repressed memories existing in the unconscious is firmly embedded in the folk psychology the experimental evidence for it—apart from cases of hysterical amnesia and fugue—is only slight (cf. Bonanno 2006; Hayne, Garry, and Loftus 2006). A pretty convincing laboratory analogue of repression was produced by Glucksberg and King (1967). Their study relied on the use of remote word associations. Glucksberg and King taught their subjects a list of nonsense syllable-word pairs (e.g. dax/window, gex/justice). Then the subjects were shown a list of words comprising the remote associates of the words learned, and some of these were accompanied by an electric shock. The subject's task was to learn which items were associated with shock. When the retention of the initial pairs was tested, there was a tendency for subjects to show poorer retention of words whose remote associates had been linked with shock. None of the subjects was able to verbalize the relation between the shocked words and the initial learning, although all of them were able to recognize which words had been accompanied by an electric shock.

other propositions implied by p. But if memories are representational items in the brain (or, metaphorically speaking, sentence tokens in the memory box), it would seem that on this interpretation we suffer from an embarrassment of riches, namely, that each individual has far too many memories for all of them to be explicitly represented in the brain. It would be a violation of the principle of clutter avoidance if all these memories were explicitly represented.

In response to this problem, some philosophers distinguish between explicit and implicit (or tacit) memory. You explicitly remember that p if this representation is actually present in your mind in the right sort of way, for example, as an item in your 'memory box' or as a trace storing a sentence in the language of thought. To implicitly remember that p your mind may not contain a representation with that content. The contents of implicit memories (unlike those of dispositional memories) have never previously been tokened and don't inhabit our long-term memory. Although at any given moment we have only a finite number of explicit memories, we implicitly remember countless things.[15]

There are two competing accounts of implicit memory (and belief). First, there are *simple-consequence* accounts according to which to implicitly remember that p is to have an explicit memory from which p swiftly and obviously follows (Dennett 1978: 39–50). Thus, to use the example from above, you may be said to remember explicitly that Caesar was assassinated in 44 BC and only implicitly that he was assassinated after 45 BC. That is an example in which the implicit memory is entailed by the explicit memory. There are also cases in which one implicitly remembers something that is swiftly inferable from one's explicit memories without being strictly implied by them. An example might be one's implicit memory that kangaroos rarely wear pajamas in the wild. Since swiftness is a matter of degree there is no sharp division

---

[15] Note that the way psychologists draw the distinction between explicit and implicit memory differs from the way philosophers draw that distinction. In the psychological sense, explicit memory involves the conscious recollection of previously presented information, while implicit memory involves the facilitation of a task, or a change in performance as a result of previous exposure to information, without, or at least not as a result of, conscious recollection. For example, if a subject memorizes a list of word pairs (e.g. window/chair) and is later cued with one word and asked to provide the other, it is the subject's explicit memory that is being tested. Once all explicit memory of the word pairs has faded, the subject's implicit memory would be revealed if he found it easier to learn the 'forgotten' pairs a second time (cf. Schacter 1987). A piece of memory that is implicit in the psychological sense may nevertheless be stored explicitly in the philosophical sense. My notions of object, property, event, and fact memory belong to the category of explicit long-term memory.

between what one remembers implicitly and what, though derivable from one's memories, one does not actually remember.

Second, there is the *formation-dispositional* account, which explains instances of implicit memory by way of hypothetical explicit memories. To implicitly remember that p is to be disposed to have an explicit memory of it in such-and-such circumstances (De Sousa 1971; Lycan 1988: 54–71; Sellars 1974). As it stands, this characterization of implicit memory is insufficient. Counterexamples suggest that to implicitly remember that p requires more than merely being disposed to explicitly remember that p, and less than representing p internally. Two strategies have been considered for supplementing the initial account. The first strategy requires the disposition to have an explicit memory be grounded in an extrapolator-deducer mechanism (i.e. a device that operates on occurrent memories and generates obvious consequences when the occasion arises), and the second strategy requires the disposition be based on reasons (good or bad).

Any merely implicit memory is merely dispositional. Yet explicit memories are not necessarily occurrent, for only some explicit memories are currently operative at any given time. Thus the distinction between implicit and explicit memories is not the same as that between occurrent and dispositional memories. In this study I will focus on explicit memory.

In sum, this investigation is primarily concerned with episodes of conscious, explicit, veridical, non-inferential, *de dicto*, propositional memory that are memory-related to past episodes of propositional representation.

1.4 METHODOLOGICAL EXTERNALISM

It is currently out of favor to acknowledge that one is engaged in conceptual analysis. There seem to be mainly three reasons for this. First, given that conceptual analysis is supposed to yield necessary and sufficient conditions, very few, if any, successful analyses have been produced—analyses, that is, of philosophically interesting concepts. The bulk of those produced have nearly always been undermined by convincing hypothetical situations that indicate that the analysandum does not mean the same thing as the analysans. Second, since conceptual analysis provides definitions and since definitions are paradigm examples of analytic statements, a defense of conceptual analysis is committed to the analytic/synthetic distinction discredited by W. V. O. Quine (1961). Third, assuming that the relation between the analysandum and the analysans is knowable a priori, the knowledge we gain through conceptual analysis is a priori knowledge—a type of knowledge many philosophers are suspicious of. One of the reasons philosophers are suspicious of a priori knowledge is because they think it is incompatible with philosophical naturalism, that is, the view that the methods of justification and explanation used in philosophy must be commensurable with those in the natural sciences.

In response to the first and second objection, I grant that reductive definitions of philosophically interesting concepts are a rare commodity and that the analytic/synthetic distinction is epistemically fruitless in that it doesn't shed light on the development of rational scientific practice. I intend to expose at best only necessary conditions for remembering. Even though a list of necessary conditions for remembering doesn't amount to a definition of memory, it goes some way towards delimiting the concept. It can bring out the content or the structure of the concept in such a way as to clarify the concept and indicate its relation to some other concepts representing its constituents.

The conditions for remembering I will expose are *at best* necessary conditions. Section 2.2 argues that the memory presupposes personal identity only as a matter of contingent fact, not as a matter of logical necessity. That memory presupposes personal identity is a contingent fact having to do with the kind of world we inhabit. And on pages 115–17 I argue that it is an empirical hypothesis as opposed to a conceptual truth that for all subjects S and all objects of memory X, S remembers X only if X is the cause of S's remembering.

What about the third objection? As will be explained in Chapter 6, I am committed to content externalism (or anti-individualism). Content externalism has it that one can have a particular concept without knowing any of its essential properties. There is a crucial difference between the possession of a concept and knowing the conditions that may be regarded as necessary to, and jointly sufficient for, the application of the concept. According to content externalism, the contents of our thoughts and the meanings of our concepts depend on relations that we bear to our physical and social environment. Since knowledge of the referents is typically empirical, it follows that a conceptual analysis may involve empirical investigations. The linguistic intuitions that guide conceptual analysis are not a priori but empirical working hypotheses (cf. Kornblith 2002). Hence I reject the view that the relation between the analysandum and the analysans must be knowable a priori.

When one examines what it takes for someone to remember something, one must do so from some point of view. One can work from the point of view of the subject, taking into account only that which is available to the subject at the given time, or one can work from the point of view of someone who knows all the relevant facts, some of which might not be available to the subject. Roughly speaking, those who adopt the subject's point of view for making these evaluations are methodological *internalists* about memory, and those who adopt a bird's-eye view are methododological *externalists* about memory. My approach is externalist. (It is important not to confuse methodological externalism with content externalism.)

The distinction between internalism and externalism about memory is modeled after the internalism/externalism distinction in epistemology. Internalism about justification is the view that all the factors required for a belief to be justified must be cognitively accessible to the subject and thus internal to his mind. Something is internal to one's mind so long as one is aware of it or could be aware of it merely by reflecting. Externalism about justification is the denial of internalism, holding that some of the justifying factors may be external to the subject's cognitive perspective. A belief is justified if it has the property of being truth-effective. The property of being truth-effective may, for example, consist in the belief being produced by a reliable method or process. No more than this is necessary for justification. Whether the subject takes his belief to be truth-effective doesn't add anything to the belief's epistemic status.

Some types of mental states are transparent to their subject in the sense that he can identify them and discriminate them from one another in any possible situation. Bodily sensations, for example, are commonly regarded as transparent. I can always identify (intense) pain and can tell it apart from (mildly) pleasurable sensations. Factive mental states, however, are not transparent. A case in point is knowledge. Knowledge is not transparent because the agent cannot discriminate true from false belief just on the basis of reflection. Similarly, whether I see something or whether it only seems to me that I see it is not something I can know by reflection.

Are memories transparent from the first-person perspective? According to an influential position in the history of philosophy the answer is 'yes'. Representative realism has it that one remembers something not by way of being directly aware of that thing, but rather a mediating image which represents that thing. To remember is to undergo a certain sort of mental experience. It is to experience a mental representation—usually called a *memory image*—which reproduces some past sense experience. The memory image provides us with the information we are then said to remember. It is a distinctive feature of representative realism that remembering involves primary awareness of memory images.

Since we have images of many things we don't remember, remembering cannot be defined simply in terms of awareness of images or experiences. The need to discern memory data from other kinds of experiences is particularly pressing if one wants to base memory knowledge on awareness of memory experiences. Representative realists maintain that one can tell, by reflection alone, whether a particular image one is having is one of memory, or one of the other faculties of the mind, such as perception or imagination. They maintain that there is a feature of memory data that stamps them as such. This feature of memory data is commonly referred to as the *memory marker*. Memory markers are a priori knowable properties of memory data by which they can be distinguished from other mental phenomena. Memory markers have been described by representative realists in a number of ways, as the feeling of warmth and intimacy (James 1890: i. 650), the feeling of familiarity and pastness (Brandt 1955: 80; Broad 1925: 271; Plantinga 1993: 59; Russell 1995: 163), the force and vivacity of memory data (Harrod 1942: 5; Hume 2000a: 12–13, 59–60; Jacoby and Whitehouse 1989), their embeddedness (Johnson 1988), and their spontaneity and involuntariness (Furlong 1951: 98).

The problem all the various proposals of memory markers have in common is that they don't offer a reliable mark. There are cases in which these alleged memory markers are present, but in which there is no inclination to speak of memory and there are instances where memories lack these alleged markers. We may seem to remember something that is really unfamiliar to us, and we may not seem to remember something that once formed part of our common experience. What is more, the properties identified as memory markers don't bear their own explanation upon their face. The association between images that strike us as familiar and memory is not an epistemic reason for anything. For the mere fact, if it is one, that we are inclined to make this association does not imply that we are *entitled* to make it. To be so entitled, we would need independent evidence suggesting that genuine memories appear familiar more often than fantasies. If such evidence exists at all, it cannot be accessed by reflection alone.

Since memories don't come with their own authentication they are not transparent to the mind in the sense that we can identify them and discriminate them from other states in any possible situation. Whether I genuinely remember p or whether it only seems to me that I remember p I cannot tell just by reflection. Incidentally this is the reason there is no logical impossibility in Russell's (1995: 159) hypothesis that the world sprang into being five minutes ago, exactly as it then was, with a population that seemed to remember a wholly unreal past.[16]

Given that memories are not transparent to their subject, method-ological internalism about memory is not an option. Memory must be analyzed from a third-person point of view. The conditions for remembering may not be identified with the conditions for saying that one remembers. The externalist approach to the study of memory is in line with my disregard for phenomenological grounds for distinguishing types of memories. The grammatical taxonomy of kinds of memory, proposed in the previous section, allows for the analysis of memory to be conducted from a third-person rather than a first-person perspective.

In the remainder of this chapter I will set forth preliminary analyses of four kinds of propositional memory: extroversive memory in the first-person mode and in the third-person mode as well as introversive memory about factive attitudes and about non-factive attitudes. The motive behind developing these tentative analyses is to identify the issues in the philosophy of memory that require and merit in-depth investigation.

1.5 EXTROVERSIVE MEMORY

As was explained in before (pp. 24–5), the content of extroversive memory can either be in the first-person mode or in the third-person mode. Let's start with extroversive memory in the first-person mode. S remembers at t_2 that p, where 'p' stands for an extroversive proposition in the first-person mode only if:

(1) S represents at t_2 that p,
(2) S represented at t_1 that p*,

---

[16] For an extensive discussion of memory markers, of skepticism regarding our ability to know that an experience of seeming to remember is a reliable guide to the past, and on Russell's skeptical hypothesis see my (2008: 81–136).

(3) p is true at t_2,
(4) p is identical with, or sufficiently similar to, p^*,
(5) S's representation at t_2 that p is suitably connected to S's representation at t_1 that p^*.

The five conditions may be labeled, respectively, the *present representation condition* (1), the *past representation condition* (2), the *truth-condition* (3), the *content condition* (4), and the *connection condition* (5).

Those who have read the introductory chapter (p. 4) already know that here and throughout the book the value of the index in the subscript to 't' determines whether the time referred to is in the past or the present: the relatively biggest number indicates the present. So here 't_2' is the present and 't_1' is the past. When there is more than one past time involved, 't_1' indicates the distant past, 't_2' the close past, and 't_3' the present.

The Representation Conditions (1) and (2)

Since to remember is to retain some previously acquired representation, the analysis of memory must include some provision for one's having had the representation in question in the past and for one's still possessing that representation. This is the motivation for the past and present representation condition.

Sometimes the occurrent cognitive state in fact-remembering is one of belief or knowledge, but it need not always be; or so Chapter 3 argues. You may have believed that p in the past and remember that p today, even though someone has in the meantime convinced you that p is false. In this case you remember that p even though you don't believe that p. And just as the present cognitive state need not be one of belief or knowledge nor does the past cognitive state. It is possible that you remember having witnessed p even though, at the time, you didn't believe that it was p you witnessed because, say, you had convincing yet misleading reasons for thinking that p is false. The cognitive verb 'to represent' in conditions (1) and (2) is meant to indicate that propositional memory requires neither the past nor the present cognitive state to qualify as belief or knowledge. 'Representing' covers all sorts of attitudes towards a proposition; believing and knowing are among these attitudes, but they are not the only ones.

Though the attitude of a memory state need not be one of believing or knowing, not any kind of cognitive attitude that stands in a memory-relation to another cognitive attitude qualifies as a memory state. For instance, an occurrent fear that p does not count as a memory—not even if it was previously formed and is now being retrieved from memory. Only cognitive attitudes with a mind-to-world (or thetic) direction of fit can qualify as memory states. Section 8.6 offers a taxonomy of attitudes.

Tokens of non-propositional awareness are remembered frequently in propositional format. Suppose that, as a small child I saw a picture of Caesar wearing a laurel wreath. I may remember this episode of non-propositional awareness by forming the belief that Caesar wore a laurel wreath. The way conditions (1) and (2) are phrased makes it clear that this study concentrates on propositional memories that are memory-related to past episodes of propositional awareness.

The Truth-Condition (3)

Though talk of 'false memory' is familiar enough it is loose talk. 'To remember' is factive in the sense that an utterance of 'S remembers that p' is true only if p is the case. If not-p, then S may think he remembers that p, but cannot actually remember that p. And it is not only propositional memory that implies truth. Non-propositional memory is also factive. For example, I cannot remember Caesar, his laurel wreath, or his being assassinated by Brutus unless there was someone called 'Caesar', he wore a laurel wreath, and was assassinated by Brutus.[17]

But, a critic might wonder, doesn't the truth-condition of memory imply that memory claims are, by definition, infallible? If memory entails truth, doesn't it follow that we can never remember things that are false? But since we obviously do remember things that are false, it seems that memory cannot be factive. This objection to the truth-condition is mistaken. Though memory entails truth, we can be mistaken in thinking that we remember something. 'What I remember is false' is shorthand for 'What I thought I remember is false'.

The truth-condition of memory can be motivated in two ways. One argument for the factivity of 'to remember' makes use of the undeniable fact that statements of the form 'I remember that p; but p is false'

---

[17] Hazlett (forthcoming) challenges the orthodox view among philosophers that 'remembers', 'knows', 'learns' etc. are factive. He argues that if the orthodox view is true, then we should expect the claim that all known propositions are true to be obvious to anyone who knows the meaning of 'knows'. However, the fact that 'remembers' or 'knows' might not be obviously factive for some competent language users is fully compatible with their being indeed factive all the same.

and 'I remember such-and-such; but such-and-such never happened' have a paradoxical ring to them. Just as G. E. Moore's famous dictum 'It's raining; but I don't believe that it is raining', though not literally contradictory, cannot be used to make coherent assertions, the statement 'I remember that p; but p is false' is pragmatically incoherent.

The crux with using Moore's paradox to motivate the factivity of memory is that one can explain the pragmatic incoherence of the statement 'I remember that p; but p is false' while maintaining that memory does *not* imply truth. When I claim to remember that p, I am convinced that p is the case. This is what the first part of the statement expresses. Yet the second part of the statement denies that p is the case. Thus 'I remember that p; but p is false' need not be incoherent because one cannot remember that p without p being the case. Instead it can be incoherent because one cannot *claim* to remember that p while *claiming* that p is false. And since the conditions for claiming to remember are distinct from the conditions for remembering it doesn't follow that remembering that p implies the truth of p just because claiming to remember that p implies the truth of p.

A better argument for the factivity of memory is based on syntax. Factive verbs are members of a class of expressions with certain syntactic features in common (cf. Kiparsky and Kiparsky 1970). First, factive verbs can always be followed by 'the fact that . . .', whereas non-factive verbs cannot (compare 'S remembers the fact that Brutus stabbed Caesar' to 'S believes the fact that Brutus stabbed Caesar' (cf. p. 21 n11)); second, factive verbs can always be followed by gerunds, while non-factive verbs cannot (compare 'S remembers having read Caesar's *Commentarii*' to 'S believes having read Caesar's *Commentarii*'); third, unlike non-factive verbs, factive verbs cannot be followed by infinitives (compare 'S remembers Brutus to have stabbed Caesar' to 'S believes Brutus to have stabbed Caesar').

According to Zeno Vendler (1972: 93–9; 1980: 280–2), the most reliable syntactic mark of factivity is the possibility of co-occurrences with wh-nominal complements, that is, clauses beginning with 'who', 'whom', 'what', 'where', 'when', and 'why'. Both factive and non-factive propositional verbs can take that-clause complements (e.g. 'S remembers that Brutus stabbed Caesar', 'S believes that Brutus stabbed Caesar'), but the that-clauses following factive verbs are different from the that-clauses following non-factive ones: only that-clauses following factive verbs can be transformed into wh-nominals. We can say 'S remembers who stabbed Caesar', 'S remembers whom Brutus stabbed', 'S remembers why Brutus stabbed Caesar', 'S remembers where Brutus stabbed Caesar', 'S remembers what Brutus did to Caesar', and 'S remembers when Brutus stabbed Caesar'. But we cannot say 'S believes who stabbed Caesar', 'S believes whom Brutus stabbed', 'S believes why Brutus stabbed Caesar', 'S believes where Brutus stabbed Caesar', 'S believes when Brutus stabbed Caesar'.[18]

There are different ways to interpret the factivity constraint on memory: the memory report must accord either with the objective reality, or with the initial perception of reality, or with both. The former interpretation of the factivity of memory is adopted by most philosophers and is widespread among psychologists. For instance, Asher Koriat and Morris Goldsmith (1996: 170) declare:

> In perception, interest lies in the correspondence between what we perceive and what is out there, that is, in the (output-bound) *veridicality* of our perceptions, and in the various ways in which they may deviate from reality (e.g., illusions). Likewise, under the correspondence metaphor, memory may be conceived as the perception of the past, and the question then becomes to what extent this perception is dependable.

Ian Newby and Michael Ross (1996), on the other hand, conceive of the direction of fit of memory as mind-in-the-present-to-mind-in-the-past, and of the accuracy of memory as the degree of correspondence between the mind at two different times. They suggest that memory reports should be evaluated 'against an individual's initial representation of the event, rather than against the supposed objective stimulus. After all, we cannot ask more of memory than that recollections reflect the person's original reality; otherwise, we confuse differences in memory with differences in perception' (ibid. 205). S. Jack Odell (1971) concurs with Newby and Ross's interpretation of the factivity constraint on memory. He imagines that he teaches a child the false statement that Columbus discovered America in 1392. When asked to remember when Columbus discovered America the child answers '1392'. 'What does [the child] remember? He remembers *what* I told him. *What* did

18 Not all non-factive verbs reject wh-nominal complements. 'What' can introduce the verb-object of 'believe': S may believe what I said as he may remember what I said. 'The possibility of "believing what" (= "that which" or "the thing which") is restricted to things that can be objects of belief. For this reason, such sentences as "I believe what he lost" are ruled out: the relevant co-occurrence set of "believe" and "lose", unlike those of "believe" and "say", do not overlap. Roughly speaking, "believe" demands that-clauses, but "lose" requires object nouns' (Vendler 1972: 98).

I tell him? That Columbus discovered America in 1392. So it follows that he remembers that p' (ibid. 593). Odell concludes that this shows that one can remember that p even when p is false.

According to the position argued for in this study, a memory report must accurately represent the objective reality *and* resemble the subject's initial perception. In other words, memory reports must not only be veridical but also authentic in the sense of reflecting the subject's original perception of reality. The correspondence metaphor of memory takes the form of representation and the form of resemblance. For this reason there needs to be a content condition (4) and past representation condition (2) in addition to the truth-condition (3). There will be more on this issue in section 8.1.

It is worth noting that, according to the account of extroversive memory proposed here, the proposition emerging from the memory process must be veridical but the proposition fed into the memory process may be false. To drive this point home consider the following example. At t_1 you came to believe that S φed. At the time, the belief was false. Unbeknownst to you, at t_2, S did in fact φ. At t_3 you claim to remember on the basis of your belief from t_1 that S φed. Do you in fact remember what you claim to remember? On my account the answer is 'yes'. The authentic reproduction of a formerly false proposition which in the meantime has become true may indeed qualify as memory.

The Content Condition (4)

The idea behind the content condition is that the memory content must be the same as, or sufficiently similar to, a content one has previously represented. One can only remember what one has previously represented. By allowing that the contents of the past and the present representation are not type-identical but only similar the content condition contradicts the widespread *identity theory of memory*. The identity theory of memory claims that for a propositional attitude token at t_2 to stand in a memory-relation to a propositional attitude token at t_1, the contents of both tokens must be type-identical. The identity theory is widespread among philosophers even though it is fundamentally at odds with what cognitive psychology tells us about the workings of human memory (cf. sect. 8.2). For our memory is not only a passive device for reproducing contents but also an active device for processing stored contents. Given the active role memory plays, there are cases where the content of a memory claim is veridical even though it contains some reconstructive elements. Yet when the reconstructive nature of memory gains the upper hand the distinction between memory and confabulation becomes blurred.

The content condition raises two questions: First, what does it mean for two diachronic content tokens to be of the same type? Second, in what respect may two diachronic content tokens differ from one another and one of them still count as sufficiently similar to the other so as to be memory-related to it? What is the permissible range of aberration between the original content and the memory content? Chapter 6 tackles the first question by setting forth an externalist account of the identity of diachronic content tokens. On this view, two diachronic content tokens are identical only if their truth-conditions supervene on the same conditions in the subject's physical and social environment. Chapter 7 defends externalism about memory contents against objections. Chapter 8 addresses the second question by arguing that two propositional content tokens are sufficiently similar for the token at t_2 to be memory-related to the token at t_1 if the token at t_2 is entailed by the token at t_1.

The Connection Condition (5)

The connection condition is meant to exclude relearning from the ranks of remembering and establish that the representation had in remembering is a retained representation. For a claim to remember something implies not merely that the subject had a past cognitive state, but that his present cognitive state is connected, in the right sort of way, to his past attitude.

To drive this point home consider the following scenario. You witness S φing. Later on, due to a severe blow to your head you permanently forget many things, including the fact that S φed. Still later, it is suggested to you, under hypnosis, that you will believe that S φed at a certain time and place. The hypnotist makes up the story of S φing but, by coincidence, it is an accurate and detailed account of the event you witnessed but forgot about. So the hypnotist produces in you an apparent memory of S φing which is intrinsically indistinguishable from the state you would be in if you had a genuine recollection of the event. Even though you meet conditions (1) to (4) we would not say that you remember that S φed. The reason you don't remember that S φed is that your past representation of S φing and your present state of seeming to remember that S φed are not suitably connected. It is sheer luck that the content of the past experience is qualitatively identical with the content of the seeming recollection.

The interpretations of the memory connection proposed in the literature fall into three categories: evidential retention theories, simple retention theories, and causal theories. Chapter 4 weighs up these accounts and argues that the causal theory of memory is the only viable one. The memory state must stand in a causal relation to the past cognitive state. Chapter 5 takes a close look at the causal relation constitutive of remembering and tries to determine what makes a causal relation 'suitable' for memory.

Having examined extroversive memory in the first-person mode, we will take a brief look at extroversive memory in the third-person mode. Extroversive memory in the third-person mode leaves open the issue of the personal identity of the rememberer. When the content of the remembered representation is 'anonymous' in the sense that it doesn't contain an indexical reference to the bearer of the past representation, remembering is consistent with the bearer of the present representation not being the same person as the bearer of the past representation.

Consider the following story adapted from Derek Parfit (1984: 221). S reads a book and comes to believe that the Venetian church of San Giorgio Maggiore was completed in 1610. Later, some of S's memory traces are surgically removed and instilled in S*'s brain. Before the operation S* did not believe that San Giorgio Maggiore was completed in 1610 (but he possessed all of the concepts necessary to form that belief). After the operation S* does believe, on the basis of the transplanted traces, that San Giorgio Maggiore was completed in 1610. Assuming that S and S* are not the same person, does S* *remember* that San Giorgio Maggiore was completed in 1610?

To be sure, granting S* memory of the year in which San Giorgio Maggiore was completed does *not* conflict with the thesis that one can remember only what is the case. The truth-condition for outwardly remembering in the third-person mode is consistent with the bearer of the memory state not being the same person as the bearer of the original belief. A critic may argue though that S* does not remember the year in which San Giorgio Maggiore was completed because he violates the connection condition for remembering. His state of seeming to remember is not caused in the right sort of way because memory traces may not be transferred from one person to another. The three stages of the causal process underlying remembering—information encoding, storage, and retrieval—must take place within a single person; or so a critic might claim. The problem with this position, however, is that there are no good reasons to support it. Provided the transplantation of memory traces doesn't affect the contiguity and counterfactuality of memory causation, surgically implanted memory traces are just as good as 'home-grown' ones. From a causal point of view, implanted memory traces are not inferior to traces brought about in the ordinary way; or so I will argue in section 5.4.

Granted that neither the factivity constraint nor the causation constraint on impersonal extroversive memory demands personal identity, it remains to be seen whether the content condition demands personal identity. Yet when the remembered content is anonymous its truth value is not affected by whether personal identity is preserved. By contrast, introversive memory and extroversive memory in the first-person mode do presuppose that the bearer of the present representation is the same as the bearer of the past representation. In section 2.2 I will explore the nature of this dependence relation and argue that introversive memory and extroversive memory in the first-person mode don't *imply* personal identity. The dependence of some kinds of memory on personal identity is of a contingent not of a logical kind.

To summarize, there are no good reasons to maintain that when memory traces encoding impersonal contents are extracted from the brain of one person and implanted in the brain of another the resulting state of seeming to remember necessarily fails to meet the criteria for extroversive memory in the third-person mode. Thus I propose the following tentative analysis of extroversive memory in the third-person mode: At t_2 S remembers that p, where 'p' stands for an impersonal extroversive proposition only if:

(1) S represents at t_2 that p,
(2') Someone represented at t_1 that p^*,
(3) p is true at t_2,
(4) p is identical with, or sufficiently similar to, p^*,
(5') S's representation at t_2 that p is suitably connected to someone's representation at t_1 that p^*.

Apart from slight differences regarding the wording of the past representation condition (2') and the connection condition (5'), the conditions of extroversive memory in the third-person mode correspond to those of extroversive memory in the first-person mode. There will be more on the relation between personal identity and memory in Chapter 2 .

1.6 INTROVERSIVE MEMORY

Introversive memories are memories about one's past propositional attitudes. Since propositional attitudes have a propositional as well as an attitudinal component, one can only represent one's past propositional attitude if one represents both its content and its attitude. Introversive memory is composed of a twofold classification. And for an introversive memory claim to be veridical both classifications need to be accurate.

Depending on whether the past propositional attitudes referred to by introversive memory is factive or non-factive the factivity constraint on introversive memory differs. Examples of factive attitudes are knowing, seeing, and remembering. The paradigm example of a non-factive attitude is believing. Let's start with introversive memory about factive attitudes: S remembers at t_2 that he represented (at t_1) that p, where 'to represent' stands for a factive attitude only if:

(1′) S represents at t_2 that he represented (at t_1) that p,

(2) S represented at t_1 that p*,

(3) p is true at t_2,

(6) p* is true at t_1,

(4) p is identical with, or sufficiently similar to, p*,

(7) The attitude that S represents at t_2 himself having taken (at t_1) towards p is the same as, or sufficiently similar to, the attitude that S took at t_1 towards p*,

(5″) S's representation at t_2 that he represented (at t_1) that p is suitably connected to S's representation at t_1 that p*.

The addendum 'at t_1' in (1′), (7), and (5″) is put in parenthesis because we frequently remember our past cognitive states without remembering the exact time at which we entertained these states. The analysis of introversive memory about factive attitudes contains the same conditions as the analysis of extroversive memory in the first-person mode, though some of these conditions are worded slightly differently. The only substantial difference is the introduction of the *past truth-condition* (6) and the *attitude condition* (7).

When the past propositional attitude is factive, as in remembering that I knew that p, the factivity constraint on introversive memory demands, first, that the content embedded in the memory content, p, be true and, second, that the content of the past representation from which the memory state causally derives, p*, be true as well. For I couldn't have known that p* unless p* was true. Introversive memory about factive attitudes requires a past truth-condition (6) in addition to the present truth-condition (3). In the case of timeless truths one truth-condition—past or present—is sufficient.

When the past propositional attitude is non-factive, however, the factivity constraint on introversive memory requires only that the content embedded in the memory content, p, be the same as, or sufficiently similar to, the content of the past representation, p*, from which the memory state causally derives. Whether p or p* are true is irrelevant to the truth of this type of remembering. For when I claim to remember that I believed that p I claim to remember the particular attitude I took towards p, not whether p is true. I claim something about how things appeared to me, not about how things were. Thus in the case of inwardly remembering non-factive attitudes the present truth-condition (3) and the past truth-condition (6) must be dropped. There will be more on the factivity condition for inwardly remembering in section 8.1.

To forestall misunderstanding I concede that talking about 'the content embedded in the memory content' is too simplistic. Suppose I remember that I believed that I saw that p. 'That I believed that I saw that p' is embedded; and so is 'that p'. So what is the target embedded content? We can't simply say that the target embedded content is expressed by what follows a 'remember that' clause. For consider: I remember that I believed that I remembered that p. In this case there are two 'remember that' clauses. Though part of the embedded content is factive, p need not be true when embedded in this way. Thus we may say that the target embedded content is the one following the 'remember that' clause that has the largest scope. Yet to not add unnecessary complications I will prescind from cases where the past propositional attitude contains further attitudes.

Regardless of whether the past propositional attitude is factive, remembering it requires faithfully representing both its content and its attitude. The memory state must be an *authentic* rendering of the past state. 'Authenticity', as I use the term, refers to the accuracy of the representation of a past propositional attitude by means of a memory judgment. Memory of factive and non-factive attitudes alike has a mind-in-the-present-to-mind-in-the-past direction of fit; memory of factive attitudes, in addition, has a mind-in-the-past-to-world direction of fit. Memory of one's factive attitudes must be true not only to one's past representation of reality but also to reality itself.

Claims to remember one's past factive cognitive states are more likely to be false than claims to remember one's past non-factive states. When I claim to remember that I saw that S φed I run a fourfold risk. First, it might be that what in fact happened was that S* φed. At the time, I mistook S* for S and formed the incorrect belief that S φed. In this case it is the past perception that is to blame. Second, at the time I was correct in thinking that what I saw was that S* φed but today I claim to have seen S φ. In this case the fault lies with the memory and not the past perception. Third, both mistakes can be combined: what in fact happened was that S* φed; at the time I took myself to be seeing that S φed; now I claim to remember having seen that S** φed. Fourth, the perceptual mistake and the memorial mistake can balance each other out. What I claim to remember is true: S* φed. But at the time I thought that it is S who φed.

Since introversive memory is governed by some of the same conditions as extroversive memory, both kinds of propositional memory give rise to the same set of issues. First, there is the question of whether remembering presupposes the diachronic numerical identity of the rememberer. Chapter 2 defends the idea that for memory contents in the first-person mode to be veridical the rememberer must be co-personal with the person who entertained the past representation. Second, there is the issue of whether remembering is a form of knowing. Chapter 3 argues that remembering implies neither knowing nor believing. Third, the connection condition for remembering calls for an explanation of the nature of the causal link between the past and present representation. This is the topic of Chapters 4 and 5. Fourth, to understand the content condition for remembering one must be able to make sense of the concept of type-identity of diachronic content tokens. Chapters 6 and 7 develop and defend an externalist account of content identity. Fifth, the content condition for remembering also raises the issue of when two diachronic content tokens are sufficiently similar for the later one to be able to be memory-related to the earlier one. An answer to this question will be given in section 8.3. Sixth, the attitude condition for inwardly remembering calls for a criterion for the similarity of psychological attitudes. Such a criterion is proposed in section 8.6.

2

Personal Identity and Memory

In sections 1.5 and 1.6 I have maintained that introversive memory and extroversive memory in the first-person mode presuppose that the bearer of the present representation is the same as the bearer of the past representation. For when a memory content involves an indexical reference to the rememberer, the veridicality constraint on memory demands that the rememberer is numerically the same as the one who had the original experience/representation. In what follows, I will investigate how the notion of personal identity is related to the notion of memory. Is the dependence of memory on personal identity of a logical or a contingent kind? I will argue that memory does not imply personal identity. The dependence relation between these two notions is of a contingent rather than a logical nature.

Section 2.1 explains the so-called *circularity objection* to the memory criterion of personal identity and explains the solution in terms of quasi-memory. Section 2.2 contains a critical discussion of the main reasons for thinking that quasi-memory is incoherent or that it is nothing but a derivative from memory. Section 2.3 discusses further objections to the memory criterion of personal identity.

2.1 THE CIRCULARITY OBJECTION

The problem of personal identity consists in the question of what it is for a person existing at one time and a person existing at another time to be one and the same person. According to the bodily criterion, personal identity is derived from the physical continuity of a single living body: a person at t_2 is co-personal with a person at t_1 only if the bodily state of the person at t_2 is a state of the same body as the state of the person at t_1. According to the psychological criterion of personal identity, the numerical identity of persons over time is due to the continuity of some mental or psychological property: a person at t_2 is co-personal with a person at t_1 only if the respective mental states are the same or suitably connected and continuous with each other. Personal identity consists in strong psychological connection and/or psychological continuity. The majority of philosophers subscribe to some version of the psychological criterion of personal identity.

What is it for a person existing at one time to be psychologically continuous with a person existing at another? This question was first posed by John Locke (1979: 328–48). Locke is customarily interpreted as claiming that experiential memory connectedness is the main ingredient of psychological continuity. On this view, a person who exists at one time is identical with a person who exists at another time if and only if the former person can, at the former time, remember an experience the latter person had at the latter time, or *vice versa*. Apart from experiential memories, psychological continuity is constituted by the suitable relation between intentions and actions as well as the persistence of beliefs, character traits, values, etc.

Remembering having experienced E at some time in the past is remembering *oneself* having experienced E at that time. A reference to oneself, now remembering, enters into the content of experiential memory. Since I can experientially remember only what has in fact occurred to me, I can experientially remember myself having had E at some time in the past only if it was in fact me who had E at that time. I can *seem* to remember experiences which are not mine but such seeming memories are no basis for claims of personal identity. Therefore, if memory connectedness is to be a criterion of personal identity, we must have some way of distinguishing between genuine and ostensible experiential memory. But this distinction, the *circularity objection* continues, is nothing but that genuine memories are ostensible memories in which the rememberer and the experiencer are the same person. Since the notion of experiential memory *implies* the notion of personal identity, experiential memory cannot be used to *define* personal identity. While someone's remembering having experienced E is a sufficient condition of his having experienced E, we cannot use the former as a criterion for the latter, since in order to establish that a person really does remember having experienced E we have to establish that he, that very person, has experienced E. Joseph Butler (1896: 388) was the first to formulate this objection to the memory criterion of personal identity.

The circularity objection rests on something like the following account of experiential memory: S remembers at t_2 an experience E only if:

(1) S is at t_2 in a state as if remembering E,
(2) S had at t_1 experience E^*,
(3) E is identical with, or sufficiently similar to, E^*,
(4) S's state at t_2 as if remembering E is suitably causally connected to S's having had E^* at t_1.

The four conditions may be labeled, respectively, the *present representation condition* (1), the *past experience condition* (2), the *content condition* (3), and the *connection condition* (4). This account of experiential memory presupposes personal identity because 'S' in condition (1) and in condition (2) refer to diachronic stages of the same person. But if experiential memory presupposes the co-personality of diachronic stages, it is circular to explain personal identity in terms of experiential memory.

Sydney Shoemaker (2003b: 23–4) and Derek Parfit (1984: 219–23) propose to solve the circularity objection by getting rid of the identity-involving conditions for experiential memory. They suggest rephrasing the past experience condition (2) thus:

(2') Someone had at t_1 experience E^*.

Moreover, the connection condition (4) is rephrased as reading:

(4') S's state at t_2 as if remembering E is suitably causally connected to someone's having had E^* at t_1.

When condition (2') is substituted for (2) and when condition (4') is substituted for (4), it is possible for one person to 'remember' an experience had by another person.[1] Shoemaker and Parfit are fully aware that this way of speaking conflicts with the ordinary usage of the term 'to remember'. They therefore introduce the notion of *quasi-memory*. S can remember only experiences had by himself, but he can quasi-remember someone else's experiences. S quasi-remembers at t_2 an experience E only if:

(1) S is at t_2 in a state as if remembering E,
(2') Someone had at t_1 experience E^*,

---

[1] Condition (5) requires that someone had at t_1 experience E^*. In sect. 5.3 I will argue that S cannot (quasi-)remember at t_2 an experience E if there was no one at t_1 who had experience E^* but if the relevant memory trace was created *in vitro* rather than transplanted from someone else. Artificially created memory traces don't give rise to (quasi-)memories.

(3) E is identical with, or sufficiently similar to, E*,
(4') S's state at t_2 as if remembering E is suitably causally connected to someone's having had E* at t_1.

Quasi-memory is supposed to be like ordinary experiential memory in all phenomenal and causal respects, except that it is not restricted to experiences of one's own past. Quasi-memory doesn't presuppose that the bearer of the past experience is co-personal with the bearer of the present state of seeming to remember having had that experience.

A world in which there is quasi-memory differs from our world in at least one of three aspects. First, in some such worlds memory traces are transplanted or copied from one person to another, as it is illustrated in Parfit's (1984: 221) story 'Venetian Memories' discussed before (pp. 41–2): S has been to Venice and remembers seeing the church of San Giorgio Maggiore. S* has never been to Venice nor has he ever seen a picture of the church of San Giorgio Maggiore. But after an operation in which some of S's memory traces are instilled in S*'s brain, S* finds himself endowed with what seems like a recollection of looking at San Giorgio Maggiore. Granted that S and S* had not been co-personal before the operation, S* quasi-remembers, rather than remembers, S's Venetian experiences.

Second, some worlds in which there is quasi-memory are worlds where there are cases of *fission*. Imagine that the hemispheres of your brain are functionally equivalent and that each on its own is capable of sustaining all your experiential memories. Imagine further that they are separated and each one is transplanted into a new body. When the anesthesia has worn off, two persons wake up apparently remembering a lot of the experiences you had before the operation. These fission-products cannot both be numerically identical with you without being numerically identical with each other. Given that memory implies personal identity, the fission-products merely quasi-remember your past.[2]

---

[2] Given fission, the psychological account of personal identity appears to have the impossible consequence that one thing could be identical with two things. There are two strategies for avoiding this consequence. First, it can be argued that, despite appearances, 'you' were really two persons all along. There were two different but exactly similar persons in the same place and made of the same matter at once, doing the same things and thinking the same thoughts. The surgeon merely separated them. This is the *multiple-occupancy view* defended by David Lewis (1983). The second strategy is to revise the original claim that mental continuity, by itself, is sufficient for persistence over time. You are identical with a past or future being who is mentally continuous with you as you are now only if no one else is then mentally continuous

Third, some worlds in which there is quasi-memory contain cases of *fusion*, where two distinct people are both psychologically continuous with a later person. Parfit (1984: 298) describes a situation of fusion, where two people are merged together with their mental attributes either both remaining (for non-conflicting attributes), or else assuming an averaged value. Given that identity is a one–one relation, fusion destroys personal identity and the fused person can merely quasi-remember past experiences. Cases of fission and fusion are commonly summarized under the heading of *branching*.

Let's examine the proposal of quasi-memory in more detail. Suppose I claim at t_2, on the basis of quasi-memory, that I φed at t_1. Further suppose that, due to my having been subjected to fission between t_1 and t_2, it wasn't me who φed at t_1 but—to use Parfit's expression—an earlier self. On most accounts of the meaning of 'I', my claim regarding my having φed at t_1 is false.[3] But then what, if anything, distinguishes quasi-memory from ostensible memory? Shoemaker's idea is that while an ostensible memory misattributes an experience one did not in fact have as one's own, a quasi-memory characterizes the experience without reference to sameness of person. To have a quasi-memory is to have a properly caused memory and to hold no view about whose memory it is. Quasi-memories don't present themselves in the first-person mode ('I φed in the past') but in the third-person mode ('someone φed in the past'). As Shoemaker (2003*b*: 24) explains, 'the claim to quasi-remember a past event implies only that someone or other was aware of it'. The notion of quasi-memory is like ordinary memory in providing us with information about the past and unlike ordinary memory in that its content doesn't touch upon the question of whose past is concerned. Quasi-memories are memories without a 'nametag'.[4]

---

with you. If your cerebral hemispheres are transplanted into different bodies, that is the end of you, even though you would persist if only one were transplanted and the other destroyed. This is the *non-branching view* defended by Wiggins (1967: 55).

[3] It might be argued that when 'I' occurs in the content of a state of seeming to remember it refers to any earlier self rather than to the very person-stage that is co-personal with the person-stage occupying the state of seeming to remember. Discussing this proposal would take us too far afield.

[4] There are subtle differences between Shoemaker's and Parfit's explication of quasi-memory. According to Parfit, the content of a quasi-memory is egocentrically indexded. In having a quasi-memory one is mistaken in taking the experience to have been one's own. I will focus on Shoemaker's explication of quasi-memory whereupon quasi-memories are experienced in the third-person mode of presentation. Giberman (2009: 300–3), however, argues that Shoemaker too conceives of quasi-memories as having *de se* form.

The concept of quasi-memory is introduced to aid a reductive analysis of the concept of personal identity. But how can personal identity be defined without circularity in terms of quasi-memory? Personal identity is said to consist in having quasi-memories that are linked by a non-branching causal chain with the relevant past experiences. More precisely, S at t_1 is identical to S* at t_2 only if S* is strongly psychologically connected and continuous with S, where this involves the existence of quasi-memory connections and there exists at t_2 no other S** who has equal or stronger psychological continuity with S.

Given that the circularity objection concerns the notion of memory, not that of quasi-memory, how does the introduction of quasi-memory help with the circularity objection? Shoemaker's and Parfit's idea is that experiential memories are a 'sub-class', a 'special case' of quasi-memories: they are quasi-memories in which the experiencer and the rememberer are the same person. Anyone who is in a state of remembering having had experience E is in a state of quasi-remembering having had experience E. And because quasi-memory doesn't imply personal identity, memory doesn't either. Whenever we remember having an experience, then, as a matter of fact, the memory experience corresponds to, and is causally related to, an experience that we ourselves had. But such an exceptionless empirical uniformity, Shoemaker and Parfit think, should not be confused with logical necessity. That memory presupposes personal identity is a contingent fact having to do with the kind of world we inhabit rather than a necessary fact. In our world, all quasi-remembering is remembering. But if branching did occur in our world, there would be cases of quasi-remembering that are not cases of remembering.

2.2 A DEFENSE OF QUASI-MEMORY

For the concept of quasi-memory to provide a solution to the circularity objection quasi-memory must be conceptually independent both from genuine memory and ostensible memory. Yet the conceptual independence of quasi-memory has come under attack: there are objections from constitutive holism, from the causal theory of memory, and from the immunity to error through misidentification. To anticipate my conclusion, I think that the notion of quasi-memory is indeed coherent and is not a derivative from the concept of memory. Introversive memory and extroversive memory in the first-person mode depend on personal identity, but it is a mistake to think that this dependence is of a logical nature.[5]

Constitutive Holism

One way to argue for the logical dependence of memory on the diachronic quantitative identity of the rememberer is to assume what Mark Slors (2001: 193) calls 'constitutive holism', a position advocated by Marya Schechtman (1990), Slors himself, and Richard Wollheim (1984: 113). Constitutive holism has it that if a brain state bearing a memory trace is transferred from you to me then, due to the difference in mental context, the content of my quasi-memory may be substantially different from the content of your memory. A memory trace in your brain undergoes a change of content when it is implanted in my brain, for the trace's content depends both on the presence of other mental states which are possessed by you but not by me, and on the absence of mental states that are possessed by me but not by you. Cases of quasi-memory are not just cases in which the quasi-memory differs qualitatively from the experience that caused it; rather, they are cases in which there is no similarity in content between the newly inserted brain state and its causal origin. For if inferential and evidential connections co-constitute mental content, as the holist claims, the clash between a quasi-memory and its newly acquired psychological context will result in the quasi-memory's having a very different content or, rather, no content at all. And if a mental state could somehow be transferred without the content being affected, the transferred state would lose the 'identity-neutrality' essential to its being a quasi-memory and would thus collapse into delusional memory. So, Schechtman (1990: 84–5) declares: 'The fact . . . that presuppositions about who has a memory are inseparable from its content means that one cannot, as Parfit claims, specify nondelusionality impersonally by keeping the content of a memory and simply deleting presuppositions about whose memory it is.' Schechtman's point is that the whole frame of mind by which a recollection is co-constituted is linked to the whole frame of mind by which the original experience was co-constituted, without it being possible to single out the causal connection that link individual mental states.

---

[5] I will not discuss the question of whether the notion of quasi-memory can figure in explanation only by presupposing an explanatory function for memory and by presupposing individual identity over time. For this see Burge (2003: 309–22).

Wollheim illustrates the point of constitutive holism in terms of an example. He asks us to imagine what it would be like for him to quasi-remember his father as a boy walking to school through the streets of Breslau. Wollheim claims that the hypothetical quasi-memory is not intelligible. Many other dispositions, such as beliefs, emotions, desires, fears, and other memories, would have to be transferred along with the original quasi-memory if it were to transfer from one person to another. If he were to quasi-remember his father's childhood walks he would have to have

a native speaker's knowledge of German: a capacity to imagine intense cold: a sense of the aspirations of a late nineteenth-century Central European schoolboy: a familiarity . . . with the details of [his] father's family, with the books he would have read, with the thoughts he would be inclined to have when he looked up into the sky, or smelled the smell of soup, with the religion, if any, in which he was brought up, and many other such dispositions which would be backgrounded, if not foregrounded, in the quasi-memory.

(1984: 113–14)

In addition, he would have to lose many of his own dispositions in order to accommodate these quasi-memories, such as his ignorance and subsequent curiosity about his father's family. Wollheim concludes that what he calls 'centered event-memories' cannot cross to another life.

In response to Wollheim's and Schechtman's objections to the conception of memory-trace copying, I shall raise three concerns. First, neuropsychological research suggests that the quasi-memory of an experience can indeed be detached from the psychological context it used to be a part of and that the constitutive holist's argument from inseparability is problematic. People suffering from retrograde amnesia frequently lose their memories of some period of their lives and then gradually recover their memories in bits and pieces. The recovered memories arrive devoid of the psychological context that was present when the experience was originally encountered (cf. Schnider et al. 1996).

Second, dissociative disorders such as schizophrenia and multiple personality disorder speak against Schechtman's claim that the mineness of a psychological state cannot be separated from its content (Northoff 2000: 207–8). People suffering from these dissociative disorders manage to integrate 'memories' from a seemingly foreign psychology into their mind frame. The personalities of someone suffering from multiple personality disorder can differ from one another in their psychology (character traits, preferences, attitudes, values, etc.), behavioral characteristics (voice, mannerisms, handwriting, etc.) and even their brain-wave patterns (Gillett 1991: 105). Consider the following fragment from the case history of a person with multiple personality disorder:

Although Martha was unaware of the existence of Harriet and was amnesic for the events that occurred while Harriet dominated consciousness, Harriet was aware of all that Martha knew, thought, and did. Each was a distinct personality, different from the other in terms of attitudes, likes, and dislikes, emotions and mood. The secondary personality (Harriet) experienced herself as an individual in her own right.[6]

Harriet remembered what Martha did, even though Harriet had a 'distinct personality', as well as a whole set of memories 'of her own life' that Martha lacked. There is even a documented case of an individual who spoke with a British accent and knew Arabic, while one of his alters spoke English with a Serbo-Croatian accent and knew Serbo-Croatian (Glover 1988: 21).

To avoid misunderstanding, I should stress I do not take the psychological data to *prove* the falsity of constitutive holism. After all, the patients suffering from retrograde amnesia who report the arrival of (recovered) memories in bits and pieces may be wrong in claiming that the original psychological context is absent. The case of amnesia doesn't show that memories can exist in isolation from their psychological context, it shows only that the amnesiac patient believes that their memories can be so isolated (Roache 2006: 342). Moreover, the fact that someone can lose a given memory and later recover it devoid of psychological context does not show that another person can do the same with the same memory. But notwithstanding the fact that the psychological data don't disprove constitutive holism they do cast doubt on its empirical plausibility.

Third, even if we grant Wollheim that his example of quasi-memory is problematic, there are other examples that are perfectly intelligible. Consider Parfit's (1984: 75–80) case of a person whose brain is divided into two identical halves and each half is housed in a new body. If before division either half is psychologically redundant, then after division each

---

[6] Nemiah 1979: 311. Psychologists and psychiatrists are in dispute over whether multiple personality disorder is a genuine condition. A good source for discussion on this matter is Hacking (1995: 8–20). Hacking thinks there are reasons for thinking that multiple personality does exist.

of the resulting persons has all the psychological characteristics of the donor, including quasi-memories of the donor's life. Since each of the resulting persons inherits *all* the donor's memories—rather than merely an isolated set of them—along with his character, likes and dislikes, habits, phobias, and so on, the fission scenario escapes the objections to quasi-memory brought forward by constitutive holists.

Instead of constitutive holism, I adopt content externalism, that is, the view that the individuation of mental contents depends on systematic relations that the subject bears with certain conditions of his physical and social environment (cf. Ch. 6). Content externalism is inclined towards some kind of psychological atomism and hence allows for quasi-memory. Psychological atomism is the view that the contents of (quasi-)memories don't depend upon the memory's psychological context but instead on the causes that produce the brain state upon which they supervene. Given atomism, the transfer of memory traces from one person to another doesn't violate the content condition for remembering—provided both individuals inhabit roughly the same physical and social environment.

Memory Causation

Both memory and quasi-memory require a suitable causal relation between a present state of seeming to remember having had an experience and the having of that experience in the past. As will become clear in Chapter 5, it is quite tricky to specify the requisite causal relation. Following Shoemaker (2003*b*: 35–6), we can call the specific causal relation that must obtain between a past experience and a present state of quasi-remembering that experience the *M-type causal chain*. And let's call the causal chain constitutive of remembering the *N-type causal chain*. Shoemaker tries to make quasi-memory as much like memory as possible, consistent with quasi-memories not being restricted to experiences of one's own past. Given this goal, he defines personal identity in terms of having quasi-memories which are connected by non-branching M-type causal chains to experiences. The M-type causal chain is said to be like the N-type causal chain, except that the former allows for branching and interpersonal memory transplants.

But now the suspicion arises that the M-type causal chain is a derivative from the N-type causal chain and consequently that quasi-memory is a derivative from memory. The crucial question is whether the M-type causal chain can be characterized independently of the notion of personal identity. Harold Noonan (2003: 156–62) argues that we have reason to doubt that this can be done. To determine whether the causal link between diachronic mental states is of type M as opposed to type N, one must have reason to suspect that the bearers of the two states are not co-personal. Unless one has evidence that speaks against identifying the bearer of the present mental state with the bearer of the past mental state it is inappropriate to suggest that the causal chain in question is of type M rather than type N. What this shows then, according to Noonan (ibid.: 160), is that the notion of the M-type causal chain can be defined only in relation to the notion of the N-type causal chain.

[O]ne can determine that someone is quasi-remembering only by determining that he is (at least) an *offshoot* of the person whose life he apparently remembers . . . and one can determine that this is so only by considering the applicability of the concept of personal identity to the . . . situation in which no competing candidate for identity with that earlier person is available.

What this is supposed to show is that the concept of quasi-memory presupposes the concept of personal identity. Contrary to Shoemaker's and Parfit's contention, quasi-memory is a sub-class of genuine memory; or so Noonan thinks.

I am skeptical of Noonan's argument. The only reason we characterize M-type causal chains in terms of N-type causal chains is that we are more familiar with the former than the latter. Yet if we lived in a world where quasi-memory was a common occurrence and memory was rare, we would take M-type causal chains as explanatorily fundamental and characterize N-type causal chains in terms of them. Which of the two notions functions as explicans and which functions as explicandum has to do with contingent facts about our linguistic practice. The crux with Noonan's argument is that it seems to confuse these contingent facts for logical ones.

Immunity to Error through Misidentification

One of the most obstinate objections to Shoemaker's and Parfit's claim that the concept of experiential memory does not imply diachronic identity stems from Gareth Evans and John McDowell. The debate between Shoemaker and Parfit, on the one hand, and Evans and McDowell, on the other, comes down to the issue of whether first-person judgments based on experiential memories enjoy a logical or only a de facto immunity to error through misidentification. Shoemaker and Parfit hold that the possibility of quasi-memory shows that first-person judgments based on memories are not necessarily immune to error through misidentification.[7] Evans and McDowell, on the other hand, maintain that because first-person judgments based on memories are necessarily immune to misidentification reports of quasi-memories express nothing but memory illusions. I side with Shoemaker and Parfit in this debate.

The notion of immunity to error through misidentification was introduced by Shoemaker (2003*a*) in an effort to shed light on Wittgenstein's discussion in the *Blue Book* of the difference between the use of the first-person pronoun 'I' as subject and the use of 'I' as object. When I say 'I have a black eye' it is just possible that it is not my eye but someone else's that is black. Now in the 'subject' case this is not possible: someone who says 'I am in pain' could not be right to think that someone was in pain but wrong about who it was. This is a fact about the grammar of 'I' as a subject term. Wittgenstein declares: 'To say, "I have pain" is no more a statement about a particular person than moaning is' (1960: 67; see also 1958: §§ 404–8). In Shoemaker's terminology, first-person beliefs that would be expressed using 'I' as subject are immune to error through misidentification. Those that would be expressed using 'I' as object are vulnerable to error through misidentification. Shoemaker (2003*a*: 7–8) defines immunity to error through misidentification thus:

[T]o say that a statement 'a is φ' is subject to error through misidentification relative to the term 'a' means that the following is possible: the speaker knows some particular thing to be φ, but makes the mistake of asserting 'a is φ' because, and only because, he mistakenly thinks that the thing he knows to be φ is what 'a' refers to.

In the previous section we saw that what distinguishes quasi-memory from ostensible memory is that the former characterizes the past experience or event without reference to sameness of person. Suppose I claim to remember that someone saw a tree burn last night. In situations where I suspect or know that my own apparent memories are

---

[7] Initially Shoemaker held that memory judgments do exhibit immunity to error through misidentification: 'But the appropriate way of expressing the retained (memory) knowledge that at the time of its acquisition was expressed by the sentence "I see a canary" is to utter the past-tense version of that sentence, namely, "I saw a canary." This, if said on the basis of memory, does not involve an identification and is not subject to error through misidentification' (2003*a*: 10).

quasi-memories it can make sense for me to say, on the basis of my
apparent memories, 'Someone saw a tree burning last night, but was it
I?' I may be in a position to know that someone saw a tree burn, but not
in a position to know that I am the person who saw it. The utterance
of a quasi-memory claim, however, is only coherent if expressions of
quasi-memory are identification-dependent and thus vulnerable to error
through misidentification. An inference is required to establish myself
as the real subject of the experiences my quasi-memories report. Given
Shoemaker's and Parfit's thesis that experiential memory is a sub-class
of quasi-memory, it follows that experiential memory judgments too are
identification-dependent.

This is where Evans digs in his heels. First-person judgments based
on experiential memory, he claims, do not involve any identification
component; they are 'identification-free'. One need not go through a
process of identifying oneself as the person who in the past had the experience in question. And from the fact that first-person judgments based
on experiential memory are identification-free Evans follows that they
are, as a matter of principle, immune to error through misidentification.
He writes, '[The] operation of memory . . . seems to exemplify the phenomenon of immunity to error through misidentification. When the
first component expresses knowledge which the subject has gained . . . in
this way, it does not appear to make sense for him to say "Someone saw
a tree burning last night, but was it I?" '[8] Given that I can entertain the
possibility of quasi-memory in such a way that an inference would be
required to establish myself as the real subject of the experiences reported
by my quasi-memories, Shoemaker and Parfit assume that likewise in
the case of my genuine experiential memories an inference is required
to establish that I am the subject of the relevant past experiences. Evans
thinks this assumption is mistaken. And so his point is that advocates of
quasi-memory get things backwards: our genuine experiential memories
exhibit immunity to error through misidentification and it is only in
unusual circumstances that the self-attribution of past experiences is
based on inferences. Therefore, experiential memory is not a kind of
quasi-memory.

[8] 1982: 240–1. William James (1890: i. 273–4n3) gives the following example of someone
being confused about whose memories he is having: 'We were driving . . . in a wagonette; the
door flew open and X, alias "Baldy", fell out on the road. We pulled up at once, and then
he said "Did anyone fall out?" or "Who fell out?" . . . When told that Baldy fell out, he said
"Did Baldy fall out? Poor Baldy!" '.

If experiential memory were identification-dependent, we would have to regard a first-person judgment based on experiential memory such as 'I saw a burning tree last night' as dividable into the two components, 'Someone saw a burning tree last night' and 'That someone is me.' Parfit (1984: 222) explicitly endorses such a two-part analysis:

Because we do not have quasi-memory of other people's past experiences, our apparent memories do not merely come to us in the first-person mode. They come with a belief that, unless they are delusions, they are about our own experiences. But, in the case of experience-memories, this is a separable belief. If . . . we had quasi-memories of other people's past experience, these apparent memories would cease to be automatically combined with this belief.

The problem Evans has with analyzing 'I saw a burning tree last night' as consisting in two components is that it does not correspond to psychological and epistemic reality. Consider the identity judgment 'That someone is me.' What does 'that someone' mean? Presumably it means a description of the following sort: the man whose past informational states are causally responsible for these apparent memories. Evans (1982: 244) argues that while it might be adequate to ascribe such an idea to someone who suspects or knows that his apparent memories are only quasi-memories, 'it is surely far-fetched in the extreme to suppose that such an Idea is generally involved in our past-tense self-ascriptions'. Evans (ibid. 245–6) concludes that 'for a subject to have information (or misinformation) . . . to the effect that *someone* saw a tree, just is for the subject to have information (or misinformation) to the effect that *he* saw a tree'. In experiential memory the experience-component cannot be separated from the ownership-component.

I agree with Evans that first-person judgments based on experiential memories usually don't involve identification components. But it does not follow from this that such judgments are *in principle* immune to error through misidentification. My judgment that I saw a tree burning last night may be vulnerable to certain sorts of misidentification error, even though having justification for the judgment does not require me to consider those errors and rule them out. I need not engage in a process of identification for the justification to rely on identification. So the fact that a judgment is identification-free does not show that it is immune to errors of misidentification (Pryor 1999: 292).

John McDowell expands on Evans's critique of quasi-memory. When I don't suspect that I might be merely quasi-remembering, my apparent experiential memories present themselves in the first-person mode—their contents represent *me* as having had the experiences in question. But, McDowell (1997: 238–44) argues, even when I am informed that my memory-like states are merely quasi-memories, their contents don't become impersonal. Quasi-memories still present themselves as identity-involving memories. The only difference is that I am aware that the identity-involving component of my states of seeming to remember is illusory. Just as in the Müller-Lyer illusion the pair of lines present themselves in perception as unequal in length even after I have come to know that they are the same length, there is no switch in content when I am informed that my memory-like states are merely quasi-memories. From this McDowell concludes that it is a mistake to think of quasi-memory as an identity-free version of a genuine memory. Quasi-memories are derivative from genuine memories in the same way that illusions are derivative from veridical perceptions.

I agree with McDowell in that experiential memory presents events as having occurred in one's own past life. I even agree with McDowell in that this may not change when one is made aware of the possibility of quasi-memory. Yet from all this it does not follow that it is impossible for the identification component of a first-person judgment based on experiential memories to be incorrect and for the content component to be correct. Evans's and McDowell's arguments only establish de facto immunity. But since quasi-memory is subjectively indistinguishable from ordinary experiential memory, it follows that the latter is in principle open to error through misidentification, although contingently not actually affected by it. Experiential memory has only a circumstantial immunity to error through misidentification.

Where does all this leave us? We saw in section 2.1 that unless the notion of quasi-memory is conceptually independent from both genuine and ostensible memory the memory criterion of personal identity falls foul of Butler's circularity objection. In this section we looked at three reasons for doubting that there could be, to quote McDowell (ibid. 241), 'an autonomously intelligible faculty of knowing the past from a participant's perspective but without commitment to the participant's having been oneself'. None of these reasons held up to scrutiny. The circularity objection fails since memory presupposes personal identity only as a matter of contingent fact, not as a matter of logical necessity. Memory only contingently guarantees identity. When I seem to remember an experience it is merely an assumption I make that I am identical with the person who had the experience, an assumption justified by the contingent non-prevalence of quasi-memory. Yet if I lived in a world where fission happened on a regular basis I would not be in the habit of concluding 'I φed' on the basis of my (quasi-)memory of experiences of φing. Instead I would conclude 'I φed or one of my fission ancestors φed.' The disjunctive conclusion is true regardless of whether I remember or only quasi-remember. But the disjunctive conclusion is also superfluous since none of us has fission ancestors.

2.3 THE CONSTITUTION OF PERSONS

After having defended the psychological criterion of personal identity against the circularity objection it is time to consider some of the (alleged) weaknesses of this account of personal identity. In this section I will examine Wollheim's charge that the account of personal identity in terms of psychological continuity oversimplifies the nature of memory and Schechtman's charge that it oversimplifies what is involved in the constitution of a person.

According to Wollheim, the account of personal identity in terms of psychological continuity in general and memory connections in particular is a distortion, for it fails to adequately explain the nature of a person's life. More precisely, the psychological account of personal identity is thought to provide an inadequate explanation of the relation between a person's life and his psychology, where 'psychology' refers to the relationship among a person's mental states and mental dispositions of imagination, memory, phantasy, desires, belief, and so on. To understand how a person's psychology is related to his life, Wollheim thinks, we must take into consideration how the person's psychology brings about the life.

The standard account of personal identity—Wollheim calls it the 'relational account'—takes memory to be a cognitive relation to the past and to thereby constitute personal continuity: if two events stand in the relation of being experiential memories of the same past event, they belong to the life of one and the same person. What the relational account overlooks, according to Wollheim, is that memory not only has a role in retaining the past but also has a forward-looking function. It keeps the past alive by giving it meaning for one's ongoing relationships and projects. Furthermore, the relational account assumes that there is a sharp difference between feelings about the past and memories of the past: one's feelings about a past event may change, one's memory of the event is constant. Wollheim points out that experiential memory always involves an element of feeling or affect and that this affective element is in part responsible for both the continuities and the disturbances of memory. Memories 'preserve and transmit the influence of some earlier event . . . partly through, their psychic force' (1984: 99). By leaving out memory's affective element, the relational account of personal identity misses what enables our memories to have the influence they have on our lives and their persistence.

On Wollheim's conception, memory is not just a means for checking on the continuity of a person's life over time, but also constitutes a person's life. The past affects people in such a way that they become 'creatures with a past: creatures, that is, tied to the past in the way peculiar to persons' (1979: 224). Memories are, as Wollheim puts it, a threading of our lives, not merely threads in them; hence the title of his book *The Thread of Life*. Memories are able to act as evidence of a past only because they carry the influence of the past by giving rise to feelings and desires. He writes:

It is . . . an oversimplification to think that the survival of the influence of a past event consists solely in the establishment of a disposition, which . . . manifests itself . . . in concurrent mental states, which enforce this influence. For such is the nature of these mental states . . . that they can have the effect of modifying or refashioning the dispositions that they manifest as well as the more standard effect of reinforcing them. They can impinge not only on the strength of the dispositions, or the way in which they bind the energies of the person, but also on their content or intentionality. . . . The feedback from mental state to mental disposition is an essential element in the way in which we try to control the lives that we lead. (1984: 99–100)

The upshot of Wollheim's critique of the relational theory of personal identity is that when memory is construed as an affective-free purely backward-looking phenomenon it is too meager a basis on which to rest the identity of a person's life.

A vital assumption of Wollheim's argument is that the relational theory of personal identity is meant to explain the nature and unity of a person's life. But is this assumption correct? Presumably proponents of the psychological criterion of personal identity do not see themselves as being concerned with the explanation of a person's life. Their goal is much more modest consisting in an account of what makes a sequence of events belong to the same person. Yet having said that, Wollheim does have a point insofar as the project of investigating into the nature and unity of a person's life should have primacy over the project of exploring the continuity of the life of a person.

Like Wollheim, Schechtman thinks that the literature on the psychological continuity theory of personal identity narrowly focuses on the 're-identification question' (what makes someone the *same* person over time?) and largely ignores the 'characterization question' (what is it *to be* a particular person?). The characterization question is not about identity understood as 'the relation which every object bears to itself and nothing else', but rather as 'the set of characteristics that make a person who she is' (Schechtman 1996: 75–6). It is about the kind of identity that is at issue in an identity crisis. Schechtman's suggestion is that unless we consider the characterization question, we will not make progress regarding the four issues that underlie and motivate the philosophical issue of personal identity: the possibility of survival over time, compensation for past hardship, concerns for future projects, and moral responsibility.

In response to the characterization question Schechtman develops a narrative self-constitution view the main idea of which is that what makes an action, experience, or psychological characteristic properly attributable to some person (and thus a proper part of his identity) is its correct incorporation into the self-told story of his life. A person 'creates his identity by forming an autobiographical narrative—a story of his life' (ibid. 93). In these autobiographical stories past, present, and future events have a meaning that is determined by all the other elements in the story. The narrative structure, Schechtman claims, is 'an organizing principle of our lives' and 'the lens through which we filter our experience and plans for action' (ibid. 113). Persons create their identities by 'coming to think of themselves as persisting subjects who have had experience in the past and will continue to have experience in the future' (ibid. 94).

Identity constituting narratives are governed by a reality constraint and an articulation constraint. Schechtman holds that for a narrative to constitute identity it may not contain gross errors of important publicly observable facts or their interpretation. A person's narrative must 'cohere with what we might call the "objective" account of her life—roughly the story that those around her would tell' (ibid. 95). Moreover, the composition of an autobiography, Schechtman claims, need not be explicit. Rather it only requires 'organizing experience according to an implicit narrative' (ibid. 114). Nevertheless, a person must be in a position to access and articulate parts of his implicit narrative in order to make sense of his own actions and feelings.

Schechtman proposes that her narrative self-constitution view retains what is plausible about the psychological continuity theory of personal identity, namely that a person is identified with his psychological life. But she also portrays her view as an 'alternative' to the psychological continuity theory (ibid. 136). The reason is that, on her view, the ontological primitive of a person is not a time-slice or person-stage, but a self-constituting narrative. Another difference between her view and the psychological continuity theory is that the connection between a person and his body is not considered to be more or less accidental. We reidentify persons by their bodies and it is part of our concept of a person that we do so.

Though I am sympathetic to the view according to which there is a sense in which we are the authors of our lives, it strikes me that Schechtman's self-narrative account is just as one-dimensional as the traditional one. While the standard view fails to pay sufficient attention to the characterization question the narrative account seems to fail to pay sufficient attention to the reidentification question. For the question about identity over time is not addressed, let alone answered by the narrative self-constitution view. The traditional problem cases—fission, fusion, body swap, etc.—don't disappear just because we adopt the narrative self-constitution view. These are problems with which any account of personal identity must deal and the self-narrative account seems to have no way of doing so.[9]

Narrative identity cannot replace numerical identity. Instead narrative identity assumes the presence of numerical identity. For a person's narrative to render certain experiences as unified into the life of a person the narrative must be of *one and the same* individual. Narrative identity presupposes numerical identity, and what its advocates maintain is just that narrative identity accounts for our practical concerns in a way numerical identity cannot. In sum, Schechtman's proposal should be regarded as a friendly amendment rather than an alternative to the psychological continuity theory of personal identity.

[9] Mark Reid (1997: 217–18) develops a narrative fission case.

3

Remembering without Knowing

Since the publication of Gilbert Ryle's *The Concept of Mind* in the late 1940s, most philosophers have come to advocate a view of propositional memory according to which remembering that p entails knowing that p. Memory is thought to be long-standing or continuing knowledge. In his classic monograph on memory Don Locke (1971: 39) declares: 'Memory consists. . .in immediate knowledge of the past; memory is to be thought of . . . as a form of knowledge. Certainly, this has come to be the standard contemporary account of the nature of memory; to remember something is to know it, where this knowledge has been acquired in the past.' The point of this chapter is to show that despite its widespread acceptance the so-called *epistemic theory of memory* is mistaken. What passes into memory may be merely a representation or belief, not knowledge. Memory works in a myriad of ways, sometimes neither beginning with nor ending with knowledge. There are instances where memory, though hitting the mark of truth, succeeds in an epistemically defective way.

Section 3.1 explains the epistemic analysis of memory. Section 3.2 argues that it is not necessary for propositional memory that the proposition in question be justifiably believed when it was originally acquired or that it be justifiably believed when it is recalled. Sections 3.3 and 3.4 challenge the epistemic theory of memory by arguing that one can remember something without believing it. Section 3.5 deals with the analysis of inferential memory. Finally section 3.6 argues for memory being a generative source of knowledge.

3.1 THE EPISTEMIC ANALYSIS OF MEMORY

The epistemic theory of memory consists of two interrelated claims. The first claim is that to remember a proposition is to know it. Robert Audi (2003: 69), a proponent of the epistemic theory, says that 'if you remember that we met, you know that we did. Similarly, if you remember me, you know me. ' Norman Malcolm (1963: 223; 1977: 102–8) defines propositional memory thus: 'A person B remembers that p if and only if B knows that p because he knew that p.' And Avishai Margalit (2002: 14) writes: 'To remember now is to know now what you knew in the past, without learning in-between what you know now. And to know is to believe something to be true. Memory, then, is *knowing from the past*'. The identification of memory with knowledge is not confined to the field of philosophy but is just as widespread among psychologists (cf. Gardiner and Richardson-Klavehn 2000).[1]

Proponents of the epistemic theory of memory also maintain that memory is not capable of generating new justification and knowledge. Just as testimony is said to transmit knowledge from one person to another, memory is said to preserve knowledge from one time to another. Both in the case of memorial knowledge and testimonial knowledge the proposition in question must have been known when it was originally acquired and a source other than memory and testimony, respectively, must have been responsible for its original acquisition. If one justifiedly believes that p on the basis of memory, then—so proponents of the epistemic theory claim—one must have acquired this justification in a non-memorial way at some earlier time. Memory cannot make a proposition acquire an epistemic status better than the one it had at the time it was originally acquired. Michael Dummett (1993: 420–1), for example, writes: 'Memory is not a *source*, still less a *ground*, of knowledge: it is the maintenance of knowledge formerly acquired by whatever means.' Alvin Plantinga (1993: 61 n22) makes the same point when he writes:

[M]emory beliefs depend, for their warrant, upon the warrant of *earlier* beliefs. I have an orange for breakfast; if this belief has no warrant, then my later belief that I *had* an orange for breakfast will also have no warrant. Memory beliefs are like testimonial beliefs . . . the warrant they have is dependent upon the warrant enjoyed by an earlier belief.

---

[1] As well as by Audi, Malcolm, and Margalit, this aspect of the epistemic theory of memory is endorsed by Annis (1980: 324), Anscombe (1981*b*: 127), Ayer (1956: 138, 147–8), Dancy (1985: 187, 195), Dretske (1983: 361), Evans (1982: 235), Grice (1941: 344), Holland (1974: 359), Huemer (1999: 346), Landesman (1961: 59, 61), Margolis (1977: 188), Moore (1959: 214), Munsat (1967: 15–17), Owens (2000: 156), Pappas (1980: 129), Pollock (1974: 196; 1986: 55), Ryle (1949: 272-9), Shoemaker (2003*b*: 43), Squires (1969: 185), Unger (1972: 304), Williams (1973: 142), Williamson (2000: 37–8), and Zemach (1968: 529).

And Audi (1997: 410) says that 'we cannot know that p from memory unless we have come to know it in another way'. This aspect of the epistemic theory of memory is called *preservationism*.

Given that remembering that p entails knowing that p and given that memory cannot improve the epistemic status a proposition has at the time of recall vis-à-vis the epistemic status it had at the time it was originally acquired, it follows that one can remember that p only if, in the past, one knew that p. The epistemic theory of memory can be summarized like this: To remember that p is to know that p, where this knowledge was previously acquired and preserved. A source other than memory is responsible for the original acquisition of knowledge that p. Memory preserves rather than generates knowledge.

As was mentioned above, the epistemic theory is the standard contemporary account of propositional memory, drawing support from a wide variety of philosophers and only infrequent criticism. Notwithstanding its widespread acceptance, the epistemic theory of memory is mistaken. It is not necessary for memory that the representation in question be known either when it was originally acquired or when it is retrieved from memory. Furthermore, it is not the case that memory is unable to generate new justification and knowledge.

Proponents of the epistemic theory of memory analyze propositional memory in something like the following way: S remembers at t_2 that p only if:

(1) S knows at t_2 that p,
(2) S knew at t_1 that p^*,
(3) p is identical with, or sufficiently similar to, p^*,
(4) S's knowing at t_2 that p is suitably connected to S's knowing at t_1 that p^*.

Condition (1) may be labeled the *present knowledge condition*, (2) the *past knowledge condition*, (3) the *content condition*, and (4) the *connection condition*.

Three notes: first, there is at least one advocate of the epistemic theory of memory, namely Sydney Shoemaker, who thinks that memory doesn't *imply* personal identity and who might therefore object to the identity-involving formulation of the past knowledge condition and the connection condition (cf. sect. 2.1). Second, most proponents of the epistemic theory of memory also sign up to the identity theory of memory, that is, the thesis that for a propositional attitude token at t_2 to stand in a memory-relation to a propositional attitude token at

t_1, the contents of both tokens must be type-identical (cf. pp. 39–40 and sect. 8.2). Yet it is important to see that the epistemic theory of memory is not committed to the identity theory of memory. It is perfectly consistent to maintain that remembering is a form of knowing and, at the same time, allow for the memory content to be only similar to, but not identical with, the content of the relevant past knowledge. (Yet problems might arise when one also endorses the tracking theory of knowledge. I will return to this issue on pp. 79–81.) Third, proponents of the epistemic theory of memory tend to subscribe to the distinction between propositional memory and experiential memory. They use the term 'propositional memory' for those cases of remembering that p which don't involve qualitative experiences and imagery. Yet, as was explained before (cf. p. 20), I take the term 'propositional memory' to refer to *any* substituend of the schema 'S remembers that p', irrespective of whether or not 'p' refers to something one has personally experienced, and irrespective of whether the memory content consists merely of the proposition p or whether, in addition, it includes images and qualia.

The present knowledge condition (1) requires that to remember something is to occupy a state of knowing. The past knowledge condition (2) ensures that one can remember only what one previously knew. Note that since knowledge implies truth, the epistemic analysis of memory manages without a separate truth-condition. The past and present knowledge condition jointly guarantee that one can remember only what is the case. The content condition (3) ensures that the memory content is the same as, or sufficiently similar to the content of one's past knowledge state. Finally the purpose of the connection condition (4) is to exclude relearning from the ranks of remembering and to guarantee that the knowledge had in remembering is retained knowledge. The epistemic theory is compatible with a range of different conceptions of the nature of the memory connection.

Most epistemologists hold that the concept of propositional knowl-edge has three necessary conditions: justification,[2] truth, and belief. Knowledge is said to be justified true belief. The truth-condition states that if you know that p, then p is true. The belief condition claims

---

[2] I use the term 'justification' to refer to *any* factor that transforms a true belief into an instance of knowledge. Sometimes a much narrower concept of justification is used, one according to which what qualifies as a justificatory factor must be something that is cognitively accessible to the subject in such a way that he can always tell whether what he believes is justified or not.

that knowing that p implies believing that p. A person need not be absolutely certain that something is true in order to know that it is. The belief condition only requires some kind of acceptance in the interest of obtaining truth. (Whether knowledge implies belief is an issue I will come back to in sect. 3.4.)

The justification condition requires that a known proposition be evidentially supported. The justification condition is there to prevent lucky guesses from counting as knowledge when the guesser is sufficiently confident to believe his own guess. Gettier cases are paradigm examples of accidentally true beliefs. Consider this Gettier example by Keith Lehrer (1965): Two agents, S and S*, work in the same office. S* has given S evidence that justifies S in believing that S* owns a Ford. Imagine that S has seen S* driving a Ford, S has been told by persons who have in the past been reliable that S* owns a Ford, and so on. From this evidence S then infers the proposition *someone in the office owns a Ford*. The belief that someone in the office owns a Ford is true. But, unsuspected by S, S* has been shamming and the belief is only true because another person in the office, S**, owns a Ford. Does S know that someone in the office owns a Ford? The belief that someone in the office owns a Ford is true. Moreover, S is justified in believing that someone in the office owns a Ford (at least in senses of 'justification' that emphasize the internal or subjective). But we wouldn't want to say in this case that S has knowledge that someone in the office owns a Ford. The reason we deny S knowledge is that it just so happened that someone in the office owns a Ford, but not the person S thinks owns a Ford. It is merely good fortune or a happy accident that S arrives at a true belief.

Two broadly different diagnoses of Gettier cases can be distinguished—the orthodox *covariationist* diagnosis and the *identificationist* diagnosis. According to the covariationist reading, what prevents S from knowing someone in the office owns a Ford is the fact that, the truth of the proposition and S's justification for believing the proposition are not only independent (as it always is the case with fallibilist knowledge) but that they are not even suitably related. There are a number of possible scenarios which are epistemically indistinguishable vis-à-vis S's evidential situation but where the proposition is false because, say, S** has recently traded his Ford for a BMW. S doesn't know that p because, given his reasons for believing p, the belief that p fails to covary with p through a sphere of possibilities. Gettier cases result from a failure of the belief in p, the truth of p, and the evidence for believing p to covary in close possible worlds.

On the identificationist reading, the crux with Gettier cases is not covariation-failure in close possible worlds but identification-failure in the actual world: the subject's reasons for holding the belief true misidentify the belief's truth-maker. What prevents S from knowing p is the fact that his reasons for holding p true have nothing to do with what makes p true. S clearly has reasons for believing that someone in the office owns a Ford, namely that S* has claimed to own a Ford. Yet if we were to explain why this belief is true—what makes it true—we would refer not to S*, but rather to S**. The truth-maker for S's belief is (mereologically) disjoint from the state of affairs that the justification is grounded in. The justification does not direct us to what accounts for the truth of the belief. S's reason for believing that someone in the office owns a Ford is true misidentifies the actual truth-maker of the proposition. He doesn't know because he takes the target proposition to have a truth-maker other than it has.

Given that knowledge implies belief, truth, and unGettierized justification (however construed) and given the transitivity of implication, the present knowledge condition (1) entails three conditions:

(5) S believes at t_2 that p,
(6) p is true at t_2,
(7) S is justified at t_2 in believing that p.

Likewise the past knowledge condition (2) implies three conditions:

(8) S believed at t_1 that p^*,
(9) p^* was true at t_1,
(10) S was justified at t_1 in believing that p^*.

Conditions (5) and (8) are *belief conditions*, (6) and (9) are *truth-conditions*, and (7) and (10) are *justification conditions*. If any one of these conditions is false or untenable, the epistemic theorist of memory is forced to conclude that S does not remember that p.

It is beyond doubt that both knowledge and memory imply truth. Just as you can know that p only if p is true, so you can remember only what is the case. 'S remembers that p' entails that p is true. If not-p, then S may think he remembers that p, but cannot actually remember that p. Truth is a component of both knowledge and memory; conditions (6) and (9) are therefore unproblematic. The task of evaluating the epistemic account of memory is thus a matter of determining the tenability of the belief conditions (5) and (8) and the justification conditions (7) and (10).

Section 3.2 challenges the justification conditions by arguing that not only is it possible to remember something one did not justifiably believe in the past but also one might acquire between t_1 and t_2 some plausible yet misleading evidence that destroys the status as justified belief of the once-genuine justified belief that one still remembers. Section 3.3 challenges the present belief condition by arguing that S can remember at t_2 that p without believing at t_2 that p.

3.2 MEMORY WITHOUT JUSTIFICATION

Given that memory implies knowledge and that knowledge implies justification, I cannot remember that p unless I am justified in believing that p and have been justified in believing that p^* in the past. Audi (2003: 69), for example, claims that 'if I remember that I met you, I am justified in believing I met you'. And Malcolm (1963: 224) writes: '[b]eing unsure whether p is true counts both against knowing that p and against remembering that p.' The task of this section is to show that one can remember that p without being justified in believing that p.

Counterexamples to the justification condition of memory can be divided along three lines. First, counterexamples may challenge the present justification condition (7) or the past justification condition (10). Second, a rememberer might lack awareness of his being justified in believing p (*absent justification cases*), his justification for believing p might be gettierized (*gettierized justification cases*), or he might lack the relevant justification for believing p due to the presence of some counterevidence or defeating information (*defeated justification cases*). Third, counterexamples may presume an internalist or an externalist account of epistemic justification. When the epistemic theory of memory is coupled with internalism about justification, S remembers at t_2 that p only if he has cognitive access at t_2 to the factors that justify his belief at t_2 that p and if he had cognitive access at t_1 to the factors that justified his belief at t_1 that p^*. Internalists explicate this cognitive access in terms of the route by which one has access: whether one is justified in believing p is wholly determined by factors that one is in a position to know by reflection alone, where 'reflection' covers a priori reasoning, introspection, and memory. Externalism about justification is simply the denial of internalism. So when the epistemic theory of memory is combined with externalism, S remembers at t_2 that p if his belief at t_2 that p and his belief at t_1 that p^* have the property of being truth-effective; whether or not S takes these beliefs to be truth-effective doesn't add anything to their respective epistemic status.

Absent justification cases pose a problem to the internalist construal of memorial justification. There are numerous justified memory beliefs for which a person has forgotten his subjective evidence, assuming he had such evidence. Yet if the subjective evidence is not accessible because it has been forgotten, then the internalist is not in a position to say of these memory beliefs that they are justified or amount to knowledge. That is why bare factual memories pose a challenge to internalism about justification. This is how Timothy Williamson (2007: 110–11) states the problem:

> Many of our factual memories come without any particular supporting phenomenology of memory images or feelings of familiarity. We cannot remember how we acquired the information, and it may be relatively isolated, but we still use it when the need arises. Although few if any memories stand in total isolation from the rest of our conscious lives, very many memories are too isolated to receive impressive justification from other internal elements.

Williamson is surely right in that there are numerous memory beliefs that enjoy a positive epistemic status even though the subject is unable to say how he acquired the information that is called up by memory. The internalist cannot appeal to the past acquisition to explain why these bare factual memories are justified. For internalism has it that the only facts that count as justifiers are one's current conscious states or the retrieved memory contents.

In light of the problem of absent justification (or forgotten evidence) the majority of proponents of the epistemic theory of memory subscribe to epistemic externalism. Externalists about memory hold that one's initial justification for a belief continues, so long as one merely continues to hold this belief—regardless of whether one is aware of one's initial grounds. The doctrine according to which a belief may inherit its justificatory status can be called the *principle of continuous justification*: at t_2, S's belief from t_1 that p^* is continuously justified if S continues to believe at t_2 that p—even if S forgot his original knowledge-producing evidence and has acquired no fresh evidence in the meantime.[3]

---

[3] Among the proponents of the principle of continuous justification are Owens (2000: 153), Pappas (1980; 1983), Pollock (1974: 175–203; 1986: 26–65), Senor (1993), and Shoemaker (1967: 271–2). For a discussion of continuous justification see my (2008: 117–26).

And there is a further problem with internalism about memorial justification. The internalist, it seems, cannot give an adequate account of the epistemic condition of higher animals, small children, and unsophisticated adults. Though it is natural to attribute knowledge to such creatures, it is far from clear whether they have *reasons* for their beliefs—something that would amount to internalist justification. Thus when the epistemic theory of memory is combined with internalism, we may not be entitled to speak of such subjects as being able to remember things; an absurd consequence.[4]

Given that absent justification cases affect only internalism and given that internalism is problematic also for other reasons, there is no need to dwell on absent justification cases. Instead I will focus on cases of gettierized and defeated justification. Let's examine gettierized justification cases first.

As was explained in the previous section (cf. pp. 69–70), a belief is gettierized if it is justified, at least in the internalist sense, but veritically lucky. A belief is veritically lucky if it is true in the actual world, but in some close possible worlds in which the subject forms the same belief on the basis of the same evidence or via the same method of belief formation, the belief is false. To see that memory is fully compatible with the violation of the present justification condition (10) due to gettierization consider this example: at t_1 you came to justifiably believe that S has borrowed Caesar's *Commentarii de Bello Gallico* from the library. From this belief you inferred that S has borrowed a book by Caesar. This belief was true. But, unsuspected by you, the belief was true because S has borrowed another book by Caesar, the *Commentarii de Bello Civili*. Granted that gettierization is incompatible with knowledge, you were not genuinely justified in believing and hence didn't know that

---

[4] Malcolm (1963: 239 n21), however, declares: 'I do not believe there is any sense in which a dog or infant can be said to know that it has some sensation. I accept the consequence that a dog cannot be said to remember that he had a painful ear, and also the more interesting consequence that a human being cannot be said to remember that he had one, if he had it at a time before he knew enough language to be able to tell anyone that he had it.' Malcolm's reasons for drawing this conclusion are independent of internalism about epistemic justification. He claims, following Wittgenstein, that it is senseless to speak of someone *knowing* his sensations. Granted this and granted that memory is a form of knowledge, one cannot speak of someone remembering his sensations. Malcolm realizes that this conclusion is too counterintuitive to be acceptable. He therefore concedes 'that *a* sense can be given to saying that a person knows that he has a sensation at the time he has it. He knows it in the sense that *he can tell you* that he has it.' The reason animals and children cannot be said to know or remember their sensations is due to their lack of a language in which to describe their sensations.

S has borrowed a book by Caesar. But now suppose that you seem to remember at t_2 what you believed at t_1, namely that S borrowed a book by Caesar. Can you in fact remember what you seem to remember? I don't see any good reasons for answering in the negative. I find it hard to imagine that anyone would deny your memory that S borrowed a book by Caesar just because the book that makes your belief true is not the one you had in mind. After all the factivity constraint on memory is satisfied.

After having suggested that memory is compatible with the past belief being gettierized, consider this counterexample to the present justification condition (7): At t_1 you came to justifiably believe that the library's copy of Caesar's *Commentarii de Bello Gallico* is checked out by S. The belief is false at the time. Unbeknownst to you, S did check out Caesar's *Commentarii de Bello Gallico* at t_2 and holds on to it through t_3. At t_3 you seem to remember, on the basis of your belief at t_1, that S has borrowed Caesar's *Commentarii de Bello Gallico*. Given the fact that your belief at t_1 wasn't true, it is merely good fortune or a happy accident that you arrive at a true memory belief. Yet despite the fact that your memory belief is veritically lucky I see no reason not to say that you can in fact remember what you seem to remember—provided, of course, the other memory conditions are met. As was already stated before (cf. p. 39), the authentic reproduction of a proposition that was false at the time it was initially entertained but which, in the meantime, has become true may qualify as memory.

Here is another counterexample to the present justification condition (7): at t_1 you came to justifiably believe that S had borrowed Caesar's *Commentarii de Bello Gallico* from the library. The belief is false. At t_2, all you can remember is that S checked out a book by Caesar; you have forgotten which book you thought S has borrowed from the library. Now it turns out that your memory belief to the effect that S has checked out a book by Caesar is true because S borrowed Caesar's *Commentarii de Bello Civili*. Can your belief qualify as memory? We should, I reckon, once again answer in the affirmative. In section 8.3 I will argue that even though the belief at t_1 that S has borrowed Caesar's *Commentarii de Bello Gallico* differs from the belief at t_2 that S has borrowed a book by Caesar, the latter belief can stand in a memory-relation to the former belief because the content of the latter belief is entailed by the content of the former belief.

Now let's turn to defeated justification cases, that is, cases where a subject remembers that p but where there is some defeating information such that, if the subject became aware of it, he would no longer be justified in believing p. The underlying thought here is that certain kinds of counterevidence contribute epistemically unacceptable irrationality to doxastic systems and, accordingly, that justification can be defeated by their presence.

Defeaters can be divided into justificational defeaters and factual defeaters (Steup 1996: 14). Justificational defeaters, in turn, come in two flavors: doxastic and normative defeaters. A doxastic defeater is a proposition that one believes to be true and that indicates that one's belief that p is either false or unreliably formed or sustained.[5] A normative defeater is a proposition that one *would* believe to be true, if one performed one's epistemic duties, and that indicates that one's belief that p is either false or unreliably formed or sustained. The difference between justificational and factual defeaters is that while justificational defeat involves propositions for which one has evidence factual defeaters are propositions for which one has no evidence. Another difference is that justificational defeaters can be either true or false but that factual defeaters must be true. Factual defeaters defeat justification in virtue of being true. The standard example is the fake barn: if you happen to see the one real barn amidst a countryside full of fakes, your belief that that's a barn is not justified. (I will return to the issue of fake barns on pp. 80–1.)

This is not the place to argue on behalf of the necessity of a no-defeater condition for justification. In addition to the sheer plausibility of the view that justification is incompatible with the presence of undefeated defeaters, the literature is dominated by endorsements of no-defeater conditions. Despite the dazzling number of different conceptions of epistemic justification, epistemologists on both sides of the internalism/externalism divide sign up to the idea that justification is incompatible with undefeated defeaters. In the case of epistemic internalism, it is obvious that the presence of undefeated defeaters undermines justification. Given that what justifies a belief is a mentally accessible item (something that one can come to know whether it obtains just by reflecting on one's mental states), being justified in believing p must exclude a person's having sufficient reasons for supposing either that p

---

[5] There are two different kinds of doxastic defeater. Rebutting defeaters are propositions that one believes to be true yet indicate that the target belief is false while undercutting defeaters are propositions that one believes to be true yet indicate that the target belief is unreliably formed or sustained.

is false or that the belief that p is not grounded or produced in a way that is sufficiently truth-indicating.

Whether the presence of undefeated defeaters is compatible with the externalist construal of justification depends on the version of externalism under consideration. Given an austere form of epistemic externalism, a subject is epistemically justified in believing something just in case the belief is truth-effective; it doesn't matter whether the subject takes his belief to be unjustified. As long as one relies on what is, in point of fact, a good reason for p, one is justified in believing that p, despite being convinced that p is false or despite being convinced that the belief that p is unreliably formed. This position is labeled 'mad-dog reliabilism' in Dretske (2000: 595). For reasons I don't have space to go into here mad-dog reliabilism is generally rejected. Several leading advocates of externalist reliabilism—Alvin Goldman, Robert Nozick, and Alvin Plantinga, to mention only a few—adopt no-defeater conditions. They hold that although a subject need not be aware of the factors that justify his belief, he may not be aware of evidence that undermines his belief. And there is no inconsistency in affirming that what confers justification on a belief is an externalist condition, but what takes justification away from a belief is an internalist no-defeater condition. The no-defeater condition ensures that for a belief to become justified it must not be incoherent with the background information the subject possesses.

Given these preliminary points, we can see that there are cases of memory where the past justification condition (10) is violated. Consider this example:[6] On a recent trip to Rome, at t_1, S signed up for a guided tour of the Museo Nuovo in the Palazzo dei Conservatori on the ancient Capitoline Hill. The museum houses the famous statue of the Capitoline Wolf feeding Romulo and Remo. S formed the true belief that the Capitoline Wolf is brown. Shortly afterwards, the tour guide fooled S by assuring him that the statue is in fact white and that, for reasons of conservation, it is illuminated by brown light. So although S's belief that the Capitoline Wolf is brown is correct, he had plausible yet misleading reasons to suppose that it is not brown. Given the incompatibility of justification with the presence of undefeated doxastic defeaters, S wasn't justified at t_1 in believing (and hence didn't know) that the Capitoline Wolf is brown. At t_2, S learns that, in spite of his

---

[6] Similar examples can be found in Martin and Deutscher (1966: 191–2) and Shope (1973: 208–9).

past evidence, the tour guide is a notorious liar. So S remembers at t_2 that the Capitoline Wolf is brown even though, at the time, he wasn't justified in believing it. The point of the example is that at t_1 S was not justified in believing that p even though at t_2 he remembers (and knows) that p. Hence memory doesn't imply past justification and the epistemic theory of memory is mistaken.

But there is a way in which one may attempt to deny that the above case provides a counterexample to the epistemic theory of memory. One may claim that the recollection S has of the Capitoline Wolf's color is inferential rather than non-inferential memory. As was explained before (cf. p. 25), inferential memory is remembering with admixture of inferential reasoning involving background knowledge or fresh evidence. The paradigm example of inferential memory is due to Malcolm (1963: 223): at t_1 you see a bird without knowing what sort of bird it is, and then later, at t_2, you discover from a book that such birds are blue jays. You claim to remember that you saw a blue jay at t_1. But it is, strictly speaking, not true because, at the time, you didn't believe that the bird you saw was a blue jay. You have only just learned that it was a blue jay. So what you claim to remember is more than what you originally knew; it contains additional pieces of information that you have acquired in the meantime. When you assert 'I remember that I saw a blue jay' you are using the verb 'to remember' in an elliptical sense. You really make two separate claims: first, 'I remember that I saw a bird of such-and-such a kind' and, second, 'I now know that it was a blue jay'. (Section 3.5 will propose a more sophisticated analysis of inferential memory.)

According to the objection at hand, when S claims 'I remember that the Capitoline Wolf is brown' this is elliptical for two claims: first, 'I remember that it looked to me as if the Capitoline Wolf is brown' and, second, 'I am now justified in believing (and know) that the Capitoline Wolf is brown.' Thus since S *inferentially* remembers that the Capitoline Wolf is brown and since the epistemic theory is supposed to hold only for non-inferential memory, this example fails to undermine the epistemic theory of memory; or so a critic might argue.

This objection fails, for there is no good reason to interpret S's memory as being based on inferential reasoning (explicit or implicit) involving background knowledge or fresh evidence. Note that the propositional content of S's memory claim—the Capitoline Wolf is brown—is the very same as the content of his original belief. By being informed that the tour guide is a notorious liar S is given no new information about what it is that he witnessed. The issue of whether S remembers having distrusted his eyes is quite distinct from the question whether he remembers seeing what he did see. Since the content of the original belief matches that of the subsequent memory claim the most straightforward interpretation of this example is as involving non-inferential memory. But if this example is an instance of non-inferential memory after all, then it *does* undermine the epistemic theory of memory.

After having seen that memory doesn't imply past justification, consider the following counterexample to the present justification condition (7):[7] at t_1, S learned that the Colosseum was completed in AD 80. He comes to know this fact about the Colosseum. At t_2, S's 'friends' play a practical joke on him. They tell him that the Colosseum was not completed until AD 90 and present him with plausible but misleading evidence to this effect. Given the incompatibility of justification with the presence of undefeated defeaters, S doesn't know at t_2 that the Colosseum was completed in AD 80, for he is unable to rule out the relevant alternative that it was not completed until AD 90. He fails to know that the Colosseum was completed in AD 80, despite the fact that he still remembers this fact. This example shows that one can know at t_1 that p, remember at t_2 everything one knew at t_1, and yet fail to know at t_2 that p—even though one continues to truly believe that p—for the reason that one isn't anymore justified in believing that p.

One way to undermine this counterexample to the epistemic theory of memory is to identify the conditions for remembering with the conditions for saying that one remembers. Given that S doesn't feel confident at t_2 to claim to remember that the Colosseum was completed in AD 80 and given that memory conditions and memory attribution conditions are the same thing it follows that S doesn't remember that the Colosseum was completed in AD 80.

The problem with this rejoinder is that it is implausible to lump together memory conditions and memory attribution conditions. As was argued in section 1.4, what makes a mental state a state of remembering is the fact that certain conditions are met; whether the subject takes himself to meet these conditions is of no importance. I may not be able to tell whether I genuinely remember something or whether it only

---

[7] Similar examples can be found in Dretske and Yourgrau (1983), Ginet (1988: 160), Naylor (1986: 298), and Saunders (1965a: 282–3).

seems to me that I remember that thing. I can take myself to remember and not remember and I can think that I don't remember when, in fact, I do remember. The reason memories don't wear their identity on their sleeves is that they imply truth and presuppose a causal chain of memory traces that are inaccessible to consciousness. Thus the fact that S doesn't feel confident to claim to remember that the Colosseum was completed in AD 80 shouldn't prevent us from attributing to him the memory that it was completed in AD 80.

It should be noted that just as the Capitoline Wolf example is not a case of inferential memory nor is the Colosseum example. The propositional content of S's memory claim—that the Colosseum was completed in AD 80—doesn't differ from the content of his original knowledge state. The two diachronic content-tokens are type-identical. Thus there is no admixture of inference or present realization involved in the process of remembering.

We can conclude that memory doesn't presuppose justification. Not only is it possible to remember something at t_2 that one didn't justifiably believe at t_1 but also one may acquire between t_1 and t_2 some plausible yet misleading evidence that destroys the status as justified belief of the once-genuine justified belief that one still remembers. What passes into memory may be merely a representation or thought, not knowledge.

The cases of memory without justification discussed so far have in common that the content of the past belief is type-identical to the (embedded) content of the memory belief. Yet it is not essential for memory that the (embedded) content of memory belief be of the same kind as the content of the past belief. Memory requires only that the diachronic content tokens be sufficiently similar. Section 8.3 is devoted to the question to what extent two diachronic beliefs may differ from one another with respect to their contents and one belief still qualify as being memory-related to the other. I argue for what I call the *entailment thesis*, whereupon a belief at t_2 is memory-related to a belief at t_1 only if the (embedded) content of the belief at t_2 is entailed by the content of the belief at t_1. In the case of non-inferential memory, the subject may not use or need additional premises to derive the (embedded) content of the belief at t_2 from the content of the belief at t_1.

The entailment thesis, in combination with certain conceptions of justification, provides further support for the view whereupon one can remember at t_2 that p, in virtue of having believed at t_1 that p*, and where the belief that p* was justified but the memory belief that p is not. One such conception of justification states that a belief that p is justified and qualifies as knowledge if it tracks the facts that make it true. Arguably the best-known tracking accounts are due to Alvin Goldman and Robert Nozick. For Goldman (1979) tracking amounts to having one's true belief formed by cognitively reliable belief formation processes (where reliability is measured by the propensity of producing true beliefs as outputs). According to Nozick (1981: 172–96), tracking amounts to having a nomically reliable method of belief formation such that one's belief that p is based upon this method, and when it is, one would not believe that p, if p were not true, and if p were true, one would believe that p. While a number of objections have been raised for tracking accounts of knowledge, the general idea of truth tracking has not been proven wrong. Quite on the contrary, there is a growing consensus among contemporary epistemologists that some version of truth tracking is likely to be true.

To see that, given tracking theories of knowledge, there can be a tension between the entailment thesis and the epistemic theory of memory consider the following counterexample to the present justification condition (7).[8] At t_1, S is driving in a part of the country where, unbeknownst to him, the inhabitants have erected a large number of fake barns, that is, papier-mâché façades looking like barns from the highway, yet lacking back walls or interiors. From the highway, these fake barns are indistinguishable from real ones. In the midst of these fake barns there are a few real barns, that are painted red. Red barns cannot be faked though barns of other colors can be faked. S is driving along the highway, looks up and happens to see a real barn, and forms the belief that there is a red barn. S couldn't have been wrong, since the fake barns cannot be painted red. Since S fulfills the tracking conditions (if p were not true, S would not believe that p, and if p were true, S would believe that p) he is justified in believing (and knows) that there is a red barn. A week later, at t_2, all S can remember about his trip to fake barn country is that he saw a barn; he has forgotten the color of the barn. He comes to believe, on the basis of his belief from t_1, that there was a barn. Given the entailment thesis, S's belief at t_2 may qualify as being memory-related to the belief he had at t_1. The reason is that

---

[8] Kripke presented a similar example in an unpublished lecture given at a session of the American Philosophical Association in the early 1980s. Kripke's example wasn't aimed against the epistemic theory of memory but against tracking theories of knowledge.

the proposition *there is a barn* is entailed by the proposition *there is a red barn*. And since no additional premisses are needed to infer *there is a barn* from *there is a red barn* S's memory is of the non-inferential kind—the very kind of memory the epistemic theory is about. Yet while S's belief at t₂ meets the conditions for non-inferential memory, it doesn't meet the tracking conditions: if there had not been a barn, S wouldn't believe that there were. S's belief that there is a barn fails the tracking conditions because he would believe of a white fake barn, for instance, that it is a barn. So memory has transformed a justified belief into an unjustified one.[9]

In the case of *inferential* memory the tension between the entailment thesis, on the one hand, and the thesis whereupon memory is a form of knowledge, on the other, is even more perspicuous. Consider this case: at t₁ you came to justifiably believe that the Colosseum was completed in AD 80. Suppose that you have read respectable books on the history of Rome, that you have checked with experts in Roman archeology, and so on. At t₂, the belief from t₁ in conjunction with other premisses makes you believe that the world didn't spring into being only five minutes ago, complete with ostensible memories, history books, fossils, etc.[10] Despite the fact that *the Colosseum was completed in AD 80* and *the world didn't come into existence five minutes ago* are different propositions your belief at t₂ may qualify as being memory-related to the belief you had at t₁ since the latter proposition is entailed by the former proposition. The Colosseum couldn't have been completed in AD 80 unless time, the succession of events, and, in particular, the past is real. However, the reality of the past is what Dretske (2005: 20–4) calls a *heavyweight implication* of your past belief content. P is a heavyweight implication if it is compelling to think that p is not the sort of thing that one can know by the exercise of reason alone and also that p cannot be known by use of one's

[9] This example is not wholly unproblematic. It might be argued that this only appears to be a case where one knows that there is a red barn but not that there is a barn. For when the belief formation method that yields S's knowledge that there is a red barn is specified, it looks as if the same method yields his knowledge that there is a barn. S is using the red barn look to detect the information both that there is something red and a barn. Since red barns cannot be faked, the look of a red barn carries both pieces of information. The red barn look method insures that S knows of a particular building that it is both red and a barn (cf. Adams and Clarke 2005: 214–16).

[10] The skeptical scenario whereupon the world sprang into being only five minutes ago, exactly as it is now, with a population that 'remembers' a wholly unreal past is owed to Russell and is discussed in my (2008: 126–33).

perceptual faculties (even aided by reason). Given that you are not justified in believing that the world didn't come into existence five minutes ago your memory has transformed a justified belief into an unjustified one.

It is empirical evidence that justifies you in believing that the Colosseum was completed in AD 80. But no empirical evidence can justify you in believing that the world didn't come into existence five minutes ago. Skeptical hypotheses such as the five-minute hypothesis are immune to empirical refutation. Neither geology, nor chemistry, nor radar astronomy can supply non-question-begging evidence that there is a past. The testimony of historians and archeologists may be good reason to believe when the Colosseum was completed, but it is not good reason to believe that there is a past.[11]

I will return to some of the issues discussed here in sections 4.1 and 5.5. Section 4.1 shows that the main problem with the evidential retention theory is that it incorrectly assumes that memory implies justification. Section 5.5 argues for a counterfactual interpretation of the causal relation that must hold between an (apparent) memory state and the corresponding past representation. Since there is a striking similarity between the counterfactual conditional that defines the causal theory of memory and the counterfactual conditionals assumed by reliabilist accounts of justification and knowledge one may get the false impression that memory is after all a form of reliabilist knowledge. This misimpression disappears, however, as soon as one takes into account three things: first, memory, unlike knowledge, is not subject to a no-defeater condition; second, the counterfactual dependence relation posited by the causal theory of memory holds between two mental items—a propositional attitude at t_1 and a propositional attitude at t_2—whereas the counterfactual dependence relation characteristic of

---

[11] A critic could adopt either of two strategies to reconcile the entailment thesis with the thesis whereupon memory is a form of knowledge: he could maintain that the belief at t_1 that p^* lacks justification because the belief at t_2 in p^*'s heavyweight implication lacks justification, or he could claim that the belief in the heavyweight implication is justified because the belief in p^* was justified. Consider the latter strategy. It could be maintained that inferential remembering should be construed as a kind of deductive reasoning process. If S competently deduces the belief that p (*the world didn't come into existence five minutes ago*) from the belief that p^* (*the Colosseum was completed in AD 80*) and if S is justified in believing p^*, then he is thereby also justified in believing p. The evidential force of the belief that p^* is transmitted via deduction to the belief that p, notwithstanding the fact that p is a heavyweight implication of p^*. This is not the place to examine the transmissibility of epistemic force.

reliabilist knowledge holds between a belief and a fact; and third, memory, unlike knowledge, doesn't imply belief.

3.3 MEMORY WITHOUT BELIEF

Granted that knowing implies believing, the epistemic theory has it that remembering too implies believing. Malcolm (1963: 224), a leading proponent of the epistemic theory, puts the point thus: 'Being unsure whether p is true counts both against knowing that p and against remembering that p.' In this section I will argue that it is indeed possible to remember that p without believing that p.

Prima facie, a proponent of the epistemic theory of memory may dismiss the possibility of memory without belief on the grounds that 'I remember that p; but I don't believe that p' is equally incoherent as G. E. Moore's famous paradoxical statement 'It is raining; but I don't believe that it is raining.' The idea is that the (alleged) incoherence of 'I remember that p; but I don't believe that p' cannot be explained unless one assumes that remembering implies believing. This objection doesn't work. It *is* possible to explain the (alleged) pragmatic incoherence of the statement 'I remember that p; but I don't believe that p' while denying that memory implies belief. When I claim to remember that p, I am convinced that p is the case and hence believe that p. This is what the first part of the statement expresses. Yet the second part of the statement denies that I believe that p. Thus 'I remember that p; but I don't believe that p' is (seemingly) incoherent not because one cannot remember that p without believing that p but because one cannot *claim* to remember that p while *claiming* to not believe that p. And since the conditions for claiming to remember are distinct from the conditions for remembering (cf. sect. 1.4), it doesn't follow that remembering that p implies believing that p because claiming to remember that p implies claiming to believe that p.

Before I can attempt to develop an argument for the possibility of memory without belief I need to say a few words about what it takes to believe something and what distinguishes believing something from merely thinking about it. Beliefs are the attitudes we have, roughly, when we take something to be the case, regard it as true, or accept it.[12]

---

[12] Here I employ what I take to be the common-sense notion of *to accept*. The verb 'to accept' has been given various technical meanings by various authors and it has been argued

The state of believing that p can manifest itself in different forms. One may be convinced by the evidence of its being true that p, one may be surprised to learn of an event that is evidence against its being true that p, one may feel pleased at its being true that p, and so on. Furthermore, an individual who believes that p, who has no reason to deceive, and who is asked, in a language he understands, whether p is the case, will generally say that it is. Believing that p involves holding p true, but it does not involve actively reflecting on p or an especially high degree of confidence with respect to p.[13]

Acceptance is a central component not only of occurrent belief but also of dispositional belief. A dispositional belief is an antecedently held but yet unarticulated occurrent belief. One possesses a dispositional belief that p if one doesn't currently believe that p but if one would hold this belief under the right sorts of circumstances. A dispositional belief can be formed without ever having been an occurrent belief.

Both occurrent and dispositional beliefs are explicit beliefs. In addition to explicit beliefs some philosophers postulate implicit (or tacit) beliefs. Implicit beliefs are not actually tokened in one's brain (in the right sort of way). According to the widespread formation-dispositional account, explained on page 30, to implicitly believe that p is to be disposed to have an explicit belief that p, in such-and-such circumstances. Since, on this account, implicit belief is explained by way of dispositional explicit belief and since explicit belief implies acceptance it follows that implicit belief also presupposes acceptance. Thus *all* forms of believing that p require that one takes p to be the case or would take p to be the case in the right sorts of circumstances.

With these preliminary remarks in mind, we can address the question whether it is possible to remember something without believing it.

that belief and acceptance (in the technical sense) are mutually independent (cf. Bratman 1999, Cohen 1992, Stalnaker 1984: 79–81). Believing something is being disposed to feel that it is true, whereas accepting something is adopting a policy of taking it as a premiss for relevant reasonings. For example, Cohen's notion of acceptance can be characterized by means of the following theses: (1) acceptance is voluntary or intentional, unlike belief; (2) belief aims at truth, but one can accept things one believes to be false; (3) beliefs come in degrees while acceptance is an all or nothing affair. The intuitive notion of acceptance employed here doesn't satisfy any of the conditions that govern Cohen's technical notion. Lehrer (1990: 20–7) argues that knowledge requires acceptance (in the technical sense of the term) rather than belief, given that acceptance may be aimed at truth, short term, and connected with decision and optionality.

[13] A subject's degree of confidence in p is usually taken to be the maximum amount he would be willing to wager on a bet that pays nothing if p is false and one unit if p is true.

There are at least four (putative) reasons why one may remember at t_2 that p without believing at t_2 that p or without having believed at t_1 that p*. One such possible reason is that at t_1 one didn't yet possess the concepts necessary to believe that p*. Such cases are a kind of *inferential memory* explained on page 25. Another reason why one may remember at t_2 that p without having believed at t_1 that p* is that one was too busy doing something else and was not paying attention to the fact that p. Lacking a better term, I will refer to this kind of remembering as *inattentive remembering*. A third reason for remembering without past believing is that p states something one didn't do or hasn't happened (e.g. I didn't lock the door). This kind of memory is usually called *negative memory*. Finally, a fourth reason why one may remember at t_2 that p without believing at t_2 that p is that one erroneously takes p to be a figment of one's imagination. I will refer to this kind of remembering as *ignorant remembering*. While cases of inferential, inattentive, and negative memory challenge the past belief condition (8), cases of ignorant remembering are directed against the present belief condition (5).[14]

The discussion of inferential memory is deferred for section 3.5. Here I concentrate on the other three kinds of memory without belief. The goal is to critically examine examples for each of the three kinds of memory without belief. The conclusion is going to be that instances of inattentive and negative memory fail to refute the past belief condition (8), but that cases of ignorant remembering are successful in casting the present belief condition (5) into doubt. Obviously, cases of memory without belief don't count against the epistemic theory of memory,

[14] Schwitzgebel argues that there are situations in which a subject is neither accurately describable as believing that p or as failing to so believe, but is rather in 'in-between states of belief'. This example is supposed to bring home the point: while being a college student S 'fully and completely believes' that the last name of Konstantin who lives across the hall is 'Guericke'. At 80, S will have no memory of Konstantin's last name. At points in the middle, S can still remember the last name provided he is given the right prompts. Against the view that the belief remains, but simply becomes less and less accessible, Schwitzgebel (2001: 77) suggests 'at some point, the belief must pass from fully present, if difficult to access, to absent . . . At some point during the course of forgetting, [S] must be between believing and failing to believe that [Konstantin's] last name is "Guericke" (or whatever).' One of the problems with this argument for the existence of in-between believing is the underlying assumption that memory implies belief. When the possibility of memory without belief is appreciated we can see that Schwitzgebel's interpretation of the example is neither the only one nor the most plausible one. Instead of S losing the belief and the memory at once it is possible that the memory remains present but becomes difficult to access and that the belief disappears in virtue of the memory's unavailability (cf. Rowbottom 2007: 2). Thus *concealed memory* seems to be yet another kind of memory without belief.

unless knowledge implies belief. In section 3.4 I will defend the idea that belief is a necessary component of knowledge.

Keith Lehrer and Joseph Richard (1975: 122) construct the following example of inattentive remembering.[15] Suppose that while S is avidly lecturing, a bell rings indicating the end of the lecture. S doesn't notice that the bell is ringing and continues his lecture. After some time, a student asks S whether he has forgotten the time. At that moment S remembers that the dismissal bell had rung, even though he didn't previously believe that it had rung. The auditory experience had failed to break into S's consciousness at the time it occurred, but passed into memory nonetheless. Lehrer and Richard take this example to show that there are instances where remembering something means believing (and knowing) it for the first time. Granted that such instances are possible, the epistemic theory of memory is mistaken in identifying memory with retained knowledge.

The problem with this alleged counterexample to the epistemic theory of memory is the implausible presumption that to believe (and know) that p one must be conscious that p. According to Lehrer and Richard, the person, not having been conscious of the dismissal bell, did not believe (or know) that the bell rang. But on a dispositional reading of 'to believe', S did believe that the bell rang since this belief was manifested in subsequent action, that is, the remembering. Moreover, if at the time the bell rang someone had asked S whether he thinks that the bell is ringing he would, no doubt, have answered in the affirmative. Since it is implausible to restrict knowledge to conscious and occurrent belief, cases of inattentive remembering fail to undermine the epistemic analysis of memory.

William James (1890: i. 649n2) develops the following case of negative memory: after having left his house and walked down the street S remembers that he didn't lock the door. He returns, verifies that the door is unlocked and locks it. This is taken by some to be an example of remembering without believing (and knowing) because if, at the time S initially left the house, he had believed that the door is unlocked he would have locked it right away. While James's example concerns

---

[15] Similar thought experiments can be found in Lackey (2005: 650), D. Locke (1971: 54), Pollock (1974: 196–7), and Traiger (1978: 111). Lackey's example is about a driver not noticing construction on a freeway, Locke's example involves a professor not noticing a certain student in a lecture hall, Pollock's example concerns a driver in a dangerous situation not noticing a billboard beside the road, and Traiger's example is about a skier during a slalom ski race not noticing a patch of blue snow.

a negative specific fact, Carl Ginet (1975: 149) gives an example of remembering a negative general fact: S can recall that during the last twenty years he has never been to a dog show without once during this period having believed that he has not been to a dog show. Thus, S is able to remember a proposition that he has never before believed or known.

Cases of negative memory fail to undermine the epistemic theory of memory for the same reason as cases of inattentive remembering. It is natural to suppose that at t_1 S had a dispositional belief to the effect that the door is unlocked or that he hasn't been to a dog show, respectively.[16] And since knowledge allows for dispositional belief, a proponent of the epistemic theory could argue that the reason S remembers at t_2 that the door is unlocked and that he hasn't been to a dog show, respectively, is because he dispositionally knew this at t_1. So cases of inattentive and negative remembering don't conflict with the belief condition of the epistemic analysis of memory for the simple reason that to believe that p and to know that p one need not be conscious that p. To avoid misunderstanding, the past belief condition of the epistemic analysis of propositional remembering:

(8) S believed at t_1 that p*

should be changed to:

(8′) S (occurrently or dispositionally) believed at t_1 that p*.

This small correction is sufficient to render the epistemic theory compatible with cases of inattentive and negative remembering (understood as counterexamples to the past belief condition).[17]

---

[16] The following objection could be pressed: A dispositional belief isn't merely a disposition to believe. To dispositionally believe p, S must either occurrently believe p, or have once occurrently believed p (and not have changed his mind about it), or believe something else that presupposes or entails p. A critic might argue that none of these ways of dispositionally believing something apply to the person who remembers having forgotten to lock the door. A detailed discussion of this point would take us too far afield (cf. Audi 1994). I just want to note though that (8′) can be revised so as to cover not only dispositional beliefs but also dispositions to believe.

[17] In my (2001: 156–7) I have claimed that the epistemic theory of memory has no way of accounting for cases of inattentive and negative remembering. I don't subscribe to this view any more.

Pollock (1974: 197) defines memory in terms of implicit rather than explicit knowledge: 'S occurrently remembers-that-p if and only if (i) S believes-that-p on the basis of recalling-that-p, (ii) S implicitly knew that p, and (iii) S's recalling-that-p is caused by his having implicitly known that p.' And implicit knowledge is defined as follows: 'S implicitly knows-that-p if

Finally let us turn to cases of ignorant remembering and the challenge they pose to the present belief condition (5). The following example is adapted from Malcolm who developed it for a different goal altogether:[18] at t_2 S suddenly finds himself with the thought that he has been kidnapped when he was a small boy (at t_1). The idea that he has been kidnapped just pops into his head; it seems to come 'out of the blue'. S can't make sense of this idea and takes it to be merely imaginary. After all the likelihood of being kidnapped is rather low. What is more, the idea in question is inferentially isolated from the large body of inferentially integrated beliefs to which S has access. Nothing of what S knows or believes about his past connects with the idea that he has been kidnapped. But now suppose that, unbeknownst to S, it is in fact the case that he has been kidnapped. The flashbulb thought is an instance of propositional memory.[19] Perhaps because of the terror of the experience S can't allow himself to even consider the possibility that he had been the victim of kidnapping but instead takes himself to be making it up.[20]

and only if the epistemologically relevant circumstances are such that he could justifiably believe-that-p, and that belief would be an instance of knowledge.' Thus, what Pollock calls 'implicit knowledge' I label 'dispositional knowledge'.

[18] Malcolm (1963: 213–14). According to Malcolm's version of the example, S has memory images of having been kidnapped rather than propositional memories to the effect that he was kidnapped. These memory images are classified by Malcolm as instances of 'perceptual memory', that is, a non-propositional version of experiential memory. According to Malcolm (1963: 215–19), S perceptually remembers X if and only if (1) S previously perceived or experienced X, (2) S's memory of X is based wholly or partly on his previous perception or experience of X, and (3) S can form a mental image of X. The point of the kidnapping example, according to Malcolm, is to show that perceptual memory implies propositional memory (see pp. 15–16). Saunders (1965*b*: 111) agrees with Malcolm that S perceptually remembers the kidnapping but denies that S propositionally remembers that he was kidnapped, on the grounds that S does not believe that he was kidnapped.

[19] A terminological note: most propositional attitude concepts insinuate that the agent accepts p or at least that he takes p to be more likely than non-p. Cases in point are *to suppose*, *to consider*, *to judge*, *to hold*, *to infer*, and *to assume*. The reason I speak of S 'thinking that p' and of him 'having the idea that p' is because these formulations do not presuppose that S accepts p.

[20] Ignorant remembering is fairly common among subjects suffering from multiple personality disorder, dissociative fugue, and post-traumatic stress disorder. For a review of empirical literature on ignorant memory see Kihlstrom and Schacter (2000).

Other examples of ignorant remembering are due to Martin and Deutscher (1966: 166–70) and Lehrer and Richard (1975: 121). Martin and Deutscher's example involves someone who paints what he takes to be an imaginary scene of a farmhouse. The person's parents see the finished painting and recognize it as an accurate representation of an actual farm, often visited by the painter as a boy. Lehrer and Richard's example is about someone who has a vivid

What distinguishes this case from the Colosseum counterexample to the present justification condition (7) discussed on pages 78–9 is that S not only lacks justification for what he remembers, but also lacks belief in what he remembers. It would be wrong to say that S *believes* at t_2 that he was kidnapped at t_1. For only after he is presented with the police record and newspaper clippings about his kidnapping does he reluctantly accept that he had been kidnapped when a small boy. It takes considerable convincing until S consents to the thesis according to which the thought in question springs from his memory rather than his imagination. At t_2 S not only remembers that p without believing that he remembers that p, but he remembers that p without believing that which he remembers, namely p. Thus the present belief condition (5) of propositional memory is mistaken.

At first sight it might seem reasonable to suppose that instances of ignorant remembering can be dealt with along the same lines as instances of inattentive and negative memory. But is it really the case that ignorantly remembering that p presupposes dispositionally believing that p? Would replacing the present belief condition:

(5) S believes at t_2 that p,

by

(5′) S (occurrently or dispositionally) believes at t_2 that p,

do the trick of rendering cases of ignorant remembering compatible with the epistemic theory? I don't think so. At t_2, that is, before S has been convinced that his flashbulb thought to the effect that he has been kidnapped springs from memory rather than imagination, there is no good reason for attributing to him a dispositional belief to the effect that he was kidnapped. For example, if S was asked at t_2 whether he thinks it more likely than not that he has been a victim of kidnapping he would, no doubt, dismiss the suggestion that he has been kidnapped. And finally when he reluctantly accepts the thesis according to which the flashbulb thought is due to him remembering having been kidnapped, rather than reviving a dormant belief, he acquires a novel (dispositional) belief.

image occur to him of an elderly woman standing by a stone well next to a red barn. The thought occurs to him that the woman is his grandmother. The rememberer doesn't consider information to support this thought, and has no feeling of conviction that the thought is true. But since the thought is actually true and caused in the right kind of way it qualifies as memory.

Granted that S doesn't dispositionally believe at t_2 that he was kidnapped, maybe he believes it implicitly. We saw that to implicitly believe that p is to be disposed to explicitly believe that p while not internally representing p. Now I don't see that the introduction of implicit belief helps to render the epistemic theory of memory compatible with ignorant-remembering counterexamples to the present belief condition. The reason is that, as was explained above, implicit belief presupposes acceptance (in the non-technical sense of the term) just as much as explicit belief does. But clearly S does not accept at t_2 that he was kidnapped. And when S does finally accept that he was kidnapped rather than saying that he had implicitly believed it all along it is much more natural to say that he acquires a new occurrent belief.

3.4 KNOWLEDGE WITHOUT BELIEF?

So far we have assumed that knowledge implies belief. Yet some epistemologists hold that you can know something without believing it. If it were possible to know that p without believing that p, then cases of memory without belief wouldn't count against the thesis that to remember that p is to know that p.

In the early 1970s, epistemologists avidly debated the question of whether knowing implies believing. Colin Radford (1966) and Zeno Vendler (1972: 89–119) answered in the negative while David Armstrong (1970) and Keith Lehrer (1970) answered in the affirmative. Radford (1966) presents the following example of knowledge without belief: S is forced to take part in a quiz on key dates of Roman history. He protests quite sincerely that he doesn't know any historical dates, but when quizzed is able to answer most questions correctly. Radford contends that S knows some history, for his answers are not just a lucky guess. The fact that he answers most of the questions correctly indicates that he has actually learned, and never forgotten, the basic facts of Roman history. But at the same time Radford maintains that S does not believe, say, that Brutus stabbed Caesar in 44 BC. The reason is that S thinks he doesn't know the answer to the question. He doesn't trust his answer because he takes it to be a mere guess. Radford (ibid. 4) writes, '[a]lthough in this situation S knows that p, he is not certain, or sure, or confident that p. Indeed he is fairly certain that his answer to the question is wrong, i.e., that not-p, since he believes it to be a pure guess in a situation where only one of many such guesses could be correct.' Radford (ibid.) concludes that knowledge without belief is indeed possible: 'a man may know that p even though he is neither sure that p, and indeed fairly sure that not-p, nor justified in being sure, etc., that p'.

The basic problem with Radford's alleged example of knowledge without belief is that it presupposes, without argument, that you can know that p without being sure that p but that you cannot believe that p without being sure that p. If belief is a necessary condition for knowledge—as I think it is—then the conditions for believing are *eo ipso* conditions for knowing. Either both knowledge and belief require subjective confidence or neither do; but it is not possible that only belief requires it. Given my commitment to epistemic externalism, I maintain that neither belief nor knowledge demand subjective confidence or certainty. So while I agree with Radford that S may *know* that Brutus stabbed Caesar in 44 BC, I think that we should also say of S that he *believes* that Brutus stabbed Caesar in 44 BC.

The idea that knowledge doesn't involve belief has again become fashionable in recent years. Timothy Williamson suggests reversing the order of explanation between knowledge and belief: instead of analyzing knowledge in terms of belief, the concept of knowledge should be used to elucidate the concept of belief. Knowledge, Williamson argues, is a simple and irreducible mental state, a mental state that cannot be explained in terms of belief plus certain other conditions.

The standard conception of knowledge has it that knowing factors into a mental and a non-mental (or environmental) component. The mental component consists of the belief that p, and the non-mental component consists of the truth of p (supposing that p concerns some aspect of non-mental reality). Williamson is aware that it seems strange to say that knowledge is an irreducible mental state, given that knowing entails believing truly which isn't a purely mental state (at least not if the truth of p is independent of the believer). He (2000: 27–8) uses an analogy from geometry to show that there is nothing structurally incoherent in the idea that the non-mental state of believing truly is 'sandwiched between' the mental state of believing and the mental state of knowing. The non-geometrical property of being a triangle whose sides are indiscriminable in length to the naked human eye is also 'sandwiched between' the geometrical property of being an equilateral triangle and the geometrical property of being a triangle. However, Jonathan Lowe (2002: 484–5) offers reasons to doubt that this analogy is pertinent. Knowing *essentially* involves the truth of what is known, which is something that is non-mental. Being an equilateral triangle, however, does not essentially involve having sides that are indiscriminable in length to the naked human eye. The reason for the latter entailment is the purely *logical* fact that if lines are of the same length, then they cannot be distinguished in respect of their length—not by the human eye and not by any other means.

Williamson develops three arguments in support of the claim that knowledge is an irreducible mental state: the non-analyzability of the concept of knowledge, the primeness of knowing, and the role of knowledge in the explanation of action.

There is widespread agreement that the project of providing non-circular necessary and sufficient conditions for knowledge has failed and that there is no reason to expect that it will ever succeed. From this Williamson (2000: 91) concludes that the concept of knowledge 'cannot be analyzed into concepts of narrow and environmental conditions' and that knowledge is an irreducible mental state. Yet this conclusion doesn't follow. First, the failure of the project of conceptual analysis can be explained in ways that are compatible with the traditional conception of knowledge as a composite condition. Second, the failure of the project of conceptual analysis doesn't show that knowledge is an irreducible *mental* state (cf. Leite 2005: 168–9).

Another argument in defense of the thesis that knowledge is an irreducible mental state involves the claim that knowing is a *prime* condition (Williamson 2000: 67–8). The thesis of primeness states that possessing knowledge is not a composite state or condition involving purely mental factors and purely environmental factors. The argument for primeness goes like this: a condition C is composite, rather than prime, if one can pluck the mental factor from one C-case, put it together with the environmental factor of a second C-case, and thereby construct a third C-case. Even if we grant Williamson that the condition of knowing doesn't allow for this kind of recombination of mental and environmental factors, it doesn't follow that knowledge is an irreducible mental state. Just because one can take a mental factor of one instance of knowing, add it to the environmental factor of another, and get something which isn't a case of knowing, doesn't mean that knowing is a prime condition. The problem with this argument is that the existence of a non-knowing-recombination is not a sufficient condition for the primeness of knowing (cf. Brueckner 2002; Magnus and Cohen 2003: 40–4).

A further reason for thinking that knowing is prime is that knowledge can sometimes provide a better explanation of action than belief can. That a person knows something may better explain his actions than merely that he believes it truly. Williamson gives the following example. You are at home when someone knocks on the door. You don't reply and wonder how the visitor reacts. If before knocking the visitor knows that you are at home, then he will (rightly) conclude that you are hiding from him and will be offended. If before knocking the visitor merely has the true belief that you are in, then he is likely to abandon this belief when you fail to reply and he will not be cross with you. Williamson (2000: 86) concludes that 'Whether [the visitor] would take offence is better predicted by whether he knows than by whether he believes. His taking offence is more highly correlated with knowing that you are in than with believing (truly) that you are in.'

The crucial premiss in Williamson's reasoning is that the visitor is less likely to revise his belief concerning your whereabouts when you fail to reply if he knows than if he merely believes truly. '[S]omeone who knows that your are in [the house] has grounds that will not be undermined just by your failure to reply' (ibid. 86). In other words, knowledge is said to be more robust than mere belief against revision upon the discovery of misleading evidence. An obvious problem with this premiss is that since knowledge doesn't necessarily involve confidence, the discovery of misleading evidence might lead the knowing subject to abandon his knowledge. In fact, Williamson allows that knowledge need not involve confidence, for he rejects epistemic internalism (cf. ibid. 164–83). And given Williamson's endorsement of epistemic externalism, his claim that knowledge is more robust than belief is at best ad hoc. According to externalism, the fact that the visitor's true belief that you are at home is based on 'grounds that are not undermined just by your failure to reply' doesn't make it more likely that he will continue to hold this belief when you fail to reply than if his true belief was not based on such grounds. For the visitor could be ignorant of the fact that his belief is based on such grounds and could therefore have no confidence in this belief.[21]

---

[21] A different objection in terms of confidence derives from Kaplan (2003). According to Kaplan, the explanation of the visitor's persistence in believing that you are at home in terms of knowledge is just as good as the explanation in terms of confidence. And since confidence is

Since, in my view, Williamson doesn't succeed in showing that one's possession of knowledge is not a complex condition comprising mental and environmental factors, I see no reason to abandon the pretheoretical conception of knowledge as implying belief.

3.5 THE ANALYSIS OF INFERENTIAL MEMORY

As was explained before (cf. p. 85), a putative reason why an agent might remember p without having believed p* in the past is because he lacked the conceptual means necessary to believe p*. To illustrate this kind of case reconsider Malcolm's blue jay example already mentioned on pages 25 and 77: at t_1 S sees a bird without knowing what sort of bird it is, and then later, at t_2, discovers from a book that such a bird is a blue jay. At t_2 he says 'I remember that I saw a blue jay at t_1.' But it is not true that S believed at t_1 that it was a blue jay. He has only just learned that it was a blue jay he saw. Does this mean that we have a counterexample to the past belief condition (8′) of the epistemic analysis of remembering? Malcolm answers in the negative. He suggests that when S asserts 'I remember that I saw a blue jay at t_1' he is using this expression in an elliptical sense. Malcolm (1963: 223) writes:

I believe that the man in our example would agree to substitute for his sentence 'I remember that I saw a [blue jay]' the *conjunctive* sentence 'I remember that I saw this bird (or: a bird of this kind) *and* now I know it was a [blue jay]'. The sentence he originally uttered was an ellipsis, in the grammarian's sense, the meaning of which is given by the conjunctive sentence. In this conjunction the first conjunct expresses factual memory, the second conjunct expresses the new information.

Since the epistemic theory of memory is intended to capture only non-inferential memory, that is, memory with no admixture of inference or present realization, the blue jay example does not count against it.

I agree with Malcolm that cases of inferential memory don't pose a threat to the epistemic analysis of memory. For this reason I have been at pains in section 3.2 to show that neither the Capitoline Wolf example nor the Colosseum example is an instance of inferential memory. Yet I

---

neither necessary nor sufficient for knowledge, the explanation in terms of confidence cannot be reduced to the explanation in terms of knowledge.

disagree with Malcolm's analysis of inferential memory. On Malcolm's reading,

(11) S remembers at t_2 that he saw at t_1 a blue jay,

amounts to saying

(12) S remembers at t_2 that he saw at t_1 a bird of this kind & S comes to know at t_2 that it was a blue jay.

The problem with this analysis of inferential memory is that it glosses over the possibility where S knows that he saw an F, knows that Fs are G, and yet fails to know that he saw a G because he doesn't draw the proper inference. But if S doesn't know that he saw a G, it follows that he doesn't inferentially remember that he saw a G. Thus to remember that he saw a blue jay S not only needs to have learned what blue jays are and what they look like, but also needs to apply this piece of knowledge to the bird he saw at t_1. (The linguistic expression of S's applying the newly acquired knowledge to the previous experience is that the indefinite pronoun 'it' in (12) refers back to 'a bird of this kind'.) If, for some reason, S failed to put his knowledge about blue jays together with the bird he saw at t_1, then it would be wrong to say that he remembers having seen a blue jay.

Against the background of what might be called the *application problem*, Eric Stiffler (1980) suggests analyzing sentence (11) as the existential generalization (13):

(13) $(\exists x)$ (x is a bird of this kind & S remembers at t_2 that he saw at t_1 x & S comes to know at t_2 that x was a blue jay).

Unlike statement (12), (13) preserves the proper application link between later knowledge and earlier memory. According to Stiffler, rather than reducing to non-inferential propositional memory plus present knowledge, inferential memory amounts to memory (and knowledge) *de re*.

Despite the advantages of (13) over (12), Stiffler's analysis of inferential memory is both too strong and too weak. The analysis is too strong because S can inferentially remember that he saw a blue jay in the garden even though he is not in a position to visualize the particular bird that he saw at t_1 in the garden. The analysis is at the same time too weak because the fact that S's earlier memory and his later knowledge concern the same object does not insure that S puts two and two together. S can remember with respect to a particular bird (*de re*) that he saw it at t_1, know now with respect to this bird (*de re*) that it is a blue jay, and yet fail to inferentially remember that he saw a blue jay at t_1. Thus, analysis (13) doesn't really solve the application problem.

Following Arnold Cusmariu (1980: 307–8), I reckon that the application problem can be solved within the confines of Malcolm's original conjunctive, *de dicto* analysis of inferential memory. All we need to do is to add a third conjunct to Malcolm's two-part analysis of statement (11):

> (14) (i) S remembers at t_2 that he saw at t_1 a bird of this kind & (ii) S comes to know at t_2 that any bird of this kind is a blue jay & (iii) S comes to know at t_2 that he saw a blue jay inferentially from (i) and (ii).

More generally, where p, q, and r are logically inequivalent propositions, S inferentially remembers that p only if:

> (15) (i) S remembers at t_2 that q & (ii) S comes to know at t_2 that r & (iii) S comes to know at t_2 that p inferentially from (i) and (ii), & (iv) the conjunction of q and r entails but is not entailed by p.

Yet, as it stands, (15) is too strict, for it assumes that inferential memory is necessarily a form of inferential knowing. Granted that my arguments against the epistemic theory of memory work, (15) must be replaced with some weaker condition (15′):

> (15′) (i) S remembers at t_2 that q & (ii) S comes to truly think at t_2 that r & (iii) S comes to truly think at t_2 that p inferentially from (i) and (ii), & (iv) the conjunction of q and r entails but is not entailed by p.

3.6 MODERATE GENERATIVISM

As was explained in section 3.1, the epistemic theory consists of two claims. The first is that remembering is a form of knowing. The second is that memory can only preserve but not generate justification and knowledge. After having dealt with the first claim I will now discuss the second. Though memory doesn't imply justification and knowledge, memory beliefs can, of course, be justified and qualify as knowledge. And so the question arises whether memory is merely a preservative source of justification and knowledge or whether it may also function as a generative source.

The epistemic theory of memory is committed to *preservationism* whereupon the only way a memory belief can have a positive epistemic status (justification, blamelessness, rationality, etc.) is if the original belief had a positive epistemic status. One is justified in believing at t_2 that p on the basis of memory only if one was justified in believing at t_1 that p^* and one acquired at t_1 the justification with respect to p^* via a source other than memory. Memory cannot improve the epistemic status a belief has at the time of recall *vis-à-vis* the epistemic status it had at the time it was originally acquired. Memory is incapable of making an unknown proposition known, an unjustified belief justified, or an irrational belief rational—it can only preserve what is already known, justified, or rational. The memory belief may be less justified than the original belief, but it may not be more justified.

The goal of this section is to show that memory can indeed function as a generative source of justification and knowledge. Given generativism, a memory belief may not only be less but also more justified than the original belief. A memory belief may be justified even if the original belief wasn't justified. Before spelling out my own view—which I call *moderate generativism*—I will briefly discuss a generativist proposal that has been put forward in the literature.

According to John Pollock, the phenomenology of recalling can provide justification for memory beliefs. He draws a parallel between memory and perception. In a standard case of perceptual belief, one is 'appeared to' in a certain way and, on the basis of this appearance, comes to justifiably believe something about the perceptual surroundings. Similarly, when one remembers something one has a recollection and, on the basis of this phenomenal state, comes to justifiably believe something about the past. ' "S recalls that p" is a prima facie justified reason for S to believe that it was true that p' (Pollock 1974: 193). So if one bases one's belief that p on one's state of seeming to remember that p, and p is undefeated, then one is at least prima facie justified in believing p. Robert Audi's position is strikingly similar to Pollock's. Audi (1995: 37) declares:

If, for any proposition p that is not obviously false, (a) S has a memorial sense that p or (b) would (other things equal) have such a sense upon considering p, then S has *prima facie* memorial justification for believing p, of a degree sufficient to make it not unreasonable for a rational person in S's position to believe p. (a) is a phenomenal condition; (b) is an accessibility condition. Each is represented as sufficient for *prima facie* justification for believing p—for *propositional justification*—not for an actual belief of p—*doxastic justification*. If, in addition, S believes p on the basis of this sense, then S has a (*prima facie*) justified memory belief that p, i.e., believes it with *prima facie* memorial justification, as opposed to simply *having* such justification for believing it.

The reason Pollock's and Audi's positions are versions of generativism is that they allow for cases where the memory belief is justified to a greater extent than the original belief.

Even if we grant Pollock and Audi that there is a distinctive memorial phenomenology that attends all the memory beliefs we are justified in holding and even if we grant that the experiential features of memory beliefs can do the epistemic work that Pollock and Audi assign to them, this version of generativism has its problems.[22] In the absence of defeating conditions, the epistemic status of a belief is said to improve simply in virtue of the belief being recalled. Every time a belief is retrieved from memory it receives an extra epistemic boost. This, I reckon, is an implausible consequence. It is implausible to suppose that, everything else being equal, a belief that is retrieved often enjoys a better epistemic status than a belief that is retrieved infrequently. There is no neat correlation between the positive epistemic status a belief has and the number of times it has been retrieved from memory. Following Matthew McGrath (2007: 19–22), we can call this the *epistemic boost problem*.

To distinguish the position Pollock and Audi subscribe to from the view for which I will argue here, I will refer to it as *radical generativism*. Radical generativism has it that memory can generate new justificatory factors, new evidence. If, for instance, I came to justifiably believe at t_1 that p^*, on the basis of a priori reasoning, and if I remember at t_2 that p, then the memory belief inherits (some of) the justification the original belief had and there will be an additional justificatory element due to the process of remembering. The justification of a memory belief has two parts: there is a preserved component and a new component due to the act of recalling.

Moderate generativism, by contrast, agrees with preservationism in that the memory process generates no new elements of justification or evidence. Memory cannot make justification and knowledge from nothing. Instead, the only way for memory to function as a generative

---

[22] For a critical discussion of the idea that remembering has a distinctive phenomenology see my (2008: 81–104).

source of justification is by removing defeaters and thereby unleashing the justificatory potential that was already present at the time the belief was initially entertained. All the elements required for a memory belief to be justified must already have been present when the belief was encoded. If the original belief had no justificatory potential because, say, it was gettierized, then memory cannot turn it into a justified belief. Memory generates justification only by lifting justificatory elements that were previously rebutted or undermined by defeating evidence.

Jennifer Lackey (2005) has recently provided two novel arguments for moderate generativism. Her first argument is meant to show that memory might not preserve belief. She argues that a subject might take in some information without forming a belief with the information in question as its content. The information can then be stored in memory. When the information is later retrieved, the subject can form a belief with the information as its content. Lackey illustrates this with a case that has already been mentioned on pages 22 and 86 n15: S sees construction on the road but (because his attention is elsewhere) does not come to believe that there is construction on the road; later, when asked what he saw while driving, S remembers (and so comes to believe) that there is construction on the road. Given some assumptions about the reliability of the relevant cognitive processes in cases of this sort the resulting belief is justified. Lackey takes this example to show that memory can generate justification by generating a new belief with a previously stored content.

This argument fails to support (moderate) generativism. Instead of being a case of memory without past justification it is a case of memory without past belief; more specifically it is a case of what (in sect. 3.3) I have called *inattentive remembering*. The reason Lackey's example fails to support (moderate) generativism is that the epistemic status of S's representation at t_1 is the very same as the epistemic status of his belief at t_2. What distinguishes S's propositional attitude at t_1 from his propositional attitude at t_2 is awareness or conceptualization but not justification. Just because memory generates belief doesn't mean that it generates justification. Examples of delayed awareness or conceptualization are fully compatible with preservationism.

Lackey's second argument for moderate generativism is more promising. Memory can generate justification for a belief, due to changes in the relationship of the belief to defeaters. Lackey points out that a subject's relation to defeaters can change over time (due to changes in his external environment affecting which propositions he ought to believe), thus altering the epistemic status of a belief held in memory, and argues that this implies that memory can function generatively. In the remainder of this section I will examine this line of argument for moderate generativism.

To see that memory can generate justification and knowledge consider a variation of the Colosseum example discussed on pages 78–9: at t_1, S learned that the Colosseum was completed in AD 80. He comes to know this fact about the Colosseum. At t_2, S's 'friends' play a practical joke on him. They tell him that the Colosseum was not completed until AD 90 and present him with plausible yet misleading evidence to this effect. At t_3, S still remembers what he knew at t_1, namely that the Colosseum was completed in AD 80, but he has completely forgotten about the doctored evidence to the effect that the Colosseum was not completed until AD 90.

At t_2 S is not justified in believing (and hence doesn't know) that the Colosseum was completed in AD 80. The reason is that he has an undefeated doxastic defeater for the belief in question. At t_3 the doxastic defeater has disappeared, for S has forgotten that his friends presented him with (bogus) evidence that suggests that the Colosseum was not completed until AD 90. S forgets the misleading belief that did the defeating work while retaining the belief that was originally defeated. Now if the presence of the undefeated doxastic defeater is the only reason S doesn't know at t_2, then he knows again when the defeater is forgotten at t_3. In this way the belief that was originally defeated can become knowledge via memory when the misleading evidence that functioned as a defeater is forgotten.

Against this example, however, it may be argued that what is functioning as a generative source of knowledge here is not memory but forgetting. Given that doxastic defeaters are propositions that are believed by the subject in question to be true, a subject can get rid of doxastic defeaters by forgetting the relevant beliefs. But since forgetting is the absence of remembering it is a mistake to conclude that memory (as opposed to forgetting) has the capacity to function as a generative source of knowledge.

By way of response to this objection, it is important to realize that a common reason for forgetting is interference from other remembered information. In a now-classic experiment students learned lists of nonsense syllables either in the evening just before going to bed or in the morning just after getting up (Jenkins and Dallenbach 1924). The researchers then tested the students' memories of the syllables after one, two, four, or eight hours. If the students learned the material just before bed, they slept during the time between the study session and the test. If they learned the material just after waking, they were awake during the interval before testing. The students forgot significantly more while they were awake than while they were asleep. What this experiment suggests is that what causes forgetting is not just the decay of memory traces due to the passage of time, but interference from other memories. Yet if forgetting something is frequently due to remembering something else, then it cannot be ruled out that the reason S has forgotten about the doctored evidence and is therefore able to know again that the Colosseum was completed in AD 80 is, after all, his memory.

Another way to reject the force of the above case is to argue that when S forgets about the bogus evidence presented by his 'friends' his undefeated doxastic defeater doesn't vanish but instead changes into an undefeated normative defeater. Given this line of thought, the bogus evidence still prevents S at t_3 from knowing what year the Colosseum was completed.

There is something to the idea that an undefeated doxastic defeater becomes an undefeated normative defeater if it is merely forgotten rather than defeated. Yet this consideration cannot be used to support the epistemic theory of memory, for there are examples of memory functioning as a generative source of justification and knowledge that involve normative rather than doxastic defeaters. Consider this example[23]: at t_1 S learned about the assassination of the mayor of his city by reading a report in a generally reliable newspaper. S unhesitatingly formed the belief that the mayor has been assassinated. The next day, at t_2, the mayor's allies, wishing to protect their jobs, exploited their high-powered connections in the media to cover up the mayor's death. To this end they convinced the television stations and newspapers to report that the mayor is alive and well. Most people see these reports and revise their beliefs about the mayor's health accordingly. S, however, missed the denials of the assassination and continues to hold the true belief that the mayor has been assassinated. At t_3, the devious scheme to cover up the mayor's death is exposed, and the newspapers and television stations report once again that the mayor has been assassinated. Throughout all of this, S remained ignorant of the media's attempt to cover up the mayor's death and continued to believe that the mayor had been

---

[23] The example is inspired by Harman (1973: 143–4) and is adapted from Lackey (2005: 640–1).

assassinated solely on the basis of remembering the original newspaper report from t_1.

Due to the presence of an undefeated normative defeater, S fails to know at t_2 that the mayor has been assassinated. Since every newspaper and television station was reporting that the mayor had *not* been assassinated, S would have believed that the mayor is alive if only he had turned on the television or had picked up a newspaper. At t_3, however, it is no longer the case that the only reason S believes that the mayor has been assassinated is that he fails to perform his epistemic duty. And given that the presence of the undefeated defeater was the only factor preventing S's true belief at t_2 from qualifying as knowledge, its absence at t_3 enables S to know. S knows at t_3 that the mayor is dead but he didn't know it at t_2. This example shows then that a subject's relation to normative defeaters can change over time as a result of changes in the external environment, thereby enabling memory to generate knowledge.

There are three ways in which one may attempt to deny that the assassination example undermines the epistemic theory of memory.[24] First, one might question that bogus evidence of which the subject isn't even aware is capable of preventing an otherwise epistemically impeccable belief from qualifying as an instance of knowledge. The suggestion is that S continues to know through t_2 of the mayor's death. The problem with this suggestion is, however, there are pieces of information that one is expected to be aware of by virtue of being a member of society, and the mere fact that one happens to be ignorant of such information doesn't enable one to have knowledge that everyone else lacks. Unless ignorance of 'common knowledge' is appropriately grounded, which it is not here, it is incompatible with having the knowledge in question. Otherwise one could come to know more by knowing less.

Second, it may be argued that the normative defeater S has at t_2 continues to defeat his belief about the mayor's death through t_3, regardless of the fact that the defeater no longer exists at t_3. The fact that at t_3 all of the major newspapers and television stations cease reporting the false information about the mayor doesn't alter the status of S's defeated belief formed prior to t_3. Absent evidence can function not only positively but also negatively, by continuing to defeat a belief. The

---

[24] The first and third objections are dealt with by Lackey (2005: 642–4). The second objection is discussed in Senor (2007: 204–5) and Lackey (2007: 213–16).

problem with this objection is that it doesn't take into consideration that the defeating evidence in question is misleading. Misleading evidence can function as a normative defeater for one's belief when present in one's immediate environment; but it loses its defeating power once it is replaced with veridical evidence. If we modify the example and imagine that the defeating evidence at t_2 is veridical, then it does continue to function as a defeater even after the media start spreading lies about the mayor at t_3.

Third, one may argue that what generates knowledge in the above example is the external environment and not S's memory. Since changes in the environment are responsible for the disappearance of the defeater at t_3, shouldn't we credit the external environment rather than memory with the ability to generate knowledge? The answer is 'no'. As Wittgenstein correctly notes in *On Certainty*: 'It is always by favor of Nature that one knows something' (1969: §505). Just as S couldn't have known at t_1 about the mayor's death without the environment's cooperation his knowledge at t_3 is dependent on the environment removing the defeater. Yet changes in the environment have epistemic significance only relative to some particular faculty of a given subject. And the only plausible candidate for a faculty operative in the given case is memory. Hence it is memory that should be credited with the generation of justification and knowledge.

The lesson to be learned from this chapter is that it is possible to remember something in the present that one didn't justifiably believe in the past. Likewise one may acquire in the meantime some plausible but misleading evidence that destroys the status as justified belief of the once-genuine justified belief that one still remembers. Moreover, cases of ignorant remembering show that one can remember something that one doesn't believe. In sum then, knowledge supervenes on some but not all cases of propositional remembering. Unlike knowledge, memory implies neither belief nor justification. But the epistemic theory of memory is not only wrong in holding that memory is a form of knowledge. It is also mistaken in assuming that memory cannot alter the epistemic status of a belief. We have seen that memory doesn't merely have the capacity to preserve epistemic features generated by other sources but that it is also a generative epistemic source.

4

In Defense of the Causal Theory of Memory

Though it is in principle possible for remembering and learning afresh to coincide (cf. sect. 8.4), usually there is a sharp divide between remembering a proposition and learning a proposition afresh. Given that this is so, any theory of memory must devise a condition that will guarantee that the content of a memory state is retained rather than relearned. To remember a proposition, not only must it have been represented before, but its present tokening must be suitably related to its past tokening.

Work on the connection condition of memory has proceeded in a number of different directions. The interpretations of the memory connection proposed in the literature fall into three categories: the evidential retention theory, the simple retention theory, and the causal retention theory. The aim of this chapter is to weigh up these three accounts and to argue for the causal retention theory. In the following chapter I will try to determine the kind of causal relation constitutive of remembering.

Sections 4.1 and 4.2 offer explication and criticism of the evidential retention theory and of the simple retention theory, respectively. Section 4.3 outlines the causal theory of memory. Section 4.4 looks at three arguments against the causal theory of memory and shows that none of them is successful. Sections 4.5 and 4.6 examine arguments in favor of the causal theory of memory and find them wanting. Section 4.6 also sets forth my own argument for the causal theory of memory. Anticipating the conclusion, there are, in my mind, two things that speak in favor of the causal theory of memory. First, unlike the causal theory, the evidential retention theory and the simple retention theory are afflicted with serious problems. Second, the causal theory of memory can best explain the truth of commonsensical counterfactual statements of the form 'If S hadn't represented at t_1 that p^* he wouldn't represent at t_2 that p.'

4.1 EVIDENTIAL RETENTION THEORY

The evidential retention theory presupposes the epistemic theory of memory. As was explained in section 3.1, the epistemic theory of memory analyzes propositional memory in something like the following way: S remembers at t_2 that p only if:

(1) S knows at t_2 that p,
(2) S knew at t_1 that p^*,
(3) p is identical with, or sufficiently similar to, p^*,
(4) S's knowing at t_2 that p is suitably connected to S's knowing at t_1 that p^*.

The purpose of the connection condition (4) is to make sure that the knowledge had in remembering is retained knowledge. Given (4), it is possible for S to know at t_2 that p, and to have known that p^* at t_1, and still fail to remember at t_2 that p. For S may simply have learned that p^* at t_1, forgotten it entirely in the interval between t_1 and t_2 and then learned p afresh at t_2. The formulation of (4) leaves open the exact nature of the memory connection. Condition (4) is compatible with any one of three competing accounts of the memory connection.

According to the evidential retention theory, for a present state of knowing p to be memory-related to a past state of knowing p^* the evidence or justification (however construed) must be the same. Retaining knowledge involves not only retaining known propositions but also supporting reasons. The idea is that for a piece of knowledge at t_2 to qualify as a memory state, its justificatory factors must be the same as those supporting the original piece of knowledge that has been retained from t_1. For S to remember that p he must know at t_2 that p, he must have known at t_1 that p^*, and his grounds for believing at t_1 that p^* must be the same as his grounds for believing at t_2 that p. A prototype of an evidential retention condition reads as follows:

(5) S's grounds for knowing at t_1 that p^* are the same as his grounds for knowing at t_2 that p.

(Here I intend the terms 'ground' and 'evidence' to cover both internalist and externalist conceptions of justification.) The evidential retention condition is a relatively recent development, finding first expression in Malcolm's *Knowledge and Certainty* and being worked out by Andrew Naylor (1971; 1983; 1985). Malcolm (1963: 230) writes:

> If B remembers that his friend, Robinson, was ill last year, then B previously knew of the illness. . . . B's *present* knowledge that Robinson was ill, if it is solely memory, has the *same* grounds. If the ground of his previous knowledge was testimony then the ground of his present knowledge is that same previous testimony.

Apart from Malcolm and Naylor the evidential retention theory of memory is advocated by David Annis (1980) and Alan Holland (1974).

The obvious problem with the evidential retention condition (5) is that it fails to rule out cases of relearning. That is, the evidential condition doesn't rule out instances where a person knew at t_1 that p^* on some grounds and knows at t_2 that p on the same grounds, but fails to remember that p, since he had completely forgotten that p in the interval between t_1 and t_2. There are two ways to fix the problem. One can add a proviso to the evidential retention condition whereupon the subject may not not know p at any time between t_1 and t_2:

> (6) S's grounds for knowing at t_1 that p^* are the same as his grounds for knowing at t_2 that p; and there is no time t_i (where $1 \leq i \leq 2$) when S does not know p (or p^*) on grounds that are the same as his grounds for knowing at t_2 that p.

Alternatively one can combine the evidential approach with the causal theory of memory to form a connection condition that looks like this:

> (7) S's grounds for knowing at t_1 that p^* are the same as his grounds for knowing that p at t_2; and S's knowing at t_1 that p^* is the cause of his knowing at t_2 that p.[1]

Both conditions seem to be successful in eliminating instances where a person comes to know at t_1 that p^*, completely forgets it, and then freshly acquires the knowledge that p at t_2. But since the causal theory of memory is the topic of section 4.3, I will focus here on (6) rather than on (7).

What does it mean for two pieces of knowledge to be supported by the same grounds? Should we say that a person remembers something only if

---

[1] Condition (6) is inspired by a similar condition suggested, but not endorsed, by Sherouse (1979: 149). The idea for condition (7) stems from Holland (1974: 362–3).

each and every ground supporting his belief at t_2 also supported his belief at t_1? Even if we knew how to individuate grounds, this interpretation would run into problems. For sometimes one's grounds for believing at t_1 that p^* are only a subset of one's grounds for believing at t_2 that p because one has acquired additional grounds in the meantime. But when the grounds at t_2 include items not included in the set of original grounds, the grounds for believing at t_1 that p^* and the grounds for believing at t_2 that p are not the very same and hence one couldn't be said to *remember* that p. This is obviously counterintuitive.

For the evidential retention condition to account for cases where sameness of grounds is violated because of an enlargement of the set of grounds all one has to do is to specify that the set of grounds for believing at t_1 that p^* has to be either the same as, *or a subset of*, the set of grounds for believing at t_2 that p:

> (6′) S's grounds for knowing at t_1 that p^* are identical to, or a subset of, his grounds for knowing at t_2 that p; and there is no time t_i (where $1 \leq i \leq 2$) when S does not know p (or p^*) on grounds that are identical to, or a subset of his grounds for knowing at t_2 that p.[2]

Condition (6′) demands not numerical sameness of grounds, but inclusion of the prior set of grounds within the present set. Given (6′), cases in which a person's evidence for p at t_2 outstrips his evidence for p^* at t_1 can be reckoned as cases of remembering—provided that the original grounds are part of the present set of grounds.

In addition to the problem of acquiring new grounds between t_1 and t_2 there is the problem of losing (some of) the original grounds. A great deal of the knowledge that we possess in memory we have forgotten how we came to know what we know. As was explained in section 3.2, there are several ways in which a belief may lose its justificatory status while being stored in memory. One way of losing grounds is to encounter defeating evidence (defeated justification cases). Another way of losing some of the grounds that originally supported the target belief is to simply forget them (absent justification cases).

Absent justification cases pose a challenge only to an internal-ist reading of the evidentialist approach. Given that the factors required for a belief to be epistemically justified must be cognitively accessible to the subject, as internalism claims, when an agent is not in

---

[2] Similar conditions can be found in Annis (1980: 332) and Naylor (1971: 33).

a position to rehearse the original grounds on which he acquired the belief that p, he cannot be said to remember that p. But claiming that the notion of memory applies to only those instances of retained knowledge where the subject is able to recount all his original grounds has the unbearable consequence that memory is an extremely rare commodity. Hence most epistemologists endorse the externalist principle of continuous justification: at t_2, S's belief at t_1 that p^* is continuously justified if S continues to believe at t_2 that p—even if S has forgotten his original knowledge-producing evidence and has acquired no fresh evidence in the meantime. When the principle of continuous justification is coupled with the evidential retention theory, S may be said to retain the grounds he originally possessed without having to be able to rehearse them.

As was explained before (cf. 74–6), defeated justification cases affect both the internalist and the externalist conception of the epistemic theory of memory. Even on an externalist perspective whereupon the justifying factors of a belief may be external to the subject's cognitive perspective, the acquisition of undefeated defeating evidence between t_1 and t_2 can undermine the justificatory status of the once-genuine knowledge that one still remembers. How then can the evidential retention theory block cases of defeated justification?

A natural suggestion, and the one adopted by Annis (1980: 329–30) and Naylor (1983: 279), is to add an indefeasibility clause to the evidential retention condition. On this proposal, one can remember only what one has indefeasible justification for believing. A subject's justification is indefeasible if there are no doxastic or normative defeaters which are undefeated. So we end up with the following connection condition:

(6″) S's grounds for knowing at t_1 that p^* are identical to, or a subset of his grounds for knowing at t_2 that p; there is no time t_i (where $1 \leq i \leq 2$) when S does not know p (or p^*) on grounds that are identical to, or a subset of, his grounds for knowing that p at t_2; and the grounds for knowing at t_2 that p amount to indefeasible justification.

Condition (6″) has the advantage of eliminating defeated justification cases. Yet it requires little reflection to see that (6″) is too stringent to be a convincing interpretation of the connection condition for remembering. For why should the conditions on remembering something one previously knew be any stricter than the conditions on knowing that thing for the first time? According to (6″), remembering at t_2 that p requires not only having been justified at t_1 in adopting the belief that p*, but also being justified at t_2 in retaining p.

Leaving the intricacies of the evidential retention condition aside, the main problem with the evidentialist approach is, of course, its commitment to the epistemic theory of memory criticized in Chapter 3. Since remembering that p doesn't imply knowing that p, any attempt to explicate the memory connection in evidential terms is doomed from the start. Discussing the evidential retention theory is nevertheless useful. Even if we convinced ourselves of the truth of the epistemic theory of memory the evidentialist approach would still run into problems, for it has the tendency to make the conditions for remembering too stringent.

4.2 SIMPLE RETENTION THEORY

According to the causal theory, for one's present representation that p to qualify as memory one must have represented that p* in the past and one's past representation of p* must be causally effective in producing one's present representation of p. Yet some philosophers maintain that to connect a past and present representation in the way required for memory what is required is merely that, in virtue of having represented p*, one acquired an ability or disposition that one retained and now exercises by representing p. Simple retention theorists such as Roger Squires (1969: 178) hold that 'in describing something [or someone] as having retained a quality, as having stayed the same in a certain respect, there is no forced reference to causal connections'; there need not be a causal connection between one's past and present states of representing.

We can sometimes explain the fact that someone who had a car last year has a car now by saying that he must have had it all along. But this is not a causal explanation. Similarly, when we explain that someone must be remembering we are, in general, either pointing out that what he did was a display of knowledge (rather than an accident, say) or we are saying that he has had that knowledge all along (ibid. 191).

Just as the conditional 'If S hadn't owned a particular car at t_1, he wouldn't own it today' need not be a causal conditional, 'If S hadn't known at t_1 that p*, he wouldn't know at t_2 that p' need not be causal either; or so the proponent of the simple retention theory maintains.

The simple retention interpretation of the memory connection goes back to Gilbert Ryle. According to Ryle (1949: 272), 'remembering something means having learned something and not forgotten it'. When this passage is read as an attempt to analyze the concept of memory, the following analysis emerges: S remembers at t_2 that p only if S knows at t_2 that p, S knew at t_1 that p*, and S has not forgotten that p in the interval from t_1 to t_2. Thus the archetype of a simple retention condition is:

(8) S has not forgotten that p in the interval from t_1 to t_2.

Condition (8) rules out as remembering those cases in which a person comes to know that p, forgets it, and then relearns it afresh. Yet the obvious problem with (8) is that we frequently remember something at t_2 even though we have (temporarily) forgotten it in the interval between initial learning at t_1 and t_2. One could try to fix this problem by adding the proviso that S has not *permanently* forgotten that p:

(8′) S has not permanently forgotten that p in the interval from t_1 to t_2.

Condition (8′), however, is a trivial truth. Since remembering is the absence of permanent forgetting, (8′) gives us no enlightenment whatsoever regarding the nature of the memory connection.

Unlike the evidential retention theory, the simple retention theory is not committed to the view that remembering that p entails knowing that p. Nevertheless many proponents of the simple retention theory subscribe to the epistemic theory of memory. Some of the simple retention conditions found in the literature are worded in such a way that it is assumed that memory entails knowledge. Stanley Munsat (1967: 33–6), for example, proposes this simple retention condition:

(9) There is no time t_i (where $1 \leq i \leq 2$) when S did not know that p,

and, an apparent variation on the same theme,

(10) S did not just find out that p.

Condition (9) fails for the same reason as condition (8): it doesn't account for instances where a person remembers that p but has temporarily forgotten that p in the interval between the prior and the present knowing. Yet it is an undeniable fact that we frequently forget something temporarily but are able to remember it later on. Munsat is aware of this problem and tries to get around it by distinguishing between not *knowing* at t_i (where $1 \leq i \leq 2$) that p and not being able to *think* of p at t_i.

> If I try to remember something at a certain time but cannot, and then later on *can* (do), we say I 'knew it all along'. And I think that if we now say that I remember that p, then we are committed to describing my previous inability to recall that p as 'not being able to think of it at the time' and *not* as 'not knowing at the time (when asked) that p'.   (ibid. 34 n8)

This is far from clear. Suppose S develops amnesia as a result of a blow on his forehead. Among the many things S forgets is his name and address. Suppose further that after a few months S's memory recovers. It seems problematic to say that S knew his name and address 'all along' and was just not able to think of it at the time. Instead, I reckon, we would say that, during the period of his amnesia, S did not know these things. Don Locke seems to share my intuition. He declares:

> [I]f someone reminds me of some fact I had completely forgotten, and would not have remembered if he had not reminded me, it does not seem correct to say that I possessed that knowledge continuously. Something has been retained, something that enables me to say when reminded, 'Ah yes, I remember now'. But that something does not seem to be a piece of knowledge, because, before I was reminded, I no longer knew the fact in question.
>
> (1971: 62–3; see also Annis 1980: 330)

Like (9), Munsat's condition (10)—S did not just find out that p—is too stringent, albeit for different reasons. It rules out cases where a person simultaneously finds out that p and genuinely remembers that p. As will be explained in section 5.4, most of our remembering depends on us being presented with some kind of prompt or retrieval cue. A subject is strictly prompted when he cannot reproduce more about the event or proposition than was supplied by the prompt. The prompted information is as detailed as the retained knowledge. The problem with (10) is that it doesn't account for cases where someone simultaneously finds out that p by being strictly prompted and by remembering that p.

Another proponent of the epistemic theory of memory, Eddy Zemach (1968: 529) proposes this simple retention condition:

(11) S believes at t_2 that he knew at t_1 that p*.

The problem with (11) is that it is both too stringent and too liberal. It is too stringent because it excludes cases where someone remembers that p but doesn't believe that he previously knew that p^*. Suppose S knows at t_2 that p and knew at t_1 that p^*. Yet he fails to believe at t_2 that he knew at t_1 that p^*; instead, he mistakenly believes that he has only now come to know p through logical deduction from some present occurrence. According to Zemach, S's knowledge that p doesn't qualify as memory that p—a counterintuitive result. Condition (11) is also too liberal because it counts certain instances of relearning as instances of remembering. Suppose S came to know at t_1 that p^*. Afterwards, at t_2, he completely forgot this fact. At t_3 he reads in a book and once again comes to know that p. He doesn't realize at any time that he had forgotten p^* at t_2, and so at t_3 he believes that he remembers that p from the time t_1, when he first knew that p^*. Thus S knew at t_1 that p^*, knows at t_3 that p, and believes at t_3 that he knew at t_1 that p^*. Zemach's condition for remembering is fulfilled, but, I take it, we wouldn't want to say that S remembers that p.

Even if we succeeded in formulating a simple retention condition that is neither too stringent nor too liberal, the simple retention approach would still not be convincing, for it doesn't have the resources to answer some of the most pressing questions regarding the memory connection. As Max Deutscher (1989: 62) quite rightly declares, in claiming 'the continuity of capacities, [we] are always committed to the continuity of *some* processes adequate to the continuity'. The simple retention conditions, however, appear informative only as long as one refrains from asking what is involved in the process of retaining of a representation or a piece of knowledge. When this question is raised, proponents of this approach must concede that they don't have a positive story to tell. The only thing they do say about the retention process is that it is not of a causal kind.

I have doubts whether the idea of non-causal information storage even makes sense. For how could the state of an information storage medium at a given time *not* have a causal effect on the state of the same information storage medium at some later time? I submit that if proponents of the simple retention theory tried to spell out the process underlying the retention of knowledge and representation their position would ultimately collapse into the causal theory of memory. Given that this is so, a proponent of the simple retention theory may choose to not give a positive story of what is involved in non-causal retention. Yet a theory of memory retention that intentionally leaves the retention process unexplained makes memory appear to be a magical faculty. The causal theory has the clear explanatory advantage over the simple theory in that it addresses the question of what kind of process makes memory retention possible. (I will return to this point at the end of section 4.6.)

4.3 CAUSAL RETENTION THEORY

According to the causal theory of memory, for S to remember that p his present representation of p must stand in an appropriate causal relation to his past representation of p*. The archetypical causal connection condition reads:

(12) S's representation at t_2 that p is suitably causally connected to S's representation at t_1 that p*.

Alternatively, the idea can be expressed as follows:

(13) S represents at t_2 that p because S represented at t_1 that p*,

where 'because' is understood as expressing a causal relation. These conditions are on the right track in that they demand that in remembering there is some sort of causal connection or dependence between the past and the present. The crucial issue, however, is what should count as a *suitable* causal connection. Not just any sort of causal connection will suffice for memory; some causal chains are not of the appropriate sort, they are deviant.

To appreciate the relevance of the problem of deviant causal chains consider the following case, adapted from Martin and Deutscher (1966: 180–1), in which a subject is randomly caused by a past event to believe that that event obtained. At t_1 S witnessed a car accident. At t_2, S told his friend all about the accident. Then, at t_3, S got a blow on the head as a result of which he permanently forgot everything about the accident he witnessed at t_1. When, at t_4, the friend noticed that S can no longer remember the car accident, he told S the details that S had told him at t_2. S heard the friend tell him about the car accident and appropriated the narrative as something he experienced first-hand. The appropriation of the friend's narrative causes S at t_5 to seem to recall the accident via a causal chain that includes his friend's memories and honest intentions. This causal chain even supports a counterfactual correlation between the facts S observed at the scene of the accident and his apparent memories of the accident at t_5: if S hadn't observed the accident at t_1, his friend wouldn't have told him about it and hence S wouldn't seem to recall the accident at t_5. Intuitively, however, S's retelling at t_5 of what he saw of the accident at t_1 doesn't qualify as remembering. S's retelling is caused by his having witnessed the accident, but the causal chain connecting the initial experience and the subsequent retelling is not of the right kind in that it follows an external loop. Not just any causal connection between a past representation and its subsequent recall renders the latter a piece of memory. In Chapter 5 I will attempt to refine condition (11) to the point of allowing only genuine instances of remembering.

The problem of spelling out the notion of appropriate causation is an instance of a more general problem. Causal relations are transitive: if A causes B, and B causes C, then A causes C. Every cause of a cause of C is also a cause of C; and every effect of an effect of A is also an effect of A. Since every element in a causal chain from A to C is both cause of C and effect of A, it is often difficult to say which is the relevant cause of a certain event. Take the following case. Owing to his unhappy childhood, S has become an alcoholic. One night, after having had too many drinks, S drives his car and gets into an accident. What caused S to have an accident? A judge might take S's lack of concentration due to his high blood-alcohol level as the cause of the accident, while a psychoanalyst might put the blame on his parents for it was their cruelty that brought about his drinking problem in the first place. The decision as to what is an effective cause and what is a contributing cause depends (in part) on pragmatic considerations and it is not clear that there is a non-arbitrary way of identifying effective causes.

We possess pretty good intuitive means to say in particular cases which causal paths warrant the attribution of memory and which don't. The problem, however, is to come up with a general criterion for the kind of causal relation constitutive of remembering. But before we can attempt to describe the nature of memory causation we need to concern ourselves with a more fundamental question: is it indeed necessary to analyze memory as a causal process? Is a causal condition—however it might be spelled out—indispensable for explaining remembering? This is the issue that concerns the remainder of the chapter.

4.4 THREE OBJECTIONS TO THE CAUSAL THEORY

The literature contains three arguments against the causal theory of memory: there is an argument from the contingency of causation, an argument from the nomologicality of causation, and an argument from temporal forgetting. In this section I shall discuss these arguments in turn and show that none of them is successful.

The Contingency of Causation

Hume famously held that the relation between cause and effect is not a necessary one and that causal relation cannot be known a priori. For Hume these two claims were two sides of the same coin. To say that two events are necessarily connected is just another way of saying that, if one knows that one event occurs, one can predict on the basis of a priori reasoning that the other events occurs as well. Today we know that Hume conflated analyticity with apriority. To say that it cannot be known a priori whether A caused B is quite different from saying that even if A did cause B, it might not have done so. Just as there are statements that are necessarily true without being knowable a priori, there are statements that are knowable a priori even though they are not necessarily true.

If, for the sake of the argument, we grant Hume that a logically necessary connection between two events is one that supports an a priori inference from one event to the other, then he is undoubtedly right in claiming that, in many cases at least, causes do not logically necessitate their effects. Whether there is a causal relation between A and B can only be learned a posteriori. *Any* event can be conceived to follow from the occurrence of a given cause; and the only way in which a particular effect can be inferred from a cause is on the basis of experience, in particular by observation of a regularity between events of the same type. This is the Humean requirement that a cause and its effect be distinct events:

[E]very effect is a distinct event from its cause. It could not, therefore, be discovered in the cause, and the first invention or conception of it, *a priori*, must be entirely arbitrary. And even after it is suggested, the conjunction of it with the cause must appear equally arbitrary; since there are always many other effects, which, to reason, must seem fully as consistent and natural. In vain, therefore, should we pretend to determine any single event, or infer any cause or effect, without the assistance of observation and experience. (2000*b*: 27)

When applied to the issue of memory, the Humean claim that causal relations can only subsist between distinct events demands that the past representation giving rise to an apparent memory be independent from the apparent memory in two respects: first, it is impossible to know a priori what kind of memory state the representation will give rise to or which representation gave rise to a given memory state; second, the causal relation between the past event and the memory state is not a necessary one.

Now there are some, like Wolfgang von Leyden (1961: 31), who maintain that 'it is part of the meaning of memory that, when it is correct, it is causally dependent upon a previous perception'. On this view, the memory state is *logically* dependent on the relevant past event. From 'S remembers at t_2 that p' it follows with logical necessity that 'S represented at t_1 that p*'. So there is a tension between this interpretation of the causal theory of memory and the Humean idea that causal relations are not necessary. The correctness of the description of a mental state as a memory of some past event logically requires the existence of the past event; and the logical is thought to exclude the causal connection, since only logically distinct events can be causally related. Norman Malcolm (1963: 231–2) phrases the Humean objection to the analytic interpretation of the causal theory of memory thus: 'One might object to the idea that the supposed effect is *causally* dependent on the supposed cause, for the reason that the "effect" is *logically* dependent on the "cause". It is logically impossible that one should remember having seen X unless one saw it.'

The problem with this objection to the causal theory of memory is twofold. First, it is far from clear that it is a conceptual truth as opposed to an empirical hypothesis that for all subjects S and all objects of memory X, S remembers X only if X is a cause of S's remembering. In section 5.2, I will argue that memory causation involves intracerebral occurrences generally referred to as 'traces' or 'engrams'. If the causal theory of memory were a conceptual truth, then, given that memory causation involves traces, it would follow that the existence of memory traces is an analytic truth. This, I take it, is an intolerable conclusion. I am therefore inclined to view the causal theory of memory as a piece of scientific knowledge about our physical nature rather than part of the ordinary notion of remembering.

Second, the Humean distinct-events requirement rests on a confusion of events with their descriptions. Any two causally related events can be described so that one is logically dependent on the other. To achieve this all one has to do is to include the description of the cause in the description of the effect, or *vice versa*. Instead of saying 'A causes B' we can say 'The cause of B causes B' thereby generating a statement that is analytic and knowable a priori (Davidson 1980*a*: 14). The Humean worry that if two events are related in all possible worlds there is no room left for causal efficacy among them turns out to be a pseudo-problem. We can always redescribe the effect in a way as to make it an entailment of the cause. But from this it doesn't follows that causation is a myth. For even if we chose to describe the effect-event in a different manner it would still follow the cause-event with the same regularity as before. Causation is a relation between events. Logical relations, however, hold between propositions and linguistic entities. And just because there is a logical relation between the descriptions of two events doesn't preclude that the events themselves stand in a causal relation.[3]

The Nomologicality of Causation

Hume not only believed in the contingency and aposteriority of causal relations but also held that wherever one event causes another, there is a causal law that relates the types of events of which the two particular events are instances. In Hume's words, 'we may define a cause to be an object, followed by another, and where all objects similar to the first are followed by objects similar to the second' (2000*b*: 60). Given the nomological character of causation and given that the causal theory of memory is a conceptual truth, it follows that by making causal claims about memory we commit ourselves to there being causal laws. Malcolm takes this to be counterintuitive. He writes:

> There is an important sense of 'cause' in which a singular causal statement of the form 'X caused Y' implies a general proposition of the form 'in like circumstances, whenever X then Y'. But *this* meaning of 'cause' cannot be involved in factual memory, since in saying that someone remembers that p, we are certainly not committing ourselves to the truth of the general proposition that 'In like circumstances, whenever a person has previously known that p then he knows that p.' (1963: 232)

I agree with Malcolm that in attributing memory to someone we usually don't commit ourselves to there being laws that govern the memory process. Yet I disagree with Malcolm in that this observation speaks against the causal theory of memory. First, as was explained above, it is far from clear that the causal theory is a conceptual truth as opposed

---

[3] The Humean objection to the analytic interpretation of the causal theory of memory could be restated thus: Whenever event A causes event B, there will be available descriptions of both events that don't imply one another. As far as I can see, this principle is valid.

to an empirical hypothesis. Second, given content externalism, which is endorsed in Chapters 6 and 7, one can possess a concept and use it correctly while being ignorant of any of its necessary conditions. Thus one might possess the concept *remembering* and use it correctly in describing S as remembering that p, even though one doesn't know the first thing about the nomologicality of memory.

While Malcolm questions whether the causal theory is a *conceptual* truth, Carl Ginet questions whether it is true at all. Given the causal theory of memory and given the nomologicality of causation it follows that, in like circumstances, whenever a person has previously known that p then he knows that p. Ginet (1975: 166–7), however, is skeptical that there are general causal laws that govern all instances of memory.

[I]t seems clear that a particular experience and later matching memory-impression could satisfy the [causal] condition . . . without there being any true nomic generalization of the form 'Whenever a person has such-and-such an experience, and certain further circumstances obtain (then or thereafter), then the person at such-and-such later time has such-and-such a memory-impression.'

There are two ways of interpreting Ginet's remark. On one reading, he takes the memory process to be an example of singularist causation. On another reading, Ginet assumes the nomologicality of causation and suggests that the memory process isn't causal because it's not lawlike. In any case, Ginet is skeptical that there are causal laws that warrant predictions concerning what and when someone remembers. We can at best predict for a particular individual in a particular situation whether he will later on remember a representation he is presently having.[4]

Ginet's scruples are ungrounded. He doesn't provide any reasons for why we should think that it is impossible to make predictions concerning what and when someone remembers something. What is more, psychologists have developed for more than a century the very kind of laws that Ginet claims are impossible. Herman Ebbinghaus (1913) measured the difficulty of learning a list of nonsense syllables by the number of study trials required to attain one errorless recitation of it. It turns out that the amount of learning is directly proportional to the time spent in learning. Ebbinghaus's experiments suggest that there is a regular relation between the number of trials for original

---

[4] Davidson has famously argued that though there are some kind of laws connecting psychological events, these laws are not deterministic, and therefore don't qualify as strict laws. Psychological events do not 'constitute a closed system; much happens that is not psychological, and affects the psychological' (1980b: 231).

learning and the number of later trials needed to recite the list without error. In the case of a list of 16 nonsense syllables a single repetition on the first day lasting less than 7 seconds gives a saving of over 12 seconds on relearning on the second day. The percent savings in relearning a list one has learned earlier is the difference in trials for original learning (say, 9 trials) minus those needed for later relearning (say, 3) divided by the original learning trials (so, $(9 - 3)/9 = 67\%$) (Bower 2000: 5). Ebbinghaus's results, plotted in what is known as the *Ebbinghaus forgetting curve*, reveal a lawlike correlation between forgetting and time. Initially, information is often lost very quickly after it is learned. Factors such as how the information was learned and how frequently it was rehearsed play a role in how quickly these memories are lost.

Temporal Forgetting

Frequently, we observe an event, thereby acquiring the ability to know about it, then forget it, and later remember what we had forgotten. It might look as if we have thereby regained knowledge that we had lost in the meantime. According to Roger Squires, the chief reason in favor of the causal theory of memory is that it promises to explain the appearance of discontinuity of knowledge possession. Proponents of the causal theory explain the seeming discontinuity by stipulating a causal chain (consisting of memory traces) that spans the temporal gap between the lost and regained ability to know. Squires argues, however, that the problem of temporal forgetting is spurious and contrived. The appearance of discontinuity in temporal forgetting, he maintains, depends on an ambiguity in the notion of retaining an ability. When this ambiguity is brought to light, temporal forgetting can be explained without the stipulation of a causal process that spans the gap between the lost and regained ability to know. Squires argues that the retention of knowledge need not be analyzed in terms of a causal process since remembering that p is nothing more than one's persisting ability to produce states of knowing-that-p.

When we say of someone that he remembers that p we can either say of him that he is currently engaged in propositional remembering, or that he is disposed to remember that p when suitable circumstances occur. Remembering can be understood as a disposition (ability, capacity) or as an occurrence (cf. p. 27). Squires concentrates on the dispositional use of 'to remember'.

Squires invites us to consider a teddy bear that has the capacity to squeak when pressed. Due to the age of the toy, this capacity is dependent on the atmospheric humidity. The bear can squeak in the dry summer months but not in the damp winter months. When we observe the bear throughout the course of a year, it might seem as if the bear's capacity to squeak is discontinuous, for it is lost in winter and regained in summer. But this is not the only way to interpret the case. Instead of saying that the bear has the ability to *squeak any time* and that he loses this ability in winter, we can say that the bear has the ability to *squeak in summer*. By taking the bear's ability to squeak to be time-indexed the appearance of discontinuity vanishes. For even in winter the bear can squeak in summer.

This point is then applied to the problem of temporal forgetting: the appearance of discontinuity in temporal forgetting is not due to us losing and later regaining the ability to know p; instead it is due to the temporal absence of the particular circumstances on which our ability to know p is dependent. Squires (1969: 186) declares: 'When we forget something, and then remember it, the capacity we lost is not the capacity we keep.' The capacity lost in temporary forgetting is the ability to know p given any circumstances; the retained capacity is the ability to know p given particular circumstances. Squires (ibid. 184) concludes that 'bridging the retention gap' by stipulating an intermediary causal process 'is a superfluous piece of philosophical engineering'.

Even if we grant Squires that the explanation of temporal forgetting is the prime motivation of the causal account of memory, he is mistaken in thinking that an account of temporal forgetting can manage without the postulation of memory causation. The problem with Squires's non-causal account is twofold: it rests on a vacuous account of temporal forgetting and it blurs the difference between permanent and temporal forgetting.[5] *Any* cognitive and epistemic ability we have we only have in particular circumstances. None of our abilities are such that we have them in any circumstances. But it is not informative to analyze temporal forgetting in terms of losing an ability we never have. Moreover, since our cognitive and epistemic capacities are such that we only have them in particular circumstances, Squires's non-causal account of memory has the consequence of rendering permanent forgetting indistinguishable from temporal forgetting—both consist of the temporal absence of circumstances on which the ability to know that p is dependent.

[5] The first point is inspired by Delmas Lewis (1983: 27).

The latter point can be contested. As was explained before (cf. pp. 100–1), psychologists operate with two different theories of forgetting. According to the *decay theory*, traces in long-term memory decline in strength with time. The competing *interference theory* states that forgetting occurs because of interference from other materials, both those that have been learned earlier (proactive interference) and those learned later (retroactive interference). What causes forgetting is not time itself, but the disruption and obscuration of memory traces by preceding or succeeding learning. Squires could adopt the interference theory and argue that every piece of information one ever experienced is stored, and that it is all lying there in one's memory bank waiting for the appropriate key to be turned for it to come flooding back. Then there would indeed be no genuine difference between permanent and temporal forgetting.

Even though decay (indexed by time) and interference (indexed by amount of distracting information) have historically been viewed as competing accounts of forgetting, they are in fact functionally related and complement one another (cf. Altmann and Gray 2002). Forgetting takes place by interference *and* by traces fading over time. When forgetting occurs because of interference, we may speak of 'temporal forgetting'. Yet when a piece of information has been forgotten due to the relevant trace having disappeared, it is permanently forgotten. Thus the difference between permanent and temporal forgetting seems to be genuine after all.

4.5 QUASI-RETENTION

After having examined three arguments against the causal theory of memory let's take a look at two arguments in favor of the causal theory. According to G. E. M. Anscombe (1981*b*: 127), the connection between a memory and the remembered event is 'an original phenomenon of causality: one of its types . . . No general theory about what causality is has to be introduced to justify acceptance of it. Nor does it have to be accommodated to any general theory, before it is accepted. It is just one of the things we mean by causality.' In the same vein, Martha Kneale (1972: 2) declares, 'It is involved in the ordinary notion of memory or recollection that the memory event should have as a part-cause the occurrence of the event recollected.' So the idea is that the causal theory of memory is part and parcel of the ordinary meaning of the cognitive verb 'to remember'. Anscombe and Kneale are careful not to claim that it is an analytic truth that the causation of memory is physically mediated, mediated by intracerebral occurrences. Whether or not memory causation is physically mediated is a scientific rather than a philosophical (or conceptual) issue. The concept of memory is said to imply only that there is a causal relation of some form or other connecting the witnessing of the original event and the subsequent state as of remembering this event.

Now I find it hard to believe that the causal theory of memory (however construed) is an analytic truth and that proponents of non-causal accounts of memory are committing a conceptual error. Another way of making the point is to say that I see no reason to deny that the statement 'For S to remember that p his present representation of p must stand in an appropriate causal relation to his past representation of p*' is insubstantial or carries no cognitive significance. The onus is on Anscombe and Kneale to explain why we should accept the view whereupon the concept of memory requires that there should be a causal relation between one's past witnessing and one's present seeming memory.

Another argument in favor of the causal theory is due to Sydney Shoemaker. Shoemaker (2003*b*: 43) claims that 'unless we understand the notion of retention, as well as that of memory, as involving a causal component, we cannot account for the role played by the notion of memory . . . in judgments of personal identity'. The argument is based on this case:

Let us suppose that the brain from the body of one man, Brown, is transplanted into the body of another man, Robinson, and that the resulting creature—I call him 'Brownson'—survives and upon regaining consciousness begins making memory claims corresponding to the past history of Brown rather than that of Robinson. We can also suppose that Brownson manifests personality traits strikingly like those previously manifested by Brown and quite unlike those manifested by Robinson. Although Brownson has Robinson's (former) body, I doubt if anyone would want to say that Brownson is Robinson, and I think that most people would want to say that Brownson is (is the same person as) Brown.   (Ibid.)

The fact that Brownson's memory claims correspond to the past history of Brown seems to suggest that Brownson is identical with Brown. Shoemaker's point is that the interpretation whereupon Brownson and Brown are the same person presupposes the causal analysis of memory and counts against any non-causal theory of memory. He argues by *reductio*. Suppose the reason Brownson is psychologically continuous with Brown is that Brownson somehow non-causally retains mental states that Brown had in the past. For mental states to be non-causally retained, Brown and Brownson must be the same person. But if Brownson's non-causally retaining mental states that used to belong to Brown presupposes that the two are the same person, then memory—analyzed in terms of non-causal retention—cannot, without circularity, be offered as evidence for Brownson and Brown being the same person. A non-causal account of memory, Shoemaker holds, cannot provide a non-circular explanation of the idea that Brown and Brownson are numerically identical. The commonsensical position whereupon the fact that Brownson's memory claims correspond to the past history of Brown is evidence for Brown and Brownson being the same person, therefore supports a causal connection between Brown's past mental states and Brownson's (alleged) memories thereof.

A crucial premiss of Shoemaker's argument for the causal theory of memory is the idea that a non-causal theory of memory presupposes personal identity while a causal theory of memory does not. But if the causal theory of memory doesn't imply personal identity, then, by the same token, the simple retention theory can be adjusted so as not to imply personal identity. This requires some explanation.

As was explained in section 2.1, Shoemaker attempts to neutralize Joseph Butler's circularity objection to the psychological criterion of personal identity by developing a notion of memory that, unlike the notion of experiential memory, doesn't imply personal identity. Shoemaker holds that if the notion of memory is replaced with that of quasi-memory a non-circular explanation can be given of why we are inclined to take Brownson's memory claims as evidence of his identity with Brown. The reason Brown is identical with Brownson is that Brownson's memory claims are causally related to Brown's past representations in essentially the same ways as a normal person's memory states are causally related to his past representations.

Just as one can develop a causal notion of memory that doesn't imply personal identity—quasi-memory—one can develop a notion of non-causal retention that doesn't imply personal identity. Following John Schumacher (1976: 103) we can call this notion *quasi-retention*. S's present representation is a quasi-memory if its content corresponds to the content of some past representation. The correspondence implied by quasi-retention is just like that that exists in the normal retention of

representations and pieces of knowledge. The only difference between
quasi-retention and normal retention is that the latter, unlike the former,
requires S to be the bearer of the past representation. Since the notion
of quasi-retention doesn't imply personal identity, it can, without
circularity, be employed in an account of personal identity. The upshot
is that Shoemaker's argument for the causal theory of remembering isn't
successful.

4.6 AN ARGUMENT FROM EXPLANATORY POWER

Another argument in favor of the causal theory of memory stems from
Martin and Deutscher. Given that we commonly explain the occurrence
of memory states in terms of counterfactuals of the form 'If S hadn't
represented at t_1 that p^* he wouldn't represent at t_2 that p', Martin
and Deutscher argue that we are in fact committed to there being a
causal relation between the original representation and the subsequent
recall.

Martin and Deutscher rest their case on this example. A person has
apparent memories of something from early childhood, and wonders
whether he really remembers it. Suppose that he does in fact remember
what he seems to remember. He wonders though whether his having
witnessed the event in early childhood has any connection with his
now giving the story or whether his description can be completely
explained by what he has been told by his parents in the meantime.[6]
Martin and Deutscher (1966: 176) maintain that the facts 'which
are used to decide whether or not he would have given the story
if he had *not* witnessed the event in his childhood' are the same as
the facts 'to decide that his past witnessing is causally necessary for his
present account'. In other words, the facts supporting the counterfactual
claim (14),

  (14) S wouldn't give the story at t_2, unless he had witnessed at t_1 the
        relevant events,

---

[6] In his autobiography, the German poet Goethe (2000*b*: 44) reports having recounted a
story of a time in his childhood when for some unknown reasons he gathered up the family
crockery and threw it, piece by piece, from a window in his house down to the street below. In
the recollection, smashing of the family dishes was much encouraged by some adult neighbors.
Goethe also reports being unable to decide whether he actually remembered the incident or
whether he had instead constructed a 'memory' after hearing members of his family repeat the
story over the years.

are said to be the same as the facts supporting the causal claim (15),

> (15) S having witnessed the relevant events at t_1 is the cause of his giving the story at t_2.

Martin and Deutscher hold that since (14) and (15) have the same truth-conditions if we know that (14) is the case we *eo ipso* know that (15) is the case. 'To decide that [S] would not have [given the story if he had *not* witnessed the event in his childhood] is to decide that his past witnessing is causally necessary for his present account' (ibid. 176). Sydney Shoemaker (2003*b*: 44) essentially makes the same point when he declares that he 'can see no reason for doubting that counterfactuals [of the form "If S had different experiences at t_1, there would be corresponding differences in what he seems to remember at t_2"] assert causal connections.'

As it stands, this argument for the causal theory of memory fails. The fact that S's present retelling of a past event is counterfactually dependent on his past witnessing of the event doesn't guarantee that the past witnessing is the cause of the present retelling. For the sort of dependence expressed by counterfactuals is considerably broader than strictly causal dependence and causal dependence is only one among a heterogeneous group of dependence relations that can be expressed by counterfactuals (Kim 1973). Squires (1969: 181) provides the following example of a non-causal counterfactual statement. In normal circumstances, the counterfactual statement 'If the strawberries hadn't been red at t_1, they wouldn't be red at t_2' differs in meaning from the causal statement 'The strawberries are red at t_2, because they were red at t_1.' Rather than asserting a causal connection, the counterfactual statement indicates that nothing has happened between t_1 and t_2 to change the color of the strawberries. It denies that certain kinds of causal explanation are necessary, by correcting the impression that the strawberries became red since t_1 or that the red color has faded since t_1. What this example shows is that counterfactual statements cannot be reduced to causal ones. But then it is a mistake to suppose that (14) and (15) are equivalent or that the truth of (14) implies the truth of (15).

Even though the truth of the causal statement (15) cannot be deduced from the truth of the counterfactual statement (14), Martin and Deutscher have a point. The point is that, provided counterfactuals have truth-values at all, the causal statement (15) provides the best explanation of the truth of the counterfactual statement (14). To drive home this point consider what a non-causal account of the counterfactual statement 'If S hadn't represented at t_1 that p^* he wouldn't represent at t_2 that p' would look like. The non-causal explanation denies that there is a causal connection between the representation at t_1 and the representation at t_2. The counterfactual statement is taken to reject certain kinds of causal explanations by eliminating the possibility that the ability to represent p (or p^*) has only been acquired since t_1. But note that the non-causal interpretation of the counterfactual in question doesn't explain the process underlying the retention of knowledge or representation. As was already pointed out at the end of section 4.2, the causal account has an explanatory advantage over its non-causal competitor. Both the causal and the non-causal account rule out the possibility that S acquired the ability to represent p (or p^*) since t_1. But only the causal account offers an explanation as to how it is possible that the ability to represent p (or p^*) is retained from t_1 to t_2. The non-causal account, by contrast, gives us no lead as to the kind of process responsible for the retention of the ability to represent a proposition. Hence the causal theory of memory provides a deeper and more comprehensive explanation of the truth of the counterfactual 'If S hadn't represented at t_1 that p^* he wouldn't represent at t_2 that p' than its non-causal competitor.

Conditionals present a perplexing set of linguistic phenomena which often seem to defy a simple, uniform treatment of them. This is obviously not the place to try to set forth a general account of counterfactual conditionals using causation. Nor do I want to suggest that the David-Lewis-style reductive counterfactual analysis of causation gets the order of explanation backwards and that the proper understanding of counterfactuals requires reference to causal relations. My point is much more modest. All I want to suggest is that a causal account of counterfactual statements expressing the memory connection meets more of the criteria of explanatory adequacy than a non-causal account.

Granted that the causal theory of memory does a better job than non-causal theories explaining the truth of counterfactual statements of the form 'If S hadn't represented at t_1 that p^* he wouldn't represent at t_2 that p', this doesn't *prove* that the causal theory of memory is correct. This would only be the case if the satisfaction of explanatory desiderata made a theory likelier to be true. Unfortunately, however, explanatory virtues and truth appear to be unrelated. Where does all this leave us then? We have seen that though there are no successful arguments against the causal theory of memory, there are no knock-down arguments for it either. The strongest reason in favor of the causal retention theory as opposed to the simple retention theory is that the former provides a deeper and more comprehensive explanation of the memory process.

5

The Nature of Memory Causation

After having defended the causal theory of memory against competing theories we can proceed to examine the nature of memory causation. As was explained in section 4.3, the causal connection condition for extroversive memory in the first-person mode states:

(1) S's representation at t_2 that p is suitably causally connected to S's representation at t_1 that p^*.

The aim of this chapter is to go some way toward determining the kind of causal relation constitutive of remembering. This involves identifying the vehicle of memory causation, specifying the strength of the causal relation constitutive of memory, determining what should count as a *suitable* causal connection, and ruling out deviant causal chains.

Section 5.1 discusses causal chains connecting the past and present representation that involve external loops. It is argued that such loops should not be eliminated by requesting that the causal chain continues entirely within the body of the rememberer but rather by demanding that the causal chain consists in a persisting memory trace or a contiguous series of memory traces, respectively. Section 5.2 attempts to say what memory traces are. Section 5.3 argues that a trace may give rise to a memory state despite the fact that it has temporarily been outside the body of the rememberer. Section 5.4 examines the cooperation of traces and retrieval cues in the formation of memories. The goal is to say what it is to remember an event upon being prompted rather than merely parroting the prompting itself. Section 5.5 argues for a counterfactual analysis of the causal dependence of memory states on past representations. Finally, section 5.6 discusses the issue of suggestibility and summarizes the account of memory causation.

5.1 EXTERNAL LOOPS

The basic problem facing the causal theory of memory is to eliminate cases of relearning. Relearning cases come in many different varieties. Let's start by discussing causal chains that involve external loops. To illustrate the kind of case I have in mind let's go back to the example discussed on pages 113–14. Suppose that at t_1 S witnesses a car accident. At t_2, S tells his friend all about the accident. Then, at t_3, S gets a blow on the head as a result of which he permanently forgets everything about the accident he witnessed at t_1. When, at t_4, the friend notices that S can no longer remember the car accident, he tells S the details that S had told him at t_2. S hears the friend tell him about the car accident and, at t_5, this causes S to seem to recall the accident via a causal chain that includes his friend's memories and honest intentions. Even if the causal chain supports a counterfactual correlation between the facts S observed at the scene of the accident and his apparent memories of the accident at t_5 it seems wrong to say that S *remembers* the accident. The reason is, or so it seems, that the causal chain connecting the past and present representation may not follow an external loop.

A simple and straightforward way of eliminating external loops is by requesting that the causal chain between the past representation and its subsequent recall should continue without interruption within the body of the rememberer. Yet a little thought reveals that this suggestion is both too stringent and too weak. To see that it is too weak imagine a pupil who has difficulty in memorizing what he read in a history book for an exam. In the end he helps himself by tattooing the relevant information into his palm. In the exam he writes down the correct answers by reading the tattoos on his palm. Although the causal process responsible for his recounting the information does not extend beyond the pupil's body, we would not say that the reason he passes the exam is that he *remembered* the information.[1]

The stipulation of an causally operative chain within the body of the rememberer is also too stringent since it is surely a contingent fact

---

[1] In the movie, *Memento*, the protagonist suffers from a form of anterograde amnesia that results in an inability to lay down new memories. Nonetheless, he sets out on a quest to find his wife's killer, aided by the use of notes, annotated Polaroids, and tattoos.

that remembering depends on processes in the nervous system. It is conceivable that information is stored in parts of the brain that can be detached, stored, and reattached to the brain. Just as we now have hearing-aids, there may be memory-aids—a human version of a flight recorder. These prosthetic devices in the cortex preserve information and, for purposes of maintenance, are sometimes taken out and, later on, reimplanted. To be sure, the literature on personal identity is full of thought experiments where the experiential memories of someone are extracted, stored in some other medium (e.g. a computer or magnetic tapes) and then copied back into the original brain. I will return to the issue of memory-aids in section 6.4.

The suggested criterion for ruling out external loops—that the causal chain should continue entirely within the body of the rememberer and not encompass events outside his body—is obviously too naive. The spatial location of the causal chain is inessential. But if not the location, what then distinguishes the causal processes constitutive of remembering from deviant causal chains? Most philosophers believe the mark of memory causation is that it is transmitted via memory traces or engrams. For something to be a memory state it must be caused by a past representation through memory traces. We can formulate the following *trace condition* (2):

(2) S's representation at t_1 that p^* and S's representation at t_2 that p are connected by a persisting memory trace or a contiguous series of memory traces.

According to (2), the causal process connecting a past representation and its subsequent recall involves intermediary memory traces. The stipulation of memory traces is motivated by the need to understand how a mental state can exert causal influence at a temporal distance. Between any two diachronic mental events that are causally related there must be a series of intermediary events, each of which causes the next, and each of which is temporally contiguous to the next.

The dominant philosopher of causation, David Hume (2000*a*: 54; cf. 114, 116), declares that 'nothing can operate in a time or place, which is ever so little remov'd from those of its existence'. The reason Hume is led to stipulate that spatio-temporal contiguity is a necessary condition of causation is that if cause and effect were not contiguous, some factor could intervene and prevent the effect, even though the cause had occurred. Where contiguity appears to be lacking, Hume holds that we find, upon closer examination, that cause and effect *are* connected by a chain of events such that the effect is finally caused by an event that is contiguous with it: 'Tho' distant objects may sometimes seem productive of each other, they are commonly found upon examination to be link'd by a chain of causes, which are contiguous among themselves, and to the distant objects; and when in any particular instance we cannot discover this connexion, we still presume it to exist.'[2] By drawing a distinction between remote and proximate causes, Hume maintains that the remote cause is connected with the effect through a chain of causes, the last one being the proximate cause; and that the proximate cause is contiguous with the effect and brings it about. Trying to establish that causation implies contiguity would, of course, take us too far afield. In what follows, I will simply assume that, at least in the case of memory causation, contiguity is a necessary condition.[3]

To see that the theory of memory traces can handle causal chains involving external loops consider once again the car-accident case. S's detailed and correct retelling at t_5 of the car accident he witnessed at t_1 does not qualify as remembering because the original memory traces are erased at t_3 as a result of the blow to his head. The reason S is in a position at t_5 to recount the happenings at the accident at t_1 is that hearing his friend telling him about the accident has given rise to new traces. It is these new traces that are operative for S's recounting the accident. What S remembers is what his friend told him about the accident, rather than the accident itself. The object of S's memory is not the accident itself, since it is not his experiencing of the accident that causes him to say what he does say. Hence, maintaining that the causal process leading up to the state of recall be transmitted by memory traces is a promising strategy for ruling out external loops. But we can only sign up to the trace theory once we understand what memory traces are.

5.2 MEMORY TRACES

Memory traces account both for the preservation of mental content through time and for the production of states of recall. Due to their

---

[2] 2000a: 54. Flage (1985: 179–86) and Stroud (1977: 43–4) argue that Hume doesn't take contiguity to be a necessary condition for causation. For a differing opinion see Beauchamp and Rosenberg (1981: 194–5) Regardless of where Hume stands on the issue, I am inclined to think that contiguity of cause and effect is a necessary condition of memory causation.

[3] In my (2008: 31–46) I critically discuss Russell's account of memory causation whereupon a past representation is directly causally active over a temporal distance.

twofold function memory traces go by two quite different kinds of description—a mental and a physical description. Insofar as traces bring about states of recall, they are intracerebral occurrences. To be exact, traces are said to be structural modifications at synapses (i.e. the area where the axon of one neuron connects with the dendrite of another neuron) that affect the ease with which neurons in a neural network can activate each other. Yet insofar as memory traces preserve mental content across time they are mental states.

The mind–body problem concerns the explanation of the relationship that exists between mental and physical descriptions. According to property dualism, the difference between mental and physical descriptions results from a difference in ontology. Dualism proclaims the existence of a single substance and argues that this substance has two potential properties: physical and mental states that are not reducible. Physicalism, on the other hand, is the thesis that, in some sense, everything is physical. Physical properties can be thought of as structural properties that consist in a thing's spatial and functional qualities. Reductive physicalism reduces mental states and processes into physical states and processes. The most widely accepted form of physicalism today, and the position I favor, is non-reductive physicalism. It states that all concrete particulars are physical, but certain complex structures and configurations of physical particles can, and sometimes do, exhibit properties that are not reducible to physical properties. A popular way to spell out non-reductive physicalism is to hold that mental properties supervene upon physical neurobiological processes in the brain. To supervene means that the higher level mental property depends upon the neurobiological process in order to exist, it is irreducible to the neurobiological process and remains ontologically distinct even though it has no direct causal effect on those physical processes.

The main objection to non-reductive materialism is that it renders mental states causally inert or epiphenomenal. If mental states supervene on physical states and if any piece of physical behavior has a complete physical causal history, then it seems that mental states are condemned to be causally inefficient. The *causal exclusion argument* has been endlessly dissected. For reasons I don't have the space to explain here I believe that the causal exclusion argument trades on one or other false assumption and that the non-reductive physicalism is indeed compatible with mental states playing a causal role (see e.g. Kallestrup 2006; Menzies 2003).

Granted that memory causation involves traces and that traces supervene on intracerebral occurrences, it follows that a disembodied mind cannot remember. And given that the ability to remember is an essential aspect of our mental life, it also follows that it is impossible for a mind to be disembodied. Another consequence of physicalism about memory traces is that the question whether someone remembers something or whether he is mistaken in believing that he remembers something is, in part, an empirical question. It is partly a question about the person's brain. This result should strike us as neither surprising nor disturbing. For if mental states supervene on physical states it is only natural that the difference between memories and other mental states is, among other things, a physical difference.

Since this is a *philosophical* study of memory, I will refrain from elaborating on the physical description of memory traces and instead focus on their mental description. What kind of mental states are memory traces? Anticipating my conclusion, I will argue that memory traces are dispositional beliefs or subdoxastic states, dependent on whether they store conceptual or non-conceptual content.

As was explained before (cf. pp. 21–2), what distinguishes propositional from non-propositional memory is that the former, but not the latter, requires the deployment of concepts. To remember that Caesar wore a laurel wreath (propositional memory), you must possess the concepts *Caesar* and *laurel wreath*. Yet a young child might remember Caesar's laurel wreath (property memory) long before he acquires the concept *laurel wreath*. The attribution of (dispositional) belief, like the attribution of propositional memory, presupposes that the attributee possesses the concepts necessary to entertain the attributed content. It thus stands to reason that memory traces preserving conceptual content should be construed along the lines of *dispositional beliefs*. Besides the presupposition of conceptualization, dispositional beliefs and traces (giving rise to propositional memory) have in common that the doctrine of first-person authority applies to neither of them.

Insofar as traces play a role in the proximate causal history of non-propositional memories they are *subdoxastic states*.[4] Two characteristic features of subdoxastic states is that they are inaccessible to consciousness

---

[4] Other labels for subdoxastic states are 'implicit knowledge', 'tacit knowledge', 'proto-knowledge', 'unconscious knowledge', and 'subpersonal states'. The problem with characterizing subdoxastic states as knowledge states is that the information transmitted by the former may be false while knowledge implies truth. The idea that memory traces are subdoxastic states is prominent in Siebel (2000: 258–70).

and that their contents are not constrained by the conceptual abilities of the subject. While the contents of (dispositional) beliefs are necessarily conceptualized by the believer, the contents of subdoxastic states don't require conceptualization. Moreover, subdoxastic states are inaccessible to awareness. This is important, for we cannot become aware of memory traces as such. What we are aware of are the states of seeming to remember they give rise to. Though traces are themselves opaque they can bring about conscious representations and behavior.[5]

How can memory traces store mental contents? The traditional answer to this question is to conceive of memory traces as images, ideas, or wax-tablet-like impressions somehow directly resembling their objects. A slightly more sophisticated conception of memory traces that has survived to this day is *structural isomorphism*. Structural isomorphism has it that the reason a memory trace can preserve the mental content of a past experience is that it is a structural analogue of the event represented by the past experience. A memory trace is said to be 'an analogue which contains at least as many features as there are details which a given person can relate about something he has experienced' (Martin and Deutscher 1966: 190). The structural analogy between the past event and the persisting trace is conceived along the lines of the relation between sounds and the grooves in a vinyl record. For each variation in the pitch, tempo, or volume of the music there is a variation in the grooves of the record.

Even though the notion of a structural mapping between traces and worldly features is sufficiently abstract to allow for the possibility of devising formal accounts of memory processing, structural isomorphism is wholly implausible. First, to say of something that it has a structure is to say that it consists of parts and that these parts are configured in a certain way. But what are the parts of the world and of mental states which, according to the structuralist view of traces, resemble one another? Second, neither the mind nor the world have a single, natural, non-arbitrary structure of elements. Rather the world and the mind have as many different structures as there are different ways of describing them—which is to say an infinite number of structures. Third, claiming that traces need to be structural analogues of past events to be able to carry information about those events contradicts the multiple realizability of mental states. The multiple realizability

---

[5] Searle (1990) argues that the notion of a mental state that is inaccessible is incoherent. For a response to Searle's qualms see Davies (1995).

thesis contends that a single mental kind can be realized by many distinct physical kinds. Organisms of different species can share the same types of memory traces even if their anatomical and physiological differences are so great that they cannot share the relevant types of physical structures.[6]

According to externalism about memory content, set forth in Chapters 6 and 7, memory traces have the content they do in virtue of systematic relations the subject bears to certain aspects of his physical and social environment. Externalism denies local supervenience by arguing against the thesis that any two physically indistinguishable organisms are also psychologically indistinguishable. But externalism is committed to global supervenience for, in the case of physical duplicates with different thoughts, there must be something different about them, namely their social or physical environment.

If we reject the idea that traces take the form of wax-tablet-like impressions or grooves in a vinyl record, then what form *do* traces take? What are the mechanisms by which traces store contents? There is basic disagreement about what kind of computations the brain performs. The debate here is between *classical computationalism* and *connectionism*. According to the language-of-thought hypothesis—the most worked-out version of the classical approach—just as sentences are made up of meaning-bearing parts put together according to certain rules, mental representations are rule-governed structures that have semantically evaluable constituents. Memory traces and other representational states are sentences in the language of thought. This view lends itself particularly well to account for metarepresentations of past mental states or what I call *introversive memories*. If representations are syntactically structured, we can conceive of memorial metarepresentation in analogy to linguistic metarepresentation. Inwardly remembering is like quoting one's past representations.

According to connectionism, what is stored in memory is not full-blown representations or formulae in an internal code (such as the language of thought) but a set of changes in the instructions neurons send to each other. When an object is experienced a stimulus enters the system and gives rise to a pattern of activity over a network of neurons. This pattern of activity is taken to be the representation of the object. The formation of this activity pattern finds reflection in the

---

[6] For a discussion of structural isomophism see Goldberg (1968); Hark (1995); Heil (1978); Rosen (1975); Stern (1991); and Sutton (1998: 307–10).

strengths of connections between the neurons. The next time a similar stimulus enters the system it results in the construction of an activation pattern that can be viewed as an attempted reconstruction of the pattern that represented the previously represented object. Remembering occurs when an input 'travels' through an already established activation pattern and thereby recreates a representation. Since many items of information can be represented over the same set of neurons and connections, connectionist networks 'store' more efficiently than symbolic networks (cf. Collins and Hay 1992; McClelland 2000).

Connectionism is motivated mainly by a consideration of the architecture of the brain, which consists of layered networks of interconnected neurons. This sort of architecture is unsuited to carrying out classical serial computations. Processing in the brain is typically massively parallel. Another advantage of the connectionist model of memory over its traditional counterpart is that connectionist systems exhibit *graceful degradation*. Graceful degradation is degradation of a system in such a manner that it continues to operate, but provides a reduced level of service rather than failing completely. Brain damage, for example, usually doesn't result in a sudden complete loss of memory, rather the performance of the memory system slowly becomes worse. Connectionist models also exhibit graceful degradation in the face of 'brain damage', that is, the removal of processing nodes and alteration of connection weights (McClelland, Rumelhart, and Hinton 1986).

The connectionist and the symbolic model of memory can be viewed as complementary rather than rival theories, provided one adopts what Steven Pinker and Alan Prince (1988) call *implementational connectionism*. Implementational connectionism uses connectionism as a tool for trying to understand how symbol-manipulating processes could be implemented in the brain. The brain is a neural net; but it is also a symbolic processor at a higher level of description. The role for connectionist research is to discover how the machinery needed for symbolic processing can be forged from neural network materials, so that classical processing can be implemented in the neural-network account.

The overall picture shows that unless there are memory traces it wouldn't be possible for an experience to exert causal influence at a temporal distance by giving rise to a state of recall. It is plausible to conceive of memory traces as higher level mental states that supervene on intracerebral occurrences. Depending on whether the content of a trace is conceptual or non-conceptual in nature the trace can either be thought of as a dispositional belief or a subdoxastic state. It is a mistake to think of the way information is stored in traces by analogy to impressions on a wax tablet or grooves on a vinyl record. Instead psychologists tell us that information is stored in the strengths of connections between neurons. On this picture traces are distributed rather than local: what can be distinctly remembered need not be held distinctly or independently, since each memory item is spread or 'superposed' across many elements in a neural network.

5.3 MEMORY TRANSPLANTS

Section 5.1 dealt with one type of wayward causation: causal chains following an external loop. The example used in section 5.1 involves someone who correctly reports what he saw at a car accident. He can report of the happenings at the accident not because he remembers them but because he gives a report that he had told a friend and that the friend had retold him when he had forgotten everything about the accident due to a blow on the head. The causal chain connecting the person's past and present representations includes the friend's memories and honest intentions. It was argued that such external loops should not be eliminated by requesting that the causal chain continues entirely within the body of the rememberer. The spatial location of the causal chain is not essential for memory causation. A more promising strategy for ruling out external loops is to demand that the causal chain consists in a persisting memory trace or a contiguous series of memory traces, respectively. For something to be a memory state it must be caused by a memory trace that itself derives from the relevant past representation.

In principle, a trace may give rise to a memory state even if it has temporarily been outside the body of the rememberer. Assuming that trace implants and transplants are possible, five scenarios can be distinguished.[7] First, memory traces are created *in vitro* and implanted into someone's brain. I will refer to this case as *trace creation*. Second,

---

[7] It is uncertain whether memory transplants will ever become a medical possibility. Brain transplants, however, are not only possible but real. Heads of monkeys have successfully been transplanted from one to another and brain tissue implantation is being explored in patients suffering degenerative disorders such as Parkinson's disease, Huntington's chorea, and Alzheimer's disease. Research on brain transplantation in humans is still very much in its

someone's memory traces are surgically extracted, kept 'alive' for a couple hours, and implanted back into the brain of the very person from whom they had been taken. This may be called an *intrapersonal trace transplant*. Third, traces are extracted from one person and implanted in the brain of another person. Let's refer to this case under the label of *interpersonal trace transplant*. Fourth, a memory trace is removed, destroyed, rebuilt out of new material and implanted into the brain of the very person from whom it had been taken. I will call this case *intrapersonal trace replication*. Fifth, there is *interpersonal trace replication*. Let's discuss these cases of external traces one after the other.

An example of trace creation is provided by the movie *Total Recall*. The lead character cannot afford his dream vacation to the planet Mars. So he contacts the company Rekall Incorporated to have artificially created memories of traveling to Mars implanted into his brain. Rekall Incorporated prides itself in creating low-cost vacation memories; as an added bonus, there is no chance that one's luggage will be lost. Unfortunately for the protagonist, things don't work out as planned. He discovers that he has already lived on Mars, where he worked in a corrupt government. As a result, part of his memory traces have been removed to keep the corruption secret. Due to the implantation of artificially created memory traces, the lead character becomes thoroughly confused about what is real and what is not.

Artificially created and surgically implanted memory traces don't give rise to memories (or quasi-memories)—not even if the content of the implanted trace is true and if it happens to match a mental content the subject had entertained in the past. The reason is that there is no causal relation between the implanted artificial trace and the relevant past representation. Suppose that while living on Mars, at t_1, S thought that p. Upon his return to Earth, at t_2, the relevant memory traces are removed from his brain. Once S is fitted with artificial memories from Rekall Incorporated, at t_3, it seems to him as if he remembers having thought that p. S's state of seeming to remember is not a state

infancy, but some experiments suggest that Parkinson patients who receive fetal brain tissue grafts improve (cf. Stein and Glasier 1995). But even if, some day, fetal brain tissue grafts should become a standard treatment for degenerative disorders, this, by itself, wouldn't prove the possibility of memory transplants. For when fetal brain tissue is extracted it seems to be free of memory traces so that by implanting it into an adult's brain no memories are being transmitted. The implanted tissue serves only the function of supplying additional storage space.

of remembering, for there is no suitable causal connection between his having thought at t_1 that p and his possession at t_3 of a memory trace to the effect that he thought that p.

Next consider intrapersonal trace transplants. Given what has been said in section 5.1 about causal chains involving external loops, there is no reason not to classify instances of intrapersonal memory transplants as cases of genuine memory. Removing a trace from someone's brain and implanting it back into the same brain doesn't violate the causal condition for remembering—provided the transplantation doesn't cause a spatio-temporal gap in the causal chain.

Whether interpersonal memory transplants can give rise to genuine memories depends on the kind of content preserved by the traces. As was explained before (cf. pp. 41–2), when the content of the recalled representation contains no indexical reference to the thinker, the truth-condition for remembering is consistent with the bearer of the present representation not being co-personal with the bearer of the past representation. But when the memory content involves an indexical reference to the thinker—as is the case in introversive memory and in extroversive memory in the first-person mode—remembering presupposes personal identity and hence interpersonal memory transplants are ruled out of court. Anyhow, from a purely causal point of view, memory traces transplanted from one person to another are not inferior to stationary traces—provided the transplantation doesn't affect the contiguity of the causal chain.

Finally consider trace replication. To illustrate this case consider a story by Derek Parfit (1984: 199) involving a 'teletransporter', that is, a machine facilitating interplanetary travel at the speed of light. The machine consists of a scanner at the departure point X that destroys one's body and brain while recording the exact states of all one's cells. The encoded information is transmitted by computer at the speed of light to a replicator at point Y, which then creates, out of new matter, a brain and body exactly like the one one used to have. Once the scanner is activated one loses consciousness at X and wakes at Y as if emerging from a short nap. One wakes in a new body that is fitted with the replication of one's old states of seeming to remember. Do these states of seeming to remember qualify as memories? Since it might be thought that teletransportation destroys personal identity, let's focus on memory contents that leave open the issue of the personal identity of the rememberer. Do replicated traces give rise to extroversive memory in the third-person mode? There are two issues that bear on this question:

the content of the memory state must be sufficiently similar to the content of the original experience and the causal chain connecting past and present needs to be contiguous.

In sect. 6.4 I argue for content externalism about memory, that is, the view that the individuation of memory contents depends on systematic relations that the subject bears to certain conditions of his past physical and social environment. As will be explained in Ch. 7, a consequence of externalism is that an environmental shift may rob us of the ability to access some of our past representations. Hence if the environment at the location of the replicator is sufficiently different from the environment at the location of the scanner, instances of trace replication could violate the content condition for remembering.

Trace replication is compatible with remembering only when the causal chain connecting the past and present representations is contiguous. And whether a causal chain involving replicated traces is contiguous depends on the way the story is spelled out. If the trace replication involved in teletransportation consists in something like downloading information from a trace onto a computer, emailing a file to another computer, and copying the information into an 'empty' trace, there is no good reason to deny that the causal chain is temporally and spatially contiguous.

In sum, the elements of the causal chain connecting a past representation and its subsequent recall need not be located within the body of the rememberer. Memory traces may be situated outside the body of the rememberer, provided there is no spatio-temporal gap in the causal chain and the content of the traces is the same as, or sufficiently similar to, the contents both of the past representation and the state of recall.

5.4 PROMPTED RECALL

The causal process underlying remembering consists of three elements: encoding, storage, and retrieval. In encoding, experiences and thoughts bring about memory traces. In storage, the content is preserved by a memory trace persisting through time or by the content being communicated from one trace to another, respectively. In retrieval, memory traces bring about states of remembering.

Memory traces are rarely causally sufficient for the production of occurrent memories. Most of the time a memory state is the joint product of the trace and an appropriate prompt or retrieval cue. Some evidence for this lies in the tip-of-the-tongue phenomenon. Cues may aid retrieval either through a controlled process in which the subject deliberately makes use of them (e.g. a knot in a handkerchief), or through an automatic process in which the cue directly facilitates the retrieval of the target representation. A person is, for example, involuntarily prompted when he encounters someone who happens to resemble an old friend whom he has not seen for years. Visual prompts can be single images or sequence of images. Apart from visual prompts there are verbal, auditory and olfactory prompts. The encoding specificity principle states that the cues presented during encoding serve as the best cues for memory retrieval (see sect. 7.5).

Martin and Deutscher (1966: 182–3) distinguish between complete (or full) and strict verbal prompts. A subject is fully prompted when he cannot correctly reproduce more about the relevant past event than was supplied by the prompt; the prompted information is identical with the stored information. Psychologists call complete prompts 'copy cues' or 'identity cues'. A subject is in need of strict prompting if he needs to be told not only what happened in the past but also that he has experienced before what he is now being informed about. A prompt can be complete without being strict, but all strict prompts are complete. Remembering due to strict prompting is what psychologists call *recognition*.[8]

The fact a subject is in need of strict prompting to be able to report some past event does not rule out that he is genuinely remembering the event. Consider this example adopted from Martin and Deutscher (ibid. 184). S is unable to remember what he did the previous afternoon. His friend tells him about driving through certain villages, eating certain dishes, visiting gothic churches, etc. Then S says, 'Now it all comes back' and retells the whole story. The point of the example is that notwithstanding the fact that S is unable to provide any information over and above the story provided by his friend it is possible that he genuinely remembers the excursion. That a person requires strict

---

[8] Martin and Deutscher (1966: 182–3) point out that verbal but not visual prompts can be in the impersonal mode. In the case of verbal prompts, the state of seeming to remember an event caused by prompting may contain no recognitional factor—we may be unable to learn from the prompt whether it was us who previously experienced that event. Sensory cues, however, are never impersonal because whenever we see something that we have seen before the representation brought about by the prompt contains the idea that we have seen something like this before. This is even the case if we cannot give any detail of what we saw that wasn't provided by the prompt. 'No matter how much detail is supplied by observation of a replica of what has been previously observed, there is always, in such cases, the *additional* "detail" of recognition.'

prompting before he can recount certain events shouldn't be ruled out as inadmissable for genuine memory.

Given that we may remember only after being strictly prompted, what is it for us to remember an event upon being prompted rather than merely parroting the prompting itself? In other words, where lies the difference between a memory being jogged by a prompting and a prompting imparting the information afresh? The answer to this question depends on the retrieval cue's causal contribution to the production of the memory state vis-à-vis the memory trace's causal contribution. Anticipating the conclusion, for a memory trace to give rise to genuine remembering it must be an independently sufficient condition (that is not preempted by another independently sufficient condition) of a state of seeming to remember or at least a necessary component of such an independently sufficient condition.

There are four ways in which retrieval cues and memory traces can collaborate in the formation of seeming memories.[9] First, there are cases of *causal overdetermination* where the trace and the cue operate independently of each other and each is a sufficient condition for the production of the seeming memory. Two kinds of overdetermination can be distinguished. The first is the concurrent-cause cases: the trace and the retrieval cue *simultaneously* cause the seeming memory but are unrelated. This is like the case of someone who gets blown up at the same time as suffering a fatal heart attack. Since there is no straight answer as to which of the two independently sufficient causes—the memory trace or the retrieval cue—is responsible for the production of the seeming memory, the production is shared without being divided between them. Thus cases of simultaneous overdetermination do count as instances of genuine remembering.

The *preemptive* kind of overdetermination cases are different. Here the two putative causes are not simultaneous but are temporally ordered. While in simultaneous overdetermination the two putative causes operate and actually issue in the overdetermined event, in preemptive overdetermination the event is actually caused in only one way, and would have been caused in a different way had the actual cause not taken place. Now, if it is the seeming memory that is due to the retrieval cue and if the causation via the trace is preempted, then it is not a genuine memory. However, if the production of the seeming memory is due to the trace acting as an independently sufficient condition and if the

---

[9] The fourfold distinction is inspired by Pears (1975: 34).

causal efficacy of the retrieval cue is preempted, then it may be a genuine memory. The fact that the seeming memory could have been caused in a deviant way should not worry us. Evaluations of whether seeming memories are genuine memories should be based on the causation that is actually operative rather than on whether there is independent sufficient causation held in reserve on a deviant route.

Frequently a memory trace is not sufficient to produce a state of seeming to remember. When the causation of the trace and that of the cue are only jointly sufficient to produce the seeming memory two cases need to be distinguished: the two causal chains either do or don't interact before they jointly bring about their effect. The former case may be called *causal reinforcement*, the latter *causal supplementation*. Either mechanisms can give rise to genuine memories—provided the memory trace is an indispensable part of the jointly sufficient condition responsible for the production of the seeming memory. Another way of making the point is to say that the memory trace needs to be at least an insufficient but non-redundant factor of an unnecessary but sufficient condition for the seeming memory. John Mackie (1965) calls such a factor an *inus condition*.

According to Mackie, causes are inus conditions. If we say that a short circuit causes the house fire, the occurrence of the short circuit must be a component of a complex condition which is, in the circumstances, sufficient for the house fire to start. The short circuit is an insufficient component because it cannot cause the fire on its own; other components such as oxygen and inflammable material must be present as well. But conjoint with these other components the short circuit is sufficient for the house fire. Though the short circuit, by itself, is not sufficient it is nonetheless a non-redundant component because, without it, the other components are not sufficient for the fire. The complex condition (short circuit, oxygen, inflammable material) need not be a necessary condition for the house fire to start. For instance, if there was no short circuit, but the house was hit by lightning, that might also have set the house on fire. Mackie's notion of an inus condition is, I think, a compelling method for distinguishing between those cases of causal reinforcement and supplementation that do and those that don't qualify as instances of genuine memory. The idea is that when a trace is not strong enough to bring about the seeming memory by itself but has to rely on help from a retrieval cue, the trace has to be a non-redundant component of the complex condition that brings about the seeming memory.

We have seen that there are a number of ways in which traces and cues can cooperate in the production of seeming memories so that the seeming memory may qualify as a genuine memory. When traces and cues are independently sufficient conditions of the seeming memory, the causation by the traces has to occur either before, or simultaneous with, the causation of the cues. When traces and cues are only jointly sufficient conditions, the resulting state of seeming to remember counts as remembering if the trace is at least an insufficient but non-redundant factor of the jointly sufficient condition. In sum, for a memory trace to give rise to a representation that potentially qualifies as a memory the following *causal strength condition* must be met:

(3) The memory trace is at least an inus condition for S's representation at t_2 that p. If the memory trace is an independently sufficient condition, it is not preempted by another independently sufficient condition.

5.5 COUNTERFACTUAL DEPENDENCE

After having discussed the causal dependence of memory states on traces vis-à-vis prompts it is time to examine the causal dependence of memory states on past representations. There is a crucial difference between the causal dependence of memory states on traces, on the one hand, and the dependence of memory states on past representations, on the other. As was shown in section 5.4, the causal dependence of memory states on traces vis-à-vis prompts can be analyzed in terms of necessary and sufficient conditions. Yet the causal dependence of memory states on past representations cannot be analyzed in the same fashion. Instead I will argue for an analysis of memory causation in terms of counterfactuals. But before I set forth my position, it is instructive to get an idea of the options available. The main alternatives to a counterfactual account of memory causation are analyses in terms of necessary and sufficient conditions, inus conditions, and conditional probabilities.

A little thought reveals that the causal chain connecting a past representation and its subsequent recall cannot be analyzed in terms of sufficient conditions. The reason a past representation isn't causally sufficient for its subsequent recall is that there are frequently other factors which are necessary for the recall. Often we remember something only after being prompted. Likewise an account of memory causation in

terms of necessary conditions is too narrow. A past representation of
X is frequently not necessary for the state of seeming to remember X,
for the state may also depend on some retrieval cue which is causally
sufficient to bring about the apparent memory of X. When the prompt
is a sufficient condition, the past representation can't be a necessary
condition for the state of seeming to remember X.

Another approach to memory causation in terms of necessary and
sufficient conditions is Mackie's inus condition explained on page 143.
To see that the inus-analysis of causation is still too strict to cover the
causal dependence of a memory state on a past representation, consider
the following example. Suppose you are taking part in a televised history
quiz and are asked for the year in which Brutus killed Caesar. At the
moment when you are about to remember that Caesar died in 44
BC someone in the televison studio blurts out '44 BC'. Your memory
that Caesar died in 44 BC is causally overdetermined by your previous
knowledge of this fact and by the person's blurting. Now suppose
that the exclusively sufficient condition of your present knowledge that
Caesar died in 44 BC is a conjunction consisting of four elements:
(1) your previous knowledge that Caesar died in 44 BC, (2) various
neurophysiological conditions having to do with remembering, (3) the
person in the studio blurting out the date '44 BC', and (4) your ears
working correctly. Neither (1) nor (3) are necessary conditions of the
exclusively sufficient condition. Thus, according to the inus-analysis,
neither the previous knowledge nor the person's blurting qualifies as
the cause of your remembering that Caesar died in 44 BC. I reckon this
conclusion is too counterintuitive to be acceptable.

Yet another possible account of the causal dependence of memory
states of past representations is in terms of conditional probabilities.
An event A is a probabilistic cause of an event B if the probability
of the occurrence of B, given that A has occurred, is greater than the
antecedent probability of B: $P(B/A) > P(B)$. This implies that the effect
must be more probable given the presence rather than the absence of
the cause: $P(B/A) > P(B/\sim A)$. Deborah Rosen (1975: 6) gives the
following example to illustrate the probabilistic analysis of memory
causation. A subject is given a number between 1 and 6—say, 4—and
on the next day is told to repeat the number. The probability of the
subject's responding with the correct number, given that he has heard
the number on the previous day, is one or almost one. This probability is
definitely higher than the probability of the subject responding with the
correct number, given that he didn't hear the number on the previous

day. Since he might respond with any of the first six numbers, the probability of his responding '4' is only 1/6. Hence, the probability of B/A exceeds the probability of B.

The problem with the probabilistic analysis of memory causation is that unless we are given precise values for the probabilities in question the analysis is too vague to be of any use in distinguishing genuine memory causation from a variety of spurious causation. Being told that the connection between a past representation and its subsequent recall is such that the occurrence of the recall, given the past representation, is more likely than if the past representation hadn't occurred is not informative. We want to know by how much the conditional probability of the occurrence of the apparent memory has to exceed the probability of the occurrence of the apparent memory in general. Yet it doesn't seem likely that we will ever be in a position to give precise values for the probabilities in question.

I advocate a counterfactual account of the causal relation that holds between apparent memory states and past representations. To motivate such an account consider the following case. Due to a severe depression, S is convinced that no one likes him. Whenever S meets someone who acts friendly toward him (which happens rarely enough), the experience gets transformed in his memory, so that, later on, it seems to S as if the person had acted unfriendly toward him.[10] S is unaware of his memory's bias. Now suppose that at t_1 S has an encounter with S^* who openly displays his dislike for S. At t_2, S seems to remember having met S^* at t_1 and that S^* disliked him. Thus, the memory claim is true and, what is more, there is a causal relation between his experience at t_1 and his apparent memory of the experience at t_2. But does S *remember* that S^* disliked him? The answer, I reckon, is negative. The reason S doesn't remember that S^* acted in an unfriendly manner is that, all things being equal, if, at the time, S had thought that S^* likes him, S would still believe at t_2 that S^* had acted in an unfriendly manner. It is just a matter of luck that the content

---

[10] It is a well-known fact that our mood can taint our (apparent) memories. Psychologists differentiate between two types of effects a subject's mood can have on his ability to remember. First, there is *mood state dependency*, whereby anything experienced in a given mood will tend to be recalled more easily when that mood is reinstated, regardless of whether the material experienced in the mood is pleasant, unpleasant, or neutral. Second, there is *mood congruency*, whereby a given mood will tend to evoke memories that are consistent with that mood, hence, when sad we tend to recall sad events, even if these were encountered during a period of happiness. By and large, the experimental evidence for mood congruency is stronger than that for mood state dependency. See Bower (1981).

of S's apparent memory matches that of his past representation. Yet intuitively, to remember something, the correspondence between the contents of one's past and present representations may not be entirely by accident.[11]

We must devise a connection condition that rules out that it is just a matter of chance that the content of the memory representation corresponds to the content of the relevant past representation. For a state of seeming to remember to be memory-related to a past representation, it has to be the case that, if the past representation had been different, one wouldn't occupy the very state of seeming to remember that one does occupy. Whether the causal origin of a veridical state as of remembering meets the criteria for memory depends not only on what actually causes it, but also on how it would have been caused if things had gone slightly differently. Whether there is potential independent sufficient causation held in reserve on a deviant route bears on the question of whether the actual causal relation between a past and a present representation meets the conditions for remembering.

Consider an example adapted from Robert Audi (2003: 58–9). Suppose that my unknowingly taking a poisonous drug causes me to feel ill, and my feeling ill then causes me to believe that I have been poisoned. There is a causal link between the past event of taking poison and my believing that I have been poisoned. Moreover, this belief is veridical. But it doesn't qualify as a memory, for my feeling ill might as well have caused me to believe something else, say, that I have eaten too many candies (which may be true as well). This is how Audi explains why my belief that I have been poisoned fails to be a memory belief: 'My memory has played no role in supporting the *content* of the belief. The belief lacks a ground appropriate for suitably connecting it with the past event it represents' (ibid. 59). Another way of making the same point is to require that the dependence relation that holds between the present and past belief supports the subjunctive conditional: if the past belief had been different so would the present belief be.

---

[11] Appeals to intuitions have recently received a lot of critical attention. It has been suggested that since intuitions are far from universal they may not be used as data points for the analysis of philosophical concepts such as the concept of memory (see e.g. Machery et al. 2004; Weinberg, Nichols, and Stich 2001). It would be interesting to find out whether subjects of different cultural background and socio-economic status react differently to scenarios in which someone correctly reports some past event but fails to track the truth. Trying to defend the use of intuitions in the philosophy of memory would, however, take us too far afield.

It is useful to compare memory with perception. A representation is a memory state only if it has some causal connection to a past event, just as a representation is a perception only if there is some causal connection to the perceived object. To perceive that F is G is to be in a state that has some causal relation to F's being G. 'S sees that F is G' requires that F's being G causes S to believe that F is G. But simple causation will not do, for it allows for a situation where F's being G causes S to believe that F is G, though that belief would have been produced in S even if F hadn't been G. For S to see that F is G, the belief that F is G must be produced by a reliable mechanism, that is, a mechanism that not only produces true beliefs in actual situations, but would continue to produce true beliefs, or at least to inhibit false ones, in other relevantly different circumstances. S doesn't see that F is G if there is a relevant counterfactual situation in which the belief that F is G would be produced via an equivalent percept and in which the belief would be false.[12]

Suppose that S represented at t_1 that p^*. This representation gave rise to memory traces that in turn caused (with or without the help of prompts) S to represent at t_2 that p. For S's representation at t_2 that p to be memory-related to his representation at t_1 that p^*, the causal chain connecting the two states must be such that *counterfactual condition* (4) holds:

(4) If S hadn't represented at t_1 that p^* he wouldn't represent at t_2 that p.

This condition already played a role in section 4.6 where I argued that the virtue of the causal theory of memory over its non-causal rivals is that it does a better job of explaining why (4) is the case.

According to the standard account of the truth-conditions of subjunctive conditionals, (4) is true just in case some world where S didn't represent at t_1 that p^* and doesn't represent at t_2 that p is closer to our world than any world where S didn't represent at t_1 that p^* but does represent at t_2 that p. So to adjudicate the truth of (4) we need to determine the degree of resemblance of a possible scenario to the actual world. A notorious problem with subjunctive conditionals is that

---

[12] David Lewis (1986: 282) suggests the following theory of perception: S perceives X if and only if (1) S has an experience E, (2) E is sufficiently veridical with respect to X, and (3) E is appropriately caused by X, where an experience E is appropriately caused by an object X when the causation is part of a suitable pattern of counterfactual dependence.

remoteness and closeness of possible worlds is relative to a context in which different standards of importance are the ones that count. There is no context-independent criterion for ranking possible worlds in terms of their remoteness from the actual world.

The advantage of the counterfactual account of memory causation over an account in terms of necessary and sufficient conditions is that it allows us to correctly classify abnormal cases in which the past representation matches the apparent memory by triggering some one-off or random causal mechanism, insensitive to the details of the past representation, which just happens to produce the right apparent memory. The advantage of the counterfactual account of memory causation over the probabilistic approach is that it has greater explanatory power. The probabilistic analysis of memory is unedifying as long as we are not told by how much the probability of an apparent memory following a matching past representation has to exceed the probability of the same apparent memory without the preceding representation.

Before ending this section I should address a worry an observant reader might have regarding the coherence of my overall position. The worry is that a counterfactual account of the memory connection is committed to the thesis that memory entails knowledge—the very thesis that was rejected in Chapter 3. Let me explain.

We have seen that memory is incompatible with certain cases of epistemic luck. Now there is universal agreement that knowledge is also incompatible with luck (cf. Pritchard 2005). Nowhere is this more apparent than in the debate regarding Gettier-style counterexamples to the tripartite account of knowledge. Gettier cases are considered to be so devastating to the tripartite view precisely because they show that such an account is consistent with there being lucky knowledge. So it is the conviction that knowledge excludes luck that is the driving force behind post-Gettier epistemology. Jonathan Dancy (1985: 134), for example, remarks: 'justification and knowledge must somehow not depend on coincidence or luck. This was just the point of the Gettier counter-example; nothing in the tripartite definition [of knowledge as justified true belief] excluded knowledge by luck.'

As was explained before (cf. pp. 69–70, 73–4), a belief is veritically lucky if it is true in the actual world, but in some close possible world in which the subject forms the same belief on the basis of the same evidence or via the same method of belief formation, the belief is false. The obvious way to exclude epistemic luck is by devising a counterfactual condition that rules out possible situations in which the subject has the same beliefs as in the actual situation but where the belief goes wrong. This is precisely the strategy adopted by so-called *truth-tracking* accounts of knowledge. The best-known truth-tracking account of knowledge is due to Robert Nozick (1981: 172–96). Nozick holds that S knows that p only if (1) p is true, (2) S believes that p, (3) if p were not true, S would not believe that p, and (4) if p were true, S would believe that p. A belief in p tracks the truth if S would not believe p if p were false in the closest possible world and he would believe p if p were true in the closest possible world. There is a growing consensus among contemporary epistemologists that some version of truth-tracking is correct.

The subjunctive conditional employed by proponents of the truth-tracking account of knowledge is strikingly similar to the subjunctive conditional (4) which, on my view, the causal dependence of (apparent) memories on past representations must support. It therefore stands to reason that memory is a form of knowledge. If the same kind of condition that defines memory also defines knowledge, doesn't it then follow that remembering is a form of knowing? Thus the question arises whether the counterfactual account of memory causation is compatible with the denial of the epistemic theory of memory argued for in Chapter 3.

In response to this objection I would like to make four points. First, granted the structural analogy between the counterfactual account of knowledge, on the one hand, and my counterfactual account of memory causation, on the other, I reject the epistemic theory of memory on the grounds that remembering, unlike knowing, doesn't imply believing (cf. sects. 3.3 and 3.4). Second, truth-tracking conditions are not meant to provide an exhaustive account of epistemic justification. As was explained in section 3.2, the truth-tracking account of justification must be supplemented by a no-defeater condition that ensures that for a belief to become knowledge it must not be incoherent with the background information the subject possesses. Memory, however, is not subject to a no-defeater condition; it is fully compatible with the lack of justification due to the presence of some defeating evidence (cf. sects. 3.2 and 3.6).

Third, for a belief to qualify as knowledge it must track the facts that make it true. Memory beliefs, however, track what one took to be true. A memory must authentically report one's past representation, but the past representation need not have been true at the time it was entertained. Memory demands a present truth-condition but not a past truth-condition. As was argued on pages 38–9 and 74, the authentic reproduction of a proposition that was false at the time it was initially entertained but which, in the meantime, has become true due to good fortune may qualify as memory. Even if the content of one's past representation, p^*, was false one's present representation that p qualifies as a memory provided the following conditions hold: p is true and one wouldn't represent that p now unless one had represented that p^* in the past.

Fourth, memory, unlike knowledge, is compatible with Gettier cases. While tracking conditions exclude Gettier cases from the ranks of knowledge, the counterfactual interpretation of the causal theory of memory has it that memory is fully compatible with the original belief and the memory belief being veritically lucky (cf. pp. 73–4). Unlike epistemic tracking conditions, the counterfactual condition (4) doesn't establish the co-variation between a belief and a fact but between two mental items—a propositional attitude at t_1 and a propositional attitude at t_2.

5.6 SUGGESTIBILITY

We have seen that the causal connection constitutive of remembering can be characterized by the conjunction of the trace condition, the causal strength condition, and the counterfactual condition. In the case of extroversive memory in the first-person mode these three conditions read:

(2) S's representation at t_1 that p^* and S's representation at t_2 that p are connected by a persisting memory trace or a contiguous series of memory traces.

(3) The memory trace is at least an inus condition for S's representation at t_2 that p. If the memory trace is an independently sufficient condition, it is not preempted by another independently sufficient condition.

(4) If S hadn't represented at t_1 that p^* he wouldn't represent at t_2 that p.

Conditions (2), (3), and (4) need to be taken together to yield a plausible account of memory causation. The counterfactual condition (4), by itself, is susceptible to relearning counterexamples and cannot rule out causal chains involving external loops. For condition (4) is met even when, in between t_1 and t_2, S records p in his diary, completely forgets about it, and later learns about p by reading his diary. Yet these kinds of cases are excluded by condition (2). Condition (2), by itself, however, is susceptible to preemption counterexamples. For (2) is met even when there are two sufficient causes for the state of recall—a strict prompt and a trace—and the preempting causal process from the prompt interrupts or cuts off the preempted causal process from the trace, preventing the trace from causing the state of recall. These kinds of cases are excluded by condition (3). Now the goal of this section is to show that unless (2) and (3) are supplemented by (4), our account of the memory connection is unable to deliver the intuitively right verdict in suggestibility cases.

A person's suggestibility can be enhanced by means of hypnosis or by means of certain drugs (misleadingly called 'truth drugs') such as sodium amytal. Hypnosis produces a state of suggestibility, in which the hypnotized individual abdicates responsibility for his actions on the assumption that he is now under the control of the hypnotist. Hypnotized individuals are less likely to distinguish an instruction as coming from another person rather than themselves, and so will tend to act on another person's ideas as though they were their own. An extreme example is reported by David Spiegel (1995: 139):

A highly hypnotizable businessman was instructed in hypnosis that there was a communist plot to take over the television media, and that he would see three names on a sheet of paper. He was then interviewed on camera by a well-known television reporter. He elaborated a tale of intrigue regarding such a plot, replete with names and dates of meetings. He hallucinated three names when confronted with a blank sheet of paper, saying: 'I know him and him, but not that one in the middle.' When pushed harder by the interviewer, he stated: 'He is a terrible man—maybe he has gotten to you already', thereby elaborating a paranoid defense of his position. As soon as the hypnosis was ended, he recanted the story, viewing it as an amusing experiment.

In a recent study that examines the effect on memory reports of misinformation that is suggested during hypnosis, Jean-Roch Laurence and Campbell Perry (1983; Laurence et al. 1986) interviewed subjects to ensure that they had slept through a particular night of the previous week. Then they were hypnotized and age-regressed to the night in question. During the hypnotic reliving of the night's sleep the subjects were asked whether they had heard a loud noise that had awakened them. Seventeen of the twenty-seven subjects responded to the suggestion implicit in the question and said that they had been woken up by a loud noise. When the hypnosis was terminated, thirteen subjects still 'recalled' having been woken up by a loud noise. They remained convinced even after they were told that the noise had been suggested to them in hypnosis. What this and similar experiments show is that hypnosis can increase the acceptance of misinformation introduced during hypnosis as well as the confidence that is associated with the acceptance of such information.[13]

Now consider a thought experiment adopted from Martin and Deutscher (1966: 186). S takes a potent hypnotic drug which causes him to become suggestible to all sorts of plausible promptings—true and false—concerning his past actions. When prompted, S is unable to select true from false promptings and accepts both as pieces of autobiographical memory. When S is not prompted, the drug doesn't affect his psychology. When left alone, S's ability to access his memory traces (including the ones about his having taken the drug) is perfectly normal.

Let's first ask ourselves whether the combination of S being in a credulous state with him being prompted rules out the possibility of him having genuine memories. Is it possible for S to genuinely remember when he is prompted? Since S accepts any plausible prompting—true and false—and since memory implies truth, the interesting case is the one where our suggestible agent S is presented with a true prompt. Does S's apparent memory caused by a true prompt qualify as memory? I reckon the intuitive answer is 'no'. Condition (4) accounts for this response. According to (4), for S to remember that p it is not enough that he represented that p* in the past and that that representation causes (via traces) his present representation that p. It must also be the case that if S hadn't represented that p* in the past he wouldn't now seem to remember that p. But given that S is in a highly suggestible state and that his apparent memory of p is caused by a true prompting, condition (4) is not met. S would still seem to remember that p even if he hadn't previously represented that p*.

It's worth noting that conditions (2) and (3), without (4), fail to eliminate this case of suggestibility from the ranks of memory. Consider two scenarios. First, the suggestible state in combination with the

[13] Though the use of hypnosis to enhance memory has a long history, some psychologists question the credibility of material that is recovered in hypnosis (e.g. Kihlstrom 1997). The point is that it is unclear which processes are responsible for the malleability of memory in hypnosis. Where hypnosis appears successful, the outcome is said to be owing to the instructions and cues given during hypnosis on how to retrieve information, rather than on hypnosis per se. And when hypnotized subjects recall information that they could not previously recall in an awake state, they are said to do so at the expense of increased guessing.

true prompting, on the one hand, and the memory trace, on the other, are independently sufficient conditions of the formation of the apparent memory. If the causation by the trace occurs either before, or simultaneously with, the causation by the suggestible-state-cum-true-prompting, the apparent memory will meet condition (3). Second, the suggestible state plus the true prompting, on the one hand, and the memory trace, on the other, are only jointly sufficient conditions of the apparent memory state. As long as the memory trace is a necessary condition of the jointly sufficient condition, the resulting state of seeming to remember will meet (3). Thus, without (4), the trace theory of memory causation (consisting of (2) and (3)) is unable to eliminate suggestibility counterexamples where the subject is provided with a true prompt.

The next question is whether our suggestible agent S can have genuine memories when he is not prompted. Given that, when left alone, S's ability to access his memory traces is normal, should we say that S has the ability to remember? This is a tricky issue. According to what has been said about causal preemption (cf. pp. 142–3), S can indeed remember when not prompted. The causal process from the traces to the apparent memory state is impeccable, notwithstanding the fact that it can be sabotaged by the occurrence of a prompt. According to (4), however, S cannot remember. For even though in the actual world, where S is not prompted, his suggestible state is causally inert and he produces mostly true reports about the past, there is a nearby possible world in which S is given false promptings and therefore produces mostly false memory claims. In connection with Squires's criticism of the causal theory of memory (cf. pp. 119–21) I have argued that for every person and every ability they have, there will be some circumstances in which they are unable to exercise that ability correctly. Presumably the case of our suggestible agent S is such a one. When not prompted, he can access his memory traces normally and has the ability to remember. But in certain adverse circumstances—namely, when prompted—he cannot remember. Regardless of what is the correct verdict in this case, we can conclude that conditions (2) and (3) are needed to eliminate cases of relearning and that condition (4) is needed to rule out cases where a suggestible agent simply parrots a true prompt.

6

Pastist Externalism about Memory Content

The content condition for remembering demands that one can only remember what one has previously represented. Traditionally philosophers have taken the view that the memory content must be type-identical with the content of the relevant past state. Since the *identity theory of memory* conflicts with what cognitive psychology tells us about the workings of human memory (cf. sect. 8.2) I propose a version of the content condition which allows for the contents of the past and present representations not to be type-identical but only sufficiently similar. A representation at t_2 that p is memory-related to a representation at t_1 that p^* only if

(1) p is identical with, or sufficiently similar to, p^*.

The content condition is the same for extroversive and introversive memory.

The content condition raises two questions: First, what does it mean for two diachronic content tokens to be of the same type? Second, in what respect and to what extent may two diachronic content tokens differ from one another and one of them still count as sufficiently similar to the other so as to be memory-related to it? In this and the following chapter I will tackle the first of the two questions. The second question is the topic of Chapter 8.

One of the most provocative projects in recent philosophy of mind and language has been the development of *content externalism* (also known as 'psychological externalism' and 'anti-individualism'), that is, the view that the individuation conditions of mental content depend, in part, on external or relational properties of the subject's environment rather than only on internal properties of the subject's mind and brain. The contents of an individual's thoughts and the meanings of his words depend on relations that the individual bears to aspects of his physical or social environment. Content externalism stands opposed to *content internalism* (also known as 'individualism'), which holds that the contents of our mental states can be individuated fully in ways that don't require reference to any particular objects or properties in the environment.

It is nowadays widely accepted that some, if not all, of our thoughts are externally individuated. In fact, content externalism has been so successful that the current debate is not so much about whether it is right or wrong, but what its implications are. There is a lively discussion concerning the compatibility of externalism and privileged self-knowledge, concerning the compatibility of content externalism and epistemic internalism, concerning the compatibility of externalism and mental causation, and concerning the anti-skeptical consequences of externalism. In what follows I will argue for the compatibility of externalism and memory. I will, first, motivate and explain content externalism and, second, apply it to memory contents. According to my version of content externalism about memory, the individuation of memory contents depends on relations the subject bears to his *past* environment. What determines the content of the memory that p are certain aspects of the physical or social environment the subject lived in at the time he had the original thought that p.

Section 6.1 motivates content externalism by discussing Twin Earth thought experiments and narrow content. Section 6.2 gives an overview of different versions of externalism. Section 6.3 applies externalism to memory contents and distinguishes different kinds of externalism about memory content. Section 6.4 compares and contrasts content externalism with the hypothesis of the extended mind. In Chapter 7 externalism about memory contents is defended against objections.

6.1 MOTIVATIONS FOR EXTERNALISM

Content externalism holds that the relations that an individual bears to his physical, and in many cases social, environment figure essentially in the type-identity conditions for mental contents. A common strategy for motivating content externalism is to describe a situation in which there are two individuals who share all their intrinsic properties, but who differ in respect to some mental properties because they inhabit different environments. In recent years, a collection of thought experiments that purport to do just this have been put forward, beginning with the classic examples by Hilary Putnam (1975*b*) and Tyler Burge (2007*c*). Putnam's and Burge's examples are primarily concerned with the role the environment plays for the determination of *meaning* but they can also be used to argue for externalism about *mental content*.

In 'The Meaning of "Meaning" ' Putnam asks us to consider this thought experiment. Suppose S is an English-speaker who uses the word 'water' much as anyone in his linguistic community. He doesn't have any considerable knowledge of the chemical properties of water. Suppose that there exists somewhere in a nearby galaxy a Twin Earth, that is, a planet that is a molecule-for-molecule duplicate of Earth. The only difference between the two planets is that no water is present on Twin Earth. What is found there instead is a liquid which looks, tastes, and behaves like water but has the chemical composition XYZ and not H_2O. Like each one of us, S has a molecular duplicate on Twin Earth.[1] Twin S has endured experiences that are just like S's, except that where S has encountered H_2O, he has encountered XYZ; and neither of them is aware of the constitution of the liquids they refer to as 'water'.

At this point Putnam introduces two common assumptions about the meaning of mental states and their relation to language. First, there is the assumption that the meaning of terms in a language is determined by the mental states of the speaker who uses them. Thus the meaning of the term 'water' is determined by the speaker's concept *water*. Second, there is the assumption that reference is a component of the meaning of a term. So the meaning of 'water' contains not only an intensional description of the character or stereotype of water, but also the referent, H_2O.

The reference of S's 'water' expression is different from the reference of his twin's 'water' expression. S's expression refers to H_2O while Twin S's refers to XYZ. Given that reference is part of the meaning, the meaning of S's 'water' expressions is distinct from the meaning of Twin S's 'water' expressions. And if the meaning of an expression is determined by the concepts of the speaker, then the concept expressed by S's term 'water' is different from the concept expressed by Twin S's term 'water'. To translate the concept expressed by the Twin Earthian word 'water' into English we have to coin a new word, perhaps *twater*. Due to the difference in concepts, S and Twin S express different thoughts

---

[1] Here and elsewhere I follow the tradition in neglecting the fact that strictly speaking none of S's molecules are identical with those of his twin, for S's molecules contain H_2O while Twin S's contain XYZ. The thought experiment can be changed to accommodate this fact.

when both of them utter, for instance, 'Gee, water is wet!'—and this in spite of their molecular identity. Putnam concludes that mental states involving natural kind terms don't supervene on physical states of our brains but on the physical states of our environment. In Putnam's famous phrase, 'meanings ain't in the head'.[2]

Putnam's Twin Earth example exploits the fact that in the case of a natural kind term such as 'water', the nature of the referent plays an essential role in individuating the concept associated with the word. A notorious objection to this thought experiment states, first, that it is limited to natural kind terms and, second, that it rests on the contentious idea that just as the chemical composition (as opposed to the color, taste, density, or boiling point) is said to be the defining characteristic of water every natural kind is supposed to have an essential property. While this is still a popular criticism of the Twin Earth example, it seems pretty clear that Putnam's overall position in 'The Meaning of "Meaning" ' doesn't presuppose any substantial type of metaphysical essentialism and is intended to apply to most terms in our language.[3]

Another thought experiment aimed at motivating content externalism has been developed by Burge in 'Individualism and the Mental'. Burge asks us to imagine an agent, the ubiquitous S, who claims to believe that he has arthritis in his thigh. The belief is false, for arthritis is a disease that occurs only in joints. S is otherwise a normal speaker of English and has many true beliefs concerning arthritis, for example, that the elderly are more prone to it than the young. Burge suggests that, even though S incompletely understands the meaning of the term 'arthritis', common-sense attributions of beliefs would ascribe to him a belief about arthritis when he says 'I have arthritis in my thigh'. The reason is that the meaning of a term (here 'arthritis') is determined by the extension it has for the members of the subject's linguistic community.

---

[2] 1975*b*: 227. Twin Earth cases assume a narrow notion of environment according to which a person's content-determining environment is limited to the planet he resides on. If, however, the notion of an environment is construed broadly, then the environment is made up of everything in the person's universe. Given the broad notion of environment, Twin Earth belongs to the environment of Earth, and *vice versa*. S's word 'water' then refers to both liquids—H_2O and XYZ.

[3] Cf. Salmon (1979). Since writing 'The Meaning of "Meaning" ', Putnam (1990: 70) has become skeptical of the search for necessary and sufficient conditions. 'Is it clear that we would call a (hypothetical) substance with quite different behavior *water* in these circumstances? I now think that the question, "What is the necessary and sufficient condition for being water in all possible worlds?" makes no sense at all. And this means that I now reject "metaphysical necessity".'

Then Burge constructs a counterfactual world very much like the real one where Twin S's physical states (described in a non-intentional language) remain the same but in which there is a difference in the linguistic community (or social environment).[4] In the counterfactual situation the term 'arthritis' refers not to arthritis but to a variety of rheumatoid ailments that can occur in both muscles and joints. Let's call the concept expressed by the term 'arthritis' uttered in the counterfactual situation *tharthritis*. Burge claims that when Twin S says 'I have arthritis in my thigh' he is saying something true. The reason is that while S's concept *arthritis* includes in its extension only ailments in the joints, Twin S's concept *tharthritis* also refers to thigh ailments. The truth-conditions of their beliefs are different, hence they have different beliefs. S cannot express his twin's 'arthritis'-belief because he doesn't have the necessary concept of *tharthritis*. Thus, it is the linguistic community that determines the extension of S's and Twin S's concepts, in spite of their molecular identity.

Contrary to Putnam's example, there is no question about it that Burge's example is applicable to most terms in our language. Arthritis is not a natural kind, but a syndrome identified on the basis of symptoms that may be of varying etiology. There is a significant element of convention in fixing what counts as arthritis. The arthritis case can be easily generalized to a broad range of terms. Burge constructs analogous examples for terms of art such as 'transcendental idealism' or 'contract', for natural kind terms such as 'elm' or 'atom', and for terms we employ to describe our everyday environment such as 'sofa', 'blue', and 'weekend'. In fact, he suggests that content-externalism is true for 'virtually all concepts and meanings that are applied to public objects or events that we know about empirically' (2007e: 281).

Since Twin Earth thought experiments are an important reason in favor of content externalism they deserve careful attention. Focusing on Burge's arthritis example, the crucial question is this: is Burge right in claiming that the subject's commitment to the community practice entails that when he uses a word in a non-standard way we should still give it the meaning it has in his linguistic community and interpret his propositional attitudes on the same basis? Burge concedes that there are cases of radical misunderstandings, where the individual must be

---

[4] Burge states his thought experiment so that it's the same person who inhabits the real and the counterfactual world. I find it more congenial to speak of a twin, so as not to confuse the two protagonists.

described as using the words with a non-standard meaning. His example is that of a person who claims to have 'orangutans' for breakfast, thinking 'orangutan' is a fruit drink (2007c: 119–20). But then the question arises as to why some cases of linguistic deviation warrant reinterpretation but others don't. Why does the belief S expresses by saying 'I have arthritis in my thigh' conform to the community usage by referring to arthritis rather than to a rheumatoid ailment that can strike the thigh as well as the joints?

Burge's reason for claiming that, by and large, linguistic (and conceptual) errors have the standard meaning is that he takes it to be part and parcel of common-sense psychology. There is a linguistic convention of interpreting people's utterances literally, despite their imperfect grasp of the community's linguistic standards. And it is this convention that lies at the bottom of Burge's interpretation of the arthritis case. He declares that 'there is a methodological bias in favor of taking natural discourse literally, other things being equal . . . Literal interpretation is *ceteris paribus* preferred' (ibid. 116–17). The externalist interpretation of Twin Earth scenarios relies on the acceptance of our ordinary practice of using the community's prevailing linguistic standards when attributing conceptual contents to others. But since there is the possibility of explaining away this ordinary practice as mere loose talk, we need an argument that establishes that this practice is in fact reasonable. We need some normative consideration for maintaining that thought content is not determined individualistically.[5]

Putnam (1975a) argues that content internalism is committed to the implausible verificationist view whereby a subject must be able to grasp a criterion for applying his words which determines once and for all what belongs in their extensions. By tying reference to our current beliefs about reference, the content internalist is repudiating paradigm methods of responsible scientific inquiry. For it is part of the nature of rational inquiry that we allow for the possibility that what, at the time, we take to be the defining features of a term may turn out to be false or incomplete. Having a certain concept, or having

---

[5] In my (2000: 10–11) I have held that the externalist thesis can be known non-empirically. In support of this claim I wrote: 'The externalist interpretation of Twin Earth thought experiments relies on an arm-chair psychological picture of how we attribute meaning to beliefs and utterances—a picture that lacks any empirical grounding. . . . The assertion of content externalism comes down to nothing but brute intuition.' I do not believe any more that it is nothing but intuition that motivates the externalist interpretation of twinning scenarios.

beliefs involving that concept, is compatible with being ignorant of the defining characteristics of the concept. The natural inclination to grant S *arthritis*-beliefs, despite his medical ignorance, reveals our (implicit) knowledge of this compatibility. Hence, content externalism explains the possibility of rational inquiry into the defining characteristics of concepts.

Burge (2007*d*) provides a similar reason for interpreting linguistic (and conceptual) errors as having the standard meaning. In his view, content externalism is a precondition of the very notion of objectivity, that is, the idea that there is a mind-independent world that we can be right and wrong about in our judgments. It is a necessary feature of, for example, perceptual judgments that they can be mistaken. To account for the fallibility of perceptual judgments we need to suppose that perceptual content is determined by objective features of the physical or social environment rather than by the subject's conception of reality. The distinction between what the world is like and how it appears to us, central to the externalist interpretation of Twin Earth cases, Burge declares, 'is just a special case of our lack of omniscience with respect to any objective empirical subject matter' (2007*a*: 23).

As they stand, Putnam's and Burge's arguments from cognitive distance don't provide compelling reasons for the externalist reading of Twin Earth scenarios. The fact that there is a distinction between the world, on the one hand, and our conception of it, on the other, doesn't presuppose that there is a distinction between what an individual takes a term to mean and what the term in fact means. Incomplete knowledge of the empirical world doesn't presuppose an incomplete grasp of one's own concepts (Wikforss 2008: 168).

How does the failure of the argument from cognitive distance affect the plausibility of content externalism? The above criticism doesn't undermine the core insight of content externalism. The core insight is that the contents of an individual's thoughts and the meanings of his words depend on relations that the individual bears to aspects of his physical or social environment. The externalist interpretation of Twin Earth scenarios, however, depends not only on content externalism but also on a theory of belief ascription. This theory states that the belief a speaker expresses by uttering a sentence is identical with the meaning the utterance has in his linguistic community. More precisely, the theory states that the standard meaning of a that-clause in a speaker's *de dicto* belief ascription is identical with the content of the ascribed belief.

Both Putnam and Burge appear to subscribe to this naive theory of belief ascription. Consider the arthritis-example. Burge (2007c: 104–5) insists that, even though S mistakenly believes that arthritis is a disease that can also strike the thigh, he and his doctor think the same thought when they (sincerely) say, for example, 'arthritis is painful'. We can agree with Burge that 'arthritis' as used by S and his doctor has the same application conditions since they are members of the same linguistic community. Consequently, the sentence 'arthritis is painful' uttered by S and by his doctor has the same truth-conditions. But whereas Burge holds that S and his doctor must also *believe* the same thing, I am inclined to think that their beliefs may differ even though the meanings of their utterances coincide. From S's saying 'arthritis is painful' it doesn't automatically follow that he believes that arthritis is painful. He may instead believe that an illness that can strike the thigh as well as the joint is painful.[6]

Although there are passages that certainly suggest that Burge subscribes to the naive theory of belief ascription it would be unfair to attribute this position to him, for (in other places) he proves to be acutely aware of the complexities of *de dicto* attitudes. Moreover, as Christopher Gauker (1991) has shown, the arthritis example can be redescribed without that-clauses in an effort to avoid the criticism of confusing *de re* and *de dicto*.

I suggest that we simply reject the naive theory of belief ascription and go with content externalism proper. It is a mistake to ascribe belief contents solely on the basis of communal meanings of utterances. What a person (sincerely) says may differ from what he believes. To drive this point home independently of Twin Earth scenarios consider David Kaplan's example of giving a lecture in a hall in which a

---

[6] Loar (1988: 102) attributes the naive theory of belief ascription to Burge: 'Sameness of the *de dicto* or oblique occurrence of a general term in two belief ascriptions implies, if everything else is the same, sameness of the psychological content of the two beliefs thus ascribed.' According to Loar, Burge holds that if speakers of the same language community utter the same general terms, then, *ceteris paribus*, they express the same beliefs. Loar doesn't specify the scope of the proviso. Thus we don't know whether, according to Loar's reading of Burge, two individuals who have different background beliefs about where arthritis can occur fulfill the *ceteris paribus* condition or not. Davidson (2001a: 28) also charges Burge with confusing *de re* and *de dicto*. He attributes to Burge the 'insistence that we are bound to give a person's words the meaning they have in his linguistic community, and to interpret his propositional attitudes on the same basis'. Similarly Bach (1988: 89 n4) claims that 'one can fully understand a thought and yet . . . not fully understand a statement that expresses it'. Yet this is precisely what Burge seems to deny. See also Taschek (1995).

portrait of Rudolph Carnap has hung behind the podium for years. Kaplan, pointing behind himself but not looking there, utters: 'That man is the greatest philosopher of the twentieth century.' But someone has replaced the portrait of Carnap with one of Spiro Agnew. Has Kaplan sincerely asserted that Spiro Agnew is the greatest philosopher of the twentieth century? Obviously not. He referred to the picture of Spiro Agnew and said something false. But he doesn't believe what he said. He has an at least defensible belief that Carnap is the greatest philosopher plus a false belief that there is a picture of Carnap behind him.[7]

Even if it is granted that the failure of Putnam's and Burge's arguments from cognitive distance doesn't undermine the core insight of content externalism, we are left with the question of how to motivate content externalism independently of Twin Earth scenarios. In the end, the most compelling reason in favor of content externalism is the inconceivability of the rival view—content internalism. Let me explain.

According to content externalism, it is possible for you and your twin on Twin Earth to be physically, behaviorally, functionally, phenomenologically, and introspectively indistinguishable even though your mental contents differ. You are psychological twins, but not propositional attitude twins. Content internalism, on the other hand, holds that it is not only psychological but also semantic features that you and your twin share. The internalist notion of *narrow content* is supposed to capture the semantic property that you and your twin on Twin Earth have in common. Mental content is said to consist of two factors: one factor, narrow content, is determined solely by non-relational properties of the subject. The other factor, *broad content* (or truth-conditions), is determined by the subject's physical or social environment.

What exactly is narrow content? Normally narrow content is defined negatively, as the type of content which is independent of how subjects are related to their environment. On the other hand, narrow content is said not to be reducible to codes in the language of thought. Narrow contents are somehow context-independent modes of presentation. The problems start when one tries to give a positive account of a notion of content that is truth-conditionally irrelevant. Fodor (1982: 112) suggests treating narrow content as phenomenological: 'The present view . . . is that when someone on Earth believes that water is wet,

<hr/>

[7] Kaplan's example is reported by Perry (1993: 66–7).

he holds a . . . belief with the content: *all the potable, transparent, sailable-on, . . . etc., kind of stuff is wet.*'

Internalists claim that what makes narrow content a *semantic* feature is that it contributes to the broad content of a mental state. If we have a narrow description of a 'water'-thought as a thought about some potable and transparent stuff and if we want to find out the truth-conditions of the thought in question, all we have to do is to see which substance in the current environment fits the description contained in the narrow content: on Earth it's H_2O, on Twin Earth it's XYZ. Defined in this way, to spell out narrow content we need to first tie it to a context and then specify a broad content. Narrow content, then, is whatever you plug into a context and which yields a truth-conditional broad content. Technically, narrow content is a function (mathematically conceived) from environmental contexts to broad contents (or truth-conditions).

The problem with the positive account of narrow content is that it becomes inexpressible. Fodor (1987: 50) admits this when he declares:

Narrow content is radically inexpressible, because it's only content *potentially*; it's only what gets to be content when—and only when—it gets to be anchored. We can't—to put it in a nutshell—*say* what twin thoughts have in common. This is because what can be said is *ipso facto* semantically evaluable; and what twin-thoughts have in common is *ipso facto* not.

If what I think is both what I say and what you hear me say, narrow contents cannot figure in understanding and communication. All my thoughts and utterances express broad content. This in turn means that insofar as my beliefs are conscious and capable of being communicated in language, they are not the beliefs they are by their purported narrow contents. Narrow content is inexpressible and unthinkable.

The idea of an unthinkable component of content is pretty strange. Normally we take it that an utterance, gesture, or thought can only be said to have meaning insofar as it can be expressed. Even unconscious beliefs can be brought into consciousness and thus can be expressed. Narrow content, however, is said to be inexpressible as a matter of principle. Without being able to examine here whether this idea is ultimately viable, I suspect that, instead of being a distinct kind of content, narrow content is a derivative or a precursor of broad content. In the words of John McDowell (1998a: 221), narrow content is 'a putative *bearer* or *vehicle* of content', not a genuine '*aspect* or *ingredient* of content'.

6.2 VARIETIES OF EXTERNALISM

Externalism comes in different flavors. Apart from content externalism there is the thesis of object-dependent senses or *Fregean externalism*, as Jessica Brown (2004: 20–1) calls it, championed among others by Gareth Evans (1982) and McDowell (1998*b*). Fregean externalism takes as its starting point Russell's account of singular propositions. Russell holds that sentences containing genuinely referring expressions express propositions whose components include the individuals thereby named. From this it follows that a singular proposition is only thinkable insofar as the object referred to exists. Singular propositions are object-dependent. Evans and McDowell apply this idea to all empirical propositions: we wouldn't be able to think about the world the way we do if it wasn't the case that perceptual experiences presented us with the objects we perceive. Thoughts about particular objects are possible for a thinker only if he is acquainted with those objects. The existence of a concrete object, and its appropriate (causal) relations to the thinker, are necessary conditions for the availability of object-dependent thoughts about it. It follows from the idea of object-dependent senses that an individual may be mistaken in thinking that he thinks a thought when in fact he is not.[8]

Leaving aside Fregean externalism, the theory of content externalism is broad enough to subsume a variety of views. The different kinds of content externalism can be classified according to two criteria. First, different forms of externalism take different kinds of environmental facts as responsible for the determination of mental content. Mental content is said to supervene on different environmental conditions. Second, different forms of externalism call for different kinds of dependence relations between brain states and environmental states. The nature of the supervenience relation is spelled out in a multitude of ways.

The Supervenience Base

According to Putnam's causal-essentialist externalism, it is the hidden (e.g. chemical) structure of objects that determines the reference of natural kind terms. Burge's anti-individualism suggests that it is the

---

[8] McDowell (1998*b*: 237) endorses this consequence of Fregean externalism. In my (2000; 2004; forthcoming) I argue that content externalism too is committed to the possibility of illusions of thoughts and I endorse this consequence.

linguistic norms of society that determine thought content. Donald Davidson's version of content externalism is centered around the idea of triangulation. In this view, the kinds of things that determine thought content are physical or social properties with which both the speaker and the interpreter are in contact. The content determining cause of a belief 'is where the lines from the [speaker] to [the object] and from us [the interpreters] to [the object] converge' (1989: 198). And according to Fred Dretske's causal-informational externalism, content is dependent on the informational states. What links the belief about water to water is that, under normal conditions, water causally contributes to one's having the belief. This study doesn't presuppose any particular externalist supervenience base.

To see that different kinds of externalism yield different individuation criteria for content, consider Dretske's (1981: 225–6) modification of Putnam's Twin Earth example: on Twin Earth the same word 'water', which is used on Earth to refer to liquid with the molecular structure H_2O, is used to refer to either H_2O or XYZ. Some lakes on Twin Earth are filled with H_2O; others are filled with XYZ. By chance, my twin on Twin Earth learns the word 'water' by being exposed only to H_2O. Does he have the same concept as I do? While Putnam would presumably respond 'yes', Dretske answers in the negative. According to Dretske, my twin's concept is different from mine because the information that causes his concept is different from the information that causes mine. When he holds a belief that he expresses by saying 'this is water', what he means is 'this is either H_2O or XYZ'. Dretske (1981: 227) concludes that 'one cannot acquire the concept F by exposure to signals that carry only the information that things are F or G'.

The Strength of the Supervenience Relation

The supervenience relation between mental states and environmental states comes in different strengths. One sort of externalism holds that you need to be in direct contact with water to have water beliefs. Other externalists (e.g. Dretske) hold that for you to have beliefs about water (assuming *water* is a simple concept) you must have had some causal contact with water at some point in your lifetime. Burge (2007*a*: 3; 2007*b*: 82–3), on the other hand, grants that you could have water beliefs even though you had never in fact interacted with water. It is sufficient that water has been described to you by others who have been in contact with it or that you simply theorize about the chemical composition of an illusionary substance called 'water'. Burge's version of externalism entails only the weakest kind of supervenience. I am not going to presuppose any particular supervenience relation.

Versions of content externalism that propose a fairly strong supervenience relation are usually part of a larger picture called *the representational theory of mind* or *representationalism*, for short. While content externalism concerns only the conditions for individuating thought contents, representationalism also concerns the conditions for having thoughts. Representationalism not only accounts for the difference among propositional attitudes but also for the difference between propositional attitudes and other states lacking mental content. The representationalist idea is that whether an internal state bears any mental content, and which content it bears, depends on its lawlike relations to certain aspects of the physical or social environment. As Jerry Fodor (1990: 58) puts it, 'only nomic connections and the subjunctives they license count for meaning'.

Causal-informational relations are not sufficient to determine the content of mental representations, for a representational state can be caused by something it does not represent, and can represent something that is not among its causes. There are two main attempts to specify what renders a causal-informational state a mental representation: the *asymmetric dependence account* (Fodor) and the *teleological account* (Dretske, Millikan, Papineau). According to teleological theories, representational relations are those which a representation-producing mechanism has the selected (by evolution or learning) function of subserving. According to asymmetric dependence theories, what distinguishes merely informational relations from content-determining ones is a higher-order relation: informational relations depend upon content-determining ones, but not the other way round. For example, we would not token the mental representation type *horse* when confronted with a cow on a dark night unless we tokened the mental representation type *horse* when confronted with a horse, but not vice versa. Therefore, the mental representation tokened in the presence of horses means *horse*, in spite of the fact that there is a causal-informational relation between it and cows on a dark night.

The chief motivation of representationalism is that it is the most promising way of accounting for mental content while preserving naturalism. According to naturalism, mental content arises out of non-meaningful bits. Those non-meaningful bits must be part of the furniture of the world of natural causes and objects. If the representationalist's account of mental content is correct, a complete description of the physical properties of someone's head and of the interactions between the person and his environment suffice to account for how the person's thoughts can be about the things they are about. The relata and the relation that constitutes (or at least suffices for) mental content is purely natural and, perhaps physical.

6.3 PASTIST EXTERNALISM

After having explained and motivated content externalism it is time to apply it to memory. Externalism maintains that memory contents are individuation-dependent upon systematic relations that the individual bears with certain aspects of his physical or social environment. But since a person can move from one environment to another (perhaps without even noticing the environmental change), the question arises whether memory contents are determined by the environment he lived in at the time he had the original thought, by the environment he lives in at the time recollection takes place, or by the environment he will inhabit at some point in the future, after recollection has taken place. Do memory contents and the concepts contained in them supervene on past, present, or future environmental conditions?

According to one version of externalism, the content of a memory state is fixed, once and for all, by the environment the subject was in at the time he had the original thought. When some content is stored in memory it is inert to all subsequent environmental changes. I will refer to this form of externalism about memory contents as *pastist externalism*. *Presentist externalism* claims that memory contents are determined by past and by present environmental conditions. And *futurist externalism* is the thesis that memory contents depend not only on the past and present but also on future environmental conditions. Given futurist externalism, it is a mistake to think that what a term or a thought means at a time necessarily supervenes upon environmental events up to that time. (What I call *futurist externalism* is often labeled *temporal externalism*. Pastist and presentist externalism are often lumped together under the heading of *non-temporal* or *standard externalism*.)

Among those ascribing to pastist externalism are Paul Boghossian (2008), Jessica Brown (2000), and Tyler Burge (1998). Proponents of presentist externalism are James Baillie (1997: 327), Peter Ludlow (1995a; 1995b; 1999a), Michael Tye (1998: 81), and my ancestral self (1998: 340). Futurist externalism is defended by John Collins (2006),

Henry Jackman (1999; 2004; 2005), Peter Ludlow (1999b), and, with reservations, Tom Stoneham (2003).

The aim of this section is to weigh up the three kinds of externalism about memory content. In the end I will side with the position according to which memory contents are fixed by the past environment and remain unchanged until some later moment of recollection.

To bring out the differences between the three kinds of externalism about memory content it is instructive to apply them to so-called *slow switching scenarios* developed by Burge (1988). Suppose that S is unwittingly switched from Earth to Twin Earth where he interacts successfully over a considerable length of time with XYZ, calling it 'water'. Externalists hold that, when S has been on Twin Earth for a good while, his word 'water' comes to express the concept *twater* instead of, or in addition to, the Earthian concept *water*. So if S used to believe on Earth the proposition *water is wet*, he would then believe the proposition *twater is wet* or *water or twater is wet*, respectively. A switch of worlds leads to a switch of thought contents. And just as S is unaware of the environmental shift from Earth to Twin Earth, he is unaware of the consequent alteration of his conceptual repertoire and mental contents.[9]

Why is it important that the switching takes place slowly? Why wouldn't a quick switch bring about the adoption of new concepts? This has to do with the externalist idea that whether an internal state bears any mental content, and which content it bears, depends on the lawlike connections between it and certain extrinsic facts (cf. sect. 6.2). Just as laws usually need to be hedged with *ceteris paribus* clauses, the nomic dependence of internal states on environmental conditions depends on certain normality standards. In the quick switching case, S's usage of the Earthian term 'water' as referring to XYZ is an anomaly.[10] Most externalists agree that a conceptual shift caused by an environmental shift takes time but there is disagreement over how

---

[9] Assuming a broad notion of environment according to which Twin Earth belongs to the environment of Earth (cf. p. 154 n2) a move from Earth to Twin Earth brings about a conceptual shift only if the slow switching example is slightly modified. Instead of Earth and Twin Earth having existed side by side for some time in the past, Twin Earth springs into existence only the very second S gets there.

[10] The fact that the concept acquisition takes time also explains why Putnam's (1981: 1–21) famous brain-in-a-vat argument against external-world skepticism only works for brains that have been in a vat for a while. A recently envatted brain still has some systematic connections with the ordinary things in the outside world and is therefore capable of expressing and thinking that it is a brain in a vat.

long it takes. While the standard view has it that the incorporation of *twater* in S's conceptual repertoire takes months and years, Andy Clark and David Chalmers (1998: 9) claim that the acquisition of the *twater* concept happens right away. In what follows I will be assuming the standard view.

What effect does the slow switching of an agent have on his ability to recall representations from before the switch? The answer to this question depends on the version of externalism about memory content one adopts as well as on the assumed interpretation of slow switching scenarios. Slow switching scenarios allow for two readings. In the *conceptual replacement view*, the slow switching of an agent causes him to adopt new concepts and to eventually lose the old ones. In the *conceptual addition view*, the slow switching of an agent causes him only to adopt new concepts but not to lose the old ones. Even long after the time of switching, the agent possesses Earthian and Twin Earthian concepts and contents.

Given the conceptual replacement view, switching scenarios seem to pose a problem for pastist externalism. If memory contents are determined by past environmental conditions and if the slow switching of an agent causes him to adopt new concepts and to lose the old ones, then a switched individual may lack the concepts necessary to remember his thought contents from before the switch. For instance, if S used to think the thought that water is wet and if his *water* concept has since given way to the *twater* concept or the *water or twater* concept, respectively, then he is unable to recount his Earthian *water* thought—except by means of indexical descriptions, such as 'the stuff that I used to think was wet' or 'the stuff I used to swim in'. For reasons to be explained in sections 7.6 and 8.3, a present *water* thought is not only not identical with the corresponding past *twater* thought or *twater-or-water* thought, respectively, but also not sufficiently similar to it. Therefore, when S tries to remember his past *water* thoughts by employing the newly acquired *twater* concept he violates the content condition of memory. Pastist externalism in conjunction with the conceptual replacement view has the consequence that slow switching can rob an agent of the ability to remember some of his thought contents from before the switch.

Some philosophers find it incredible that an environmental shift should be able to rob us of the ability to access some of our past thoughts. To avoid the conclusion that slow switching can affect our memory one of two strategies can be adopted: either the conceptual addition view is substituted for the conceptual replacement view or pastist externalism is replaced by presentist or futurist externalism. In my mind, neither strategy is successful. In section 7.2, I will argue that, notwithstanding the explanatory advantages the conceptual addition view has to the conceptual replacement view, the addition view raises a host of problems. That is why it would be most unfortunate if externalists were forced to rely on the conceptual addition view to circumvent the (allegedly) counterintuitive claim that environmental switching can bring about memory failures.

What then about the other strategy? Are presentist and futurist externalism successful in blocking potential worries regarding the idea that an environmental shift can undermine our ability to access our past thought contents? Prima facie, the answer is 'yes'. In either theory, when a person moves from one environment to another the contents of his memories shift accordingly. A memory state is not identified with a single content but with a series of contents at different times. Given that the content of a memory token at t_3 has to match neither the content of the type-identical memory token at t_2 nor the content of the original representation at t_1 of which it is a memory, a switched subject can remember representations from before the switch, despite the fact that he is unable to reproduce the original contents.

On second consideration, however, it is a mistake to think that presentist and futurist externalism are not committed to the (allegedly) implausible conclusion whereby slow switching undermines our ability to remember. Given presentist or futurist externalism, the 'memory' of a switched agent is unable to play the epistemic role it is supposed to play, namely to be a reliable source of information about the past.[11] To see this, suppose that at t_1 S comes to form the correct belief that he is drinking a glass of water. Then he is unknowingly brought to Twin Earth. When, at t_2, S seems to remember the proposition *I had a glass of twater at t_1*, his 'memory' turns into a falsehood since at t_1 S had not yet encountered XYZ. So S's memory is no longer able to inform him about the past.

According to Ludlow, this objection to presentist and futurist externalism shouldn't be taken too seriously since in the majority of cases

---

[11] This objection is developed in Hofmann (1995). The relevant passages from Hofmann's paper are cited or paraphrased by Kraay (2002: 300–1), Ludlow (1995*b*: 72–3; 1999*a*: 167; 1999*b*: 154), and Nagasawa (2000: 173–4). Kraay and Nagasawa endorse Hofmann's criticism of presentist and futurist externalism. Hofmann, unlike myself, holds that remembering is a form of knowing.

the truth values of thought contents before and after an environmental switch are the same. He writes:

If I believe at t_1 that water is wet, then at t_2, memory will deliver a belief that twater is wet. If at t_1 I believed it was possible to drown in water, memory will deliver a t_2 belief that it is possible to drown in twater—and good thing, too! Twater is no less wet or dangerous than water.   (1999*a*: 167).

There are only relatively few instances, Ludlow claims, where, given presentist or futurist externalism, a veridical belief will give rise to false 'memory'. One such case is when I believe at t_1 that I drank some water and then, at t_2, 'remember' having drunk some twater. Here the 'memory' process does transform a truth into a falsehood. However, Ludlow (ibid.) notes, although this 'memory' is literally false, it is not false 'in a way that undermines my plans and actions on Twin Earth'. Ludlow (1995*b*: 74) concludes that it is not the case that presentist or futurist externalism renders memory an unreliable source of information. On the contrary, 'there is no reason at all why [transient memories] cannot be completely reliable in those environmental conditions in which they occur'.

The upshot is that, regardless which version of externalism about memory content we adopt, switching cases can have a destructive effect on our ability to remember. Given the conceptual replacement view, any instance of slow switching where the pastist externalist will have to say that the agent is no longer able to remember the past (even though his apparent memory remains perfectly clear), the presentist or futurist externalist will have to say that memory has disengaged from the past. Presentist and futurist externalism, on the one hand, and pastist externalism (in conjunction with the conceptual replacement view), on the other, yield different types of memory failure but the end result is the same: the agent is no longer able to access facts about the past through memory. Hence, pastist externalism is not at any particular disadvantage to its presentist and futurist rivals.

Where does all this leave us? What, if anything, allows us to adjudicate between the three versions of externalism about memory contents? In my mind, there are two reasons that clearly speak in favor of pastist as opposed to presentist or futurist externalism.

In any version of externalism concepts and mental content are determined by factors of which the thinker (or anyone else) may be ignorant. Prima facie it shouldn't make a difference whether these factors lie in the past or in the future. However, appearances are deceiving.

There is in fact a significant difference between one's ignorance of a fact about the future and one's ignorance of a fact about the past: while the former fact has not been actualized the latter has been. It might be deemed incredible to maintain, as pastist externalism says, that one's mental content is determined by a state of affairs that is actual but one is ignorant of. But then it must seem even more incredible to maintain, as futurist externalism does, that one's mental content is determined by a state of affairs that has not even been actualized (and of course one is ignorant of).

Second, even if we grant Ludlow that, given the determination of memory contents by the present or future environment, failures of truth preservation are rare and benign, presentist and futurist externalism lead to an absurd conception of memory. In this conception, the truth values of memories are dependent on states of affairs in the present and future rather than on states of affairs in the past. Consider a memory state expressed at t_2 by the statement 'S owned at t_1 a copy of Caesar's *Commentarii de Bello Gallico*'. Intuitively, this memory is about the past. The memory claim is true only if it is an accurate representation of the state of affairs at t_1. Presentist and futurist externalism, however, have it that the concepts used in memories are determined by the present or future environment. But if the concepts employed in memories refer to present or future affairs, then the truth values of memory beliefs are dependent on present or future states of affairs. The consequence of this view is that the memory claim in question turns out false if at t_2 (or at some future time t_3) S no longer owns a copy of Caesar's *Commentarii*. But this is surely absurd. Thus, even independently of slow switching, presentist and futurist externalism give rise to an unacceptable conception of memory.[12]

We have seen that pastist externalism is not only not at any particular disadvantage to its presentist and futurist rivals, but also that these rivals have certain problems that are absent in the case of pastist externalism. But even if the advantages of pastist externalism to presentist and futurist externalism are granted, one may still be reluctant to accept pastist externalism about memory contents. For as was explained before, it may be deemed implausible that pastist externalism

---

[12] Presentist and futurist externalists might try to defend their theories by maintaining that, while memory contents are determined by the present or the future, they somehow refer to the past: the direct objects of memories—present or future environmental conditions—somehow indicate past environmental conditions. Yet I cannot make sense of the reference of present or future environmental conditions to past ones.

(in conjunction with the conceptual replacement view) has the consequence that environmental switches rob us of the ability to remember some of our thoughts from before the switch. One way of blocking the objection in questions is to adopt the conceptual addition view instead of the conceptual replacement view. Section 7.2 is dedicated to the discussion of the two interpretations of slow switching scenarios. But even if we go with the conceptual replacement view there is no good reasons not to accept pastist externalism. In sections 7.5 and 7.6 it will be shown that there are neither psychological nor philosophical arguments to substantiate worries regarding the pastist externalist thesis that unwitting switching can bring about memory failure.

6.4 KEEPING MEMORY WITHIN ITS BOUNDARIES

Internalists are opposed to content externalism because they believe that mental content is determined by factors intrinsic to the subject. Proponents of what is known as the *hypothesis of the extended mind*, henceforth HEM (also known as 'environmentalism', 'active externalism', and 'vehicle externalism'), on the other hand, maintain that content externalism doesn't go far enough in repudiating the Cartesian picture of mentality as intrinsic to the subject. Content externalism still locates mental states inside the head or body of a subject. According to HEM, the role of the physical or social environment is not restricted to the determination of mental content. Mental states are not only externally individuated, yet internally located, but are externally located states. The reason they are externally located states is that they are realized by cognitive processes that are, in part, constituted by physical or bodily manipulations of environmental states. Cognitive processes are hybrid entities, made up in part of what is going on inside the brain of the creatures who have them, but also made up in part of what is going on in the environment of those creatures. Mental states are externally constituted in the sense that they are composed not only of the internal states of the subject in question but also of objects, properties, or events in the subject's environment together with the appropriate relation connecting the two. '[T]he human organism is linked with an external entity in a two-way interaction, creating a *coupled system* that can be seen as a cognitive system in its own right' (Clark and Chalmers 1998: 8). In slogan form: the mind is not, exclusively, inside the head.

HEM has been inspired by the work of the cognitive psychologists who maintain that as external stores (e.g. repositories of written language) become widely used, the process of cognition changes its nature: subjects begin to rely more heavily on external stores. And when external stores take on an indispensable information-bearing role in the process of cognition, as they do in the case of modern humans, they become proper parts of the cognitive system. Among the philosophers who believe that cognition is frequently continuous with processes in the environment are Andy Clark and David Chalmers (1998), Daniel Dennett (1996), John Haugeland (1998: 207–40), Ruth Garrett Millikan (1993: 135–70), and Kim Sterelny (2004).

Proponents of HEM tend to embrace content externalism. Yet it is important to see that, though mutually consistent, content externalism and HEM are distinct theories.[13] It is one thing to say, as content externalism does, that the contents of mental states are individuated by the relations those states bear to certain environmental features. And it is quite another thing to say, as HEM does, that the cognitive processes that realize mental states are constituted in part by the subject's environment. The external individuation of mental contents does not entail the external location of mental states. And just as content externalism doesn't imply HEM, the latter doesn't imply the former. Instead of embracing content externalism, proponents of HEM could endorse some other semantic theory such as conceptual-role semantics.[14]

HEM is a broad and multilayered research program that cannot be exhaustively discussed in the context of this study. I will confine myself here to discussing HEM insofar as it has been applied to beliefs embedded in memory.[15] Andy Clark and David Chalmers's

---

[13] Sometimes HEM is defined so as to include content externalism. Tollefsen (2006: 142 n4), for instance, writes: 'Content externalism holds that the content of a mental state is determined by environmental or causal factors. My twin on Twin Earth does not have the same water beliefs as me because Twin Earth contains XYZ, not H_2O. The content differs. The vehicle, however, [i.e. the pattern of neurological activity] remains . . . the same and inside the head. Active externalism argues that the vehicle of content need not be restricted to the inner biological realm. The idea is that both cognitive contents and cognitive operations can be instantiated and supported by both biological and non-biological structures and processes.'

[14] The connection between HEM and Fregean externalism is closer than between HEM and standard content externalism. If a proposition is a structured collection of individuals and properties, as Russell claims, then propositional thought contents contain the very object they refer to. And on the assumption that a subject's thought contents are part of his mind it seems to follow that that his mind extends into the environment.

[15] For the sake of the argument, I will follow Clark and Chalmers in assuming that memory implies belief. See sect. 3.3.

(1998: 12–16) argument in support of HEM takes the form of a thought experiment and a battery of responses to possible objections. S wants to visit a particular museum. At first he doesn't remember where the museum is located. He thinks for a moment and recalls that the museum is on 53rd Street. Clark and Chalmers note that it is uncontroversial to assume that S has had this belief about the museum's location all along, even if it has not always been occurrent. The belief was stored in memory, waiting to be accessed. Next consider S*, who suffers from severe amnesia. Due to his failing memory, S* always carries around a notebook in which he jots down information. He decides to go to the same museum as S, and he also doesn't remember the location of the museum. Unlike S, S* cannot retrieve the desired piece of information from his memory. Instead he consults the notebook, which says that the museum is on 53rd Street.

Clark and Chalmers argue that the information in the notebook plays the same functional role for S* that an ordinary non-occurrent, but explicitly encoded, belief plays for S. They claim that we should therefore count the notebook as part of S*'s mind, and the location of the museum as one of S*'s beliefs. This inference rests on the so-called *parity principle*: 'If, as we confront some task, a part of the world functions as a process which, *were it to go on in the head*, we would have no hesitation in recognizing as part of the cognitive process, then that part of the world *is* . . . part of the cognitive process' (ibid. 8). If 'exograms' act as engrams, then they can be treated as engrams, notwithstanding the difference in their location. Given the parity principle, S* has the (dispositional) belief that the museum is on 53rd street even before he consults his notebook because the notebook plays the same role for S* that memory traces play for S and because any alternative explanation involving intermediate beliefs about the contents of the notebook introduces 'one step too many' (ibid. 13) to our description of S*'s mental life.

Clark and Chalmers are careful not to trivialize the proposed extension of the boundaries of the mind. In response to the worry that, given HEM, there is no stopping the 'leakage' of mind into the world they require that the coupled system composed of neurological processes and external tools may not be easily decoupled. The agent's mind includes only those external tools to which he has regular, unfettered access. The external aids that can count as part of the agent's mental processing must be reliably available when needed and used or accessed pretty much as automatically as biological processing and memory. Clark and

Chalmers (ibid. 17) list four grounds for ascribing an extended belief to the amnesiac S*:

First, the notebook is a constant in [S*'s] life—in cases where the information in the notebook would be relevant, he will rarely take action without consulting it. Second, the information in the notebook is directly available without difficulty. Third, upon retrieving information from the notebook he automatically endorses it. Fourth, the information in the notebook has been consciously endorsed at some point in the past, and indeed is there as a consequence of this endorsement.

Clark and Chalmers are confident that constancy, direct accessibility, and present endorsement are constitutive of believing but they concede that it is debatable whether past endorsement belongs to the necessary conditions for belief. Without the past-endorsement condition there doesn't seem to be a difference between remembering and relearning. Yet adding this condition seems to rob HEM of its attraction. For if an extended belief requires conscious endorsement and if conscious endorsement is ultimately an internal process, then HEM is not really that different from the conservative picture whereupon the mind doesn't extend beyond the brain.

While Clark and Chalmers are primarily concerned with extended beliefs, Mark Rowlands (1999: 6) focuses on extended memories. Rowlands invites us to imagine a subject who is looking for a particular book at the library. He has seen the book before, but he cannot remember what it is called or who the author is. Moreover, he doesn't remember exactly where it is in the library, but he does remember the floor, and he also remembers that it is on a shelf with a peculiar distinguishing feature, say, a red tray at the end. Therefore, the agent goes to the correct floor, looks for the shelf with the red tray at the end, and then works his way along the shelf until he finds the book. According to Rowlands, in this case, the agent's remembering where the book is in the library is a process formed by a combination of an internal representation of the location of the book on a floor together with the physical manipulation of the bookshelf with the distinguishing feature. The library shelf is an environmental structure that carries information about the location of the book. The shelf stands in, or goes proxy, for a complex internal memory store. 'By working his way along the shelf, a person can, in effect, *process* some of the information embodied in it . . . The external information-bearing structure stands in for the internal information-bearing structure' (ibid. 122). Rowlands concludes, 'not all the information processing relevant to remembering need occur inside the skin of remembering organisms. Some of the relevant information processing can be constituted by bodily manipulations, on the part of the remembering organisms, of relevant environmental structures' (ibid. 27).

Clark's, Chalmers's, and Rowlands's arguments for HEM can be challenged in a number of ways. I will mention only four objections. First, if we ask S^*, before he consults his notebook at t_1, whether he believes the museum is located on 53rd street, he will presumably respond that he has no idea about the location of the museum. Not only does he not occurrently believe at t_1 that the museum is on 53rd street, but also he doesn't believe it dispositionally. For if S was asked at t_1, before he consults his notebook, whether he thinks it more likely than not that the museum is located on 53rd street, he would dismiss the suggestion or suspend judgment.[16] Moreover, when asked at t_1 whether he believes that the museum is on 53rd street S^* cannot say that his *notebook* believes that the museum is on 53rd street. For if S^* knew his notebook's beliefs all along, then he wouldn't need to consult the notebook. But then why should we attribute to S^* the belief that the museum is on 53rd street? The belief attribution seems to be ungrounded. Clark and Chalmers may respond by claiming that while S^*, considered in isolation, doesn't believe at t_1 that the museum is in 53rd street S^* and the notebook form a 'coupled system' that does possess the belief in question. But even if the coupled system possess the belief in question my point stands. My point is that there are no HEM-independent reasons at t_1 for attributing the belief that the museum is on 53rd street to either S^* or the coupled system consisting of S^* and his notebook. In other words, the way the thought experiment is set up already assumes the truth of HEM.

Second, according to Clark and Chalmers, S^* forms a coupled system with his notebook. S^*'s notebook functions in the same way internal memory functions and, according to the parity principle, should be considered part of S^*'s mind. While it is certainly correct that our memory frequently relies on external tools, the dynamics of the mind–notebook relation is importantly different from the mind–memory relation (cf. Sterelny 2004: 245–7). A subject's access to externally stored information is neither as reliable nor as uncontaminated as access to internally

---

[16] In sect. 3.3 I have argued that, given that believing that p involves holding p true, cases of ignorant remembering contradict the thesis that memory implies belief.

stored information. Unlike a notebook, biological memory need not be charged, may get wet, and is immune to computer viruses and worms.

Third, Adams and Aizawa (2008: 88–105) accuse HEM of what they call the *coupling-constitution fallacy*, that is, the fallacy of inferring from the fact that some external object or process is in some way causally connected to a cognitive process to the conclusion that the external object or process is thereby part of that cognitive process. The mere causal coupling of some process with a broader environment does not thereby extend that process into the broader environment. Aizawa gives the following example to bring home the point. The kidneys filter impurities from the blood. In addition, this filtration is causally influenced by the heart's pumping of the blood, the size of the blood vessels in the circulatory system, the one-way valves in the circulatory system, and so forth. Yet the fact that these various parts of the circulatory system causally interact with the process of filtration in the kidneys doesn't mean that filtration occurs throughout the circulatory system, rather than in the kidneys alone. A process may interact with its environment, but this does not mean that the process extends into the environment.

Fourth, it is questionable that the external portions of extended memory states or processes of remembering and internal memories are as functionally similar as proponents of HEM make them out to be (cf. O'Brien 1998: 80–3; Rupert 2004: 407–18). The internal memory process is not a passive storehouse, like a notebook, but a constantly active system that is both integrative and reconstructive and that is affected by desires, moods, and beliefs. For example, internal memories, but not external ones, are subject to interference effects. As was explained before (cf. pp. 100–1, 121), interference occurs when the learning of additional associations to a stimulus causes the old ones to be forgotten. Moreover, internal memories, but not external ones, exhibit the generation effect whereupon information will be better remembered if it is generated rather than simply read. For example, you are more like to remember the word 'notebook' if you generate it from the fragment 'n_t_boo_' than if you simply see the word in its entirety.

Clark offers two responses to this objection. First, whether the revision of stored information in light of new evidence occurs at the time the new evidence is received (as is the case in biological memory) or later, at the time the outdated information would have been called upon by the process of recall (as is the case in a notebook), need not result in behavioral differences. And provided that behavioral indistinguishability is the mark of identity a notebook and a biological memory traces are in fact as similar as HEM takes them to be (Clark 2005: 6). The obvious problem with this rejoinder is the uncritical assumption of behaviorism. Second, Clark argues that the objection at hand rests on a mistaken reading of the parity principle as requiring fine-grained identity of causal contribution. 'Yet just because some alien neural system failed to match our own biological memory-systems in various ways . . . we should surely not *thereby* be forced to count the action of such systems as non-cognitive, or as not an instance of memory at all' (Clark 2007: 167). The functional isomorphism of inner and outer processes which, under the parity principle, is to count as relevant is not to do with specific formats and dynamics, but with functional poise of the information in question.[17] Yet the problem with this loosening of the parity principle is that it leads to a gratuitous proliferation of cognitive systems, thereby making it impossible to determine the ontological boundaries of the mind.

I am well aware that none of these objections to HEM amount to a knock-down argument. In the end, the dispute between HEM and the orthodox view comes down to the question of which position is explanatorily more fruitful. According to advocates of HEM, realizing that the distinction between internal cognitive processes and external aids is unmotivated results in a flash of paradigm-shifting insight that reveals the greater theoretical utility to be gained by embracing HEM (cf. Clark and Chalmers 1998: 14; Rowlands 1999: 121). Exploring the explanatory issue would go beyond the scope of this study.

But even if HEM has the explanatory advantages its advocates ascribe to it, there are explanatory costs attached to the endorsement of HEM. For if all kinds of external aids and props can become proper parts of the human cognitive process, then we are forced to redraw the boundaries between stable persisting human individuals. But it is not clear how this can be done. For once we move beyond the bodily boundaries there seem to be no considerations that would allow us to draw a principled boundary demarcating the environment from the persisting subject. Moreover, HEM seems to undermine the idea of responsible agency. Terry Dartnall (2004: 145) puts the worry this way: 'If I dig a hole in my

---

[17] According to Sutton (forthcoming), proponents of HEM have moved away from the parity principle and have adopted instead the 'complementarity principle'. The complementarity principle states that exograms don't have to be functionally isomorphic to engrams but must complement them.

garden with a spade, it is not the coupled system of me-and-the-spade that does the digging. My-spade-and-I do not get the prize for "best hole in the garden". I get the prize, even though I could not have done the digging without the spade.' In order not to have to deal with the vexing issue of where the subject containing the memory system ends and the environment begins I will stick to the orthodox view whereupon the mental process of remembering is purely internal in character and environmental features such as the library shelf are merely external aids to remembering.

According to section 5.3, it is conceivable that memory traces are extracted from a brain, stored in some external medium, and, later on, implanted back into the same brain. But doesn't this view commit me to HEM, for it acknowledges that the cognitive process underlying remembering may take place outside the head? The answer is 'no'. On the causal theory of memory proposed here, the production of memory traces via an original representation and the production of a memory state via memory traces must take place 'inside the head'. The fact that a trace has been temporarily stored outside the body of the rememberer before it is reimplanted and before it gives rise to a memory state does not contradict the common-sense distinction between memories and external information stores.

6.5 COLLECTIVE REMEMBERING

The hypothesis of the extended mind can easily be widened to the hypothesis of the social mind. If external aids and props can be proper parts of an individual's cognitive process, as HEM claims, then presumably this also applies to other people's minds and memories. Consider the following adaption of Clark and Chalmers's thought experiment: S is married to S** who, though he doesn't suffer from amnesia, is absentminded and forgetful. S** has difficulty remembering names, appointments, birthdays, phone numbers, and so on. Whenever S**'s memory fails him, S provides him with the required information. In fact, S plays the same role for S** that the notebook does for S*. S acts as S**'s external memory. If we want to say of S* that his mind extends to the notebook, shouldn't we then also say that S**'s mind extends to S's mind and that they form a coupled system? After all, the dynamics of S's mind are much more similar to S**'s cognitive system than the dynamics of the notebook are to S*'s biological memory. S's and S**'s memories are, for instance, both subject to interference and generation effects. It seems then that if HEM is correct, the mind not only extends to encompass non-biological artefacts but also other minds. And when a cognitive process extends into another mind then we get a collective coupled system. Remembering via a collective coupled system may be referred to as *transactive memory*, a term coined by Daniel Wegner (1986).

The idea behind the notion of transactive memory is that agents frequently become epistemically dependent on one another and that this interdependence forms a collective memory system. When agents serve as external memory aids to each other they are able to benefit from each other's knowledge and expertise if they develop a shared understanding of who knows what in the group.[18] Transactive memory systems are built on the view of individuals playing the role of external memory for other individuals who, in turn, encode meta-memories (i.e. memories about the memories of others). Wegner (1995) proposes that there are two types of meta-memories: information about the areas of expertise of each member and information about the locations of the knowledge. Knowledge is encoded, stored, and retrieved from the collective memory through various transactions between individuals, based on their meta-memories.

Experiments indicate that that transactive memory can serve as a facilitator of group performance, where groups whose members are aware of the knowledge and expertise of other group members perform better than groups whose members do not possess such knowledge (cf. Moreland and Argote 2003). Transactive memory systems enable groups to make better use of the knowledge that their members possess and such systems are a more reliable information store than isolated individual memories.

The notion of transactive memory is a way of conceiving of what is commonly referred to as *collective memory*, a term coined by the sociologist Maurice Halbwachs at the beginning of the twentieth century. Halbwachs claims that individual memories are dependent on social

---

[18] Tollefsen (2006: 145) makes the following observation regarding the division of labor in a transactive memory system: 'individuals in a transactive memory system must know something about each other's domains of expertise. They need to be aware of where information is stored and the storage capabilities of individuals in the group. . . . When there are no clear experts other ways of assigning responsibility for the information are used. The person who first introduces the information may, by default, be held responsible for encoding, storing and retrieving the new information.'

groups for their existence and that even in the case of solitary reminisc-
ing one is recalling from a social perspective or for a social purpose. 'The
individual memory, in order to corroborate and make precise and even
to cover the gaps in its remembrances, relies upon, relocates itself within,
momentarily merges with, the collective memory' (1950: 50). There is a
striking similarity between what Halbwachs calls 'social frameworks of
memory' and what Wegner calls 'transactive memory systems'. 'There
is no point', Halbwachs (1925: 38) writes, 'in seeking where memories
are preserved in my brain or in some nook of my mind to which I alone
have access: for they are recalled to me externally.' The people around
me and the groups I am a member of 'give me the means to reconstruct'
some of my memories.

   Though it is beyond doubt that there is a social dimension to remembering theorists disagree over which phenomenon to call collective as
opposed to individual memory. There is a multiplicity of phenomena
lumped together under the heading 'collective memory'. These phenomena may be characterized as lying on a continuum running from *collected*
to *collectivistic* memories.[19] Collected memories are the aggregated or
shared individual memories of members of a group. Collectivistic memories, by contrast, are properties of groups, cultures, or societies and are
not reducible to the individual memories of their members. A group can
collectivistically remember something even if none of its members has
the corresponding individual memory.[20] Collectivistic memories therefore need not be contained 'in the head' but may consist in 'patterns
of publicly available symbols objectified in society' (Olick 1999: 336).
In this vein, researchers study the cultural artefacts (e.g. memorials,
museums, libraries, national holidays) and practices that represent the
past for a particular cultural group to examine collectivistic memory.

   Halbachs vacillates between these two notions of collective memory.
In some places he seems to assert that collective memory is nothing
but the aggregate of many individual memories. He writes: 'While
the collective memory endures and draws strength from its base in
a coherent body of people, it is individuals as group members who

---

[19] The term 'collected memory' is due to Olick (1999: 338); the term 'collectivistic
memory' is due to Wessel and Moulds (2008: 289).

[20] Edwin Hutchins, for example, argues for 'socially distributed cognition' (1995: 129)
and uses a crew's navigation of a large ship as his paradigm example. He attributes mental
states to the ship's crew as a single unit. Such mental states include remembering, perceiving,
having expertise, and entertaining hypotheses. Hutchins claims that the crew, as a whole, can
instantiate a mental state that no individual member of the crew instantiates.

remember' (1950: 78). Yet elsewhere he argues for collectivistic memory when he declares: 'One may say that the individual remembers by placing himself in the perspective of the group, but one may also affirm that the memory of the group realizes and manifests itself in individual memories' (1925: 40).

The extended mind hypothesis and Wegner's theory of transactive memory lie in between the collectivistic and the individualistic extremes of the continuum. When the mind extends beyond the skull the environment becomes integral to the individual's capacity to remember. Yet the extended mind hypothesis does not go so far as to claim that environmental memories persist after the individual has passed away. The social environment is taken to contain memories only to the extent that an individual uses it as a storehouse of information.

7

In Defense of Pastist Externalism

In the previous chapter I have argued that memory contents supervene on relations that the individual bears to past environmental conditions. The view that past environmental conditions fix the contents of our memory states (in conjunction with the conceptual replacement view) has the consequence that an environmental shift brings about a conceptual shift that, in turn, can rob us of the ability to remember some of our past thoughts. Some may find this idea rather implausible. The goal of the present chapter is to explain and defend the context-dependency of memory that follows from pastist externalism.

The starting point is the so-called *memory argument* adapted from Paul Boghossian (2008). The memory argument purports to show that externalism about memory yields the absurd consequence that a subject can know the contents of his current thoughts only if the environmental conditions determining these contents will not change in the future. Thus future events determine whether you can know what you are thinking right now. It will be argued that the memory argument fails because it mistakenly assumes that remembering is a form of knowing. This error is corrected in a *refined memory argument*, but then a further problem emerges in that the refined memory argument rests on an equivocation of the term 'forgetting'. Though neither the original nor the refined memory argument stands up to scrutiny, they rest on a prima facie reasonable worry. Given externalism, an environmental shift, by itself, can cause memory failure. But doesn't the ability to remember depend, in the first instance, on our mental condition — on factors in the head — rather than on conditions of the environment we live in? If we are unable to remember today what we knew yesterday this is due to a change within us, not a change of our surroundings; or so a critic of pastist externalism might say. On closer inspection, however, it turns out that worries concerning the externalist thesis that environmental switching can cause memory failures are misplaced because there are neither philosophical nor psychological reasons to substantiate them. In the end nothing stands in the way of accepting the context-dependency of memory that follows from pastist externalism.

Section 7.1 sets the stage and explains the memory argument. Section 7.2 critically discusses one of the premises of the memory argument. Section 7.3 develops a refined version of the memory argument that overcomes the problems of the original version. Section 7.4 shows that the refined version of the memory argument is also invalid. The two remaining sections dispel some possible remaining worries concerning pastist externalism about memory content. Section 7.5 shows that externalism about memory corresponds with psychological data and section 7.6 suggests that it is compatible with the psychological criterion of personal identity.

7.1 THE MEMORY ARGUMENT

A much-discussed question in the recent literature is whether an externalist theory of mental content is compatible with the doctrine that we have privileged knowledge of our current and conscious mental states. By the doctrine of privileged self-knowledge we can know the contents of our conscious and current thoughts just by reflection, without depending on empirical information about either external behavior or physical and social circumstances. Yet if the contents of our thoughts are partly determined by external affairs, as content externalism claims, knowledge of our thought contents seems to require information beyond what is available by reflection. In other words, if mental states are individuated according to their relational or extrinsic properties, then, since reflection can reveal only intrinsic properties of mental states, we cannot have what we think we have: non-empirical knowledge of our thought contents. Suppose I hold a belief that I express by saying 'water is wet'. Assuming content externalism, it seems that I need to know what substance I am in contact with—H_2O, XYZ, or some other liquid—to be able to know what it is I am thinking about. Thus, knowledge of my thought content requires investigation of my external content-determining circumstances. But this would mean that knowledge about my thought content is epistemically mediated, based on empirical evidence. And this flies in the face of our conviction that such knowledge is non-empirical, privileged, or authoritative.

In response to the (alleged) problem at hand, content externalists have tried to accommodate the doctrine of privileged self-knowledge. The leading externalist theory of privileged self-knowledge is the so-called *inclusion theory of self-knowledge,* which was first worked out by Tyler Burge (1988) and John Heil (1988).[1] The inclusion theory works particularly well for *cogito-like judgments,* that is, judgments about one's conscious and current first-order thoughts. Examples of cogito-like judgments are 'I am now thinking that writing requires concentration' and 'I hereby judge that examples need elaboration'. According to the inclusion theory, cogito-like judgments are authoritative because their contents are contextually self-verifying—they contain as constituent the first-order states they are about. The content of the that-clause (in the second-order thought) is inherited from the first-order thought since the intentional content mentioned in the that-clause is not merely an object of reference or cognition; it is part of the higher-order cognition itself. The first-order content is included in, or contained by, the reflexive content of the second-order thought and that is why first- and second-order contents cannot come apart and no errors are possible in cogito-like judgments.[2]

The inclusion theory of self-knowledge has met with numerous objections. One of the authors who has attempted to show that content externalism and privileged self-knowledge are incompatible after all is Paul Boghossian. Boghossian invites us to consider the following slow switching scenario. At t_1 S lives on Earth and thinks thoughts involving the concept *water,* for instance, the thought that water is wet. Moreover, he knows that he is thinking that water is wet. Some time after t_1 S is unwittingly switched from Earth to Putnam's Twin Earth. According to content externalism, S's word 'water' eventually comes to express the concept *twater* instead of the Earthian concept *water.* So if he used to believe on Earth *water is wet,* he would now believe *twater is wet.* And just as he is unaware of the environmental shift from Earth to Twin

---

[1] Advocates of the inclusion theory of self-knowledge, besides Burge and Heil, are Davidson (2001*b*), Gertler (2001), Macdonald (2007), Sawyer (2002), myself (1996), and, with reservations, Peacocke (1996).

[2] In my view, content externalism and privileged self-knowledge are only partially compatible. Although externalism is compatible with privileged self-knowledge of one's particular thought contents, it is consistent with us lacking privileged access to the attitudinal component of one's thoughts (cf. my 1996). Moreover, self-knowledge (a propositional attitude) is consistent with our lacking the ability to rule out, via reflection, the possibility that we don't have any propositional attitudes. Self-knowledge only provides us with knowledge of what is *in* our minds, but not that we have minds (cf. my 2000 and 2004).

Earth, he is unaware of the consequent alteration of his conceptual repertoire and belief contents. Now given that the slow switching of an agent causes him to adopt new concepts and to lose the old ones, at t_2, S lacks the necessary concepts to recount his earthian *water* thought. Not only is he unable to reproduce the very content of his thought at t_1 — the content he used to have privileged self-knowledge about — but he cannot even entertain a sufficiently similar content (cf. sects. 7.6 and 8.3). How can this fact be explained? Either S forgot at t_2 what he knew at t_1 or he never knew it. Since Boghossian (2008: 158) excludes straightforward memory failures by stipulation he concludes that 'the only explanation . . . for why S will not know [at t_2] what he is said to know [at t_1], is . . . that he never knew'. Following Peter Ludlow (1995*a*: 157), we can parse the argument into these steps:

(1) If S forgets nothing, then what S knew at t_1, S can know at t_2,
(2) S forgets nothing,
(3) S does not know at t_2 that p,
(4) Therefore, S did not know at t_1 that p,

where 'p' stands for a proposition involving a concept affected by a slow switch taking place between t_1 and t_2.

According to Boghossian, argument (1) through (4) is a *reductio* of content externalism. The reason content externalism is absurd is that it conflicts with the doctrine of privileged self-knowledge. The idea is that if mental contents are determined by external affairs, we have to investigate the relevant environmental conditions to know about our thought contents. The application of externalism to memory contents is nothing but a heuristic move to motivate the incompatibility of externalism with privileged self-knowledge. While this is the standard reading of the argument, it is not the only one. Boghossian's argument can also be read as a critique of pastist externalism about memory content. In this interpretation, the point of the argument is that, given pastist externalism about memory content, you can know your present thought contents only if, in the future, you will not be subjected to slow switching. Future switching determines whether you can know what you are thinking right now. Obviously, this conclusion is too strange to be credible. The moral of the argument is therefore that the price we have to pay for pastist externalism about memory content is excessively high and that we should get rid of it.

When argument (1) through (4) is understood as a critique of pastist externalism about memory contents, in the way explained above, I refer to it as the *memory argument*. The memory argument hinges on three assumptions: first, the thesis that memory contents are fixed by past (rather than present or future) environmental conditions; second, the conceptual replacement view whereupon the slow switching of an agent causes him to adopt new concepts and to lose the old ones; and, third, the epistemic theory of memory, according to which remembering is a form of knowing. The first assumption was already defended in section 6.3 and need not be discussed again. The third assumption has been rejected in Chapter 3. What then about the second assumption? If the only criterion for the correct interpretation of slow switching cases were the avoidance of the memory argument, then we ought to reject the conceptual replacement view and instead adopt the conceptual addition view. For unless switching brings about the loss of old concepts, the memory argument doesn't get off the ground. Unfortunately, however, the conceptual addition view is not without problems of its own. In section 7.2 I will argue that, irrespective of the memory argument, the conceptual addition view is not any more plausible than the conceptual replacement view. And in the subsequent sections I will argue that the memory argument is innocuous even if we stick to the conceptual replacement view.

7.2 TWO INTERPRETATIONS OF SLOW SWITCHING

Slow switching scenarios allow for two kinds of interpretations. In the *conceptual replacement view*, the slow switching of an agent causes him to adopt new concepts and to eventually lose the old ones. In the *conceptual addition view*, the slow switching of an agent only causes him to adopt new concepts but not to lose the old ones. Even long after the time of switching, the agent possesses Earthian and Twin Earthian concepts and contents. Although the conceptual replacement view represents the standard interpretation of switching scenarios, only a few philosophers openly commit themselves to this position. Explicit proponents of the replacement view are Peter Ludlow (1999*a*: 163–5), William Lycan (1996: 129–30), and Michael Tye (1998: 83–4). The claim that switching does not involve the loss of old concepts is endorsed by Tyler Burge (1998: 359), Kevin Falvey (2003: 229), John Gibbons (1996: 295), Jane Heal (1998: 108), Bernard Kobes (1996: 89), and Klaas Kraay (2002: 305–7).

The level of the debate between the conceptual replacement view and the conceptual addition view is usually quite low. The defense of the addition view is rarely more than a simple assertion. Take, for example, Heal (1998: 108), who writes: 'For a referring term to take on a new referential relation, as a result of interaction with a new kind of stuff or individual, is not necessarily for it to lose its original reference.'[3] No elaboration provided. No need for elaboration acknowledged. The defense of the replacement theory is equally ungrounded. Tye (1998: 83–4), for example, notes that the addition view is 'very implausible' because 'after many years on Twin Earth I surely am not prepared to apply both the concept *twater* and the concept *water* to the liquid that comes out of taps, fills lakes, etc. in my current environment'. No argument given.

Ludlow develops an indirect argument for the conceptual replacement view of switching scenarios by accusing the addition view of having the consequence that apparently sound inferences are transformed into unsound ones. He invites us to imagine this case:[4]

Suppose, for example, that at t_2 I fall in some twater and think a thought which I express as 'I am thinking that water is wet'. I then reason out loud as follows: 'I am thinking that water is wet, and I was thinking that water is wet at t_1, therefore I have thought that water is wet at least twice'. Here is a case where the content of the first premiss of my reasoning is causally connected to my falling into twater at t_2, and the content of the second premiss is causally connected to my falling into water at t_1. If those are the contents at work in my inference, then my inference is (contrary to appearance) unsound. (1999a: 165)

As Ludlow describes the situation, the problem is this: although each of the premisses is true and the agent's reasoning appears (introspectively, to the agent) to be deductively valid, the conclusion is in fact false because the token of 'water' in the first premiss expresses the concept *twater* and the token of 'water' in the second premiss expresses the concept *water and/or twater*. The idea is that the addition view, unlike the replacement view, undermines our ability to tell a priori whether any particular inference of ours satisfies one of the forms of valid inference.

---

[3] Gibbons (1996: 299–302) has come up with something that at least purports to be an argument in favor of the conceptual addition view.

[4] A case of this sort (involving Pavarotti) is presented in Boghossian (1992a: 21–2). While Ludlow uses the transformation of seemingly sound inferences into unsound ones as an argument against the conceptual addition view, Boghossian uses it as an argument against content externalism.

The problem with Ludlow's indirect argument for the replacement view is fourfold. First, it is far from obvious that we are able to tell a priori whether any particular inference is valid. Second, Ludlow owes us an explanation of why we should suppose that the concept expressed by 'water' in the first premiss is any different from the concept expressed by 'water' in the second premiss. A number of philosophers have criticized this hybrid view.[5] Their idea is that when an agent is engaged in explicit reasoning, he intends throughout his reasoning to be using terms in a univocal way, where the meaning of the various tokens of a single word-form are determined in something like the way that the meaning of an anaphoric pronoun is determined. Third, granted the hybrid view, it is not the case that the addition view *mistakenly* characterizes a valid inference as an invalid one. The inference in question is invalid. The agent is mistaken in applying the concept expressed by 'water' in the first premiss to his past experience on Earth. He is using the concept obtained from the first premiss to identify the liquid he remembers, as expressed in the second premiss. It is a mistake of memory identification rather than one of reasoning, but the inference is invalid nevertheless (Burge 1998: 367). Fourth, even if we grant that the addition view converts valid inferences into invalid ones, this doesn't speak in favor of the addition view. For the replacement view too converts (seemingly) valid arguments into invalid ones. The inference at hand is invalid regardless of whether the term 'water' in the second premiss expresses the concept *water and/or twater* or the concept *water*.

Boghossian (1992*a*: 18–21; 2008: 147) favors the addition view but he follows the tradition and assumes the replacement view of switching scenarios. Indeed, the conceptual replacement view is an indispensable tenet of the memory argument. For unless switching causes an agent to lose his old concepts beyond recovery, an environmental shift will not rob him of the ability to recount thoughts involving those old concepts. If switching results in the addition of new concepts, but not in the loss of old ones, nothing stops a switched agent from reactivating his past thought contents.

Since the memory argument rests on the replacement view, a critic of the memory argument only has to adopt the addition view. In fact, the avoidance of the memory argument is the chief motive for adopting the addition view. Yet the conceptual addition view has problems of its own.

---

[5] Cf. Burge (1998), Goldberg (2005; 2007), Kobes (1996: 91), Schiffer (1992). In (1992*b*) Boghossian responds to Schiffer (1992).

To understand these problems, two versions of the addition view need to be distinguished: the *ambiguity view* and the *amalgamation view*.[6] In the *ambiguity view*, slow switching causes the agent unknowingly to take on two concepts (*water* and *twater*) for disjointly different sorts of things (H_2O and XYZ). The switched agent's word 'water' is ambiguous like our word 'bank'. Just as 'bank' refers, on different occasions, to an effluvial embankment or a financial institution, the switched person's word 'water' refers, in different contexts, to H_2O or XYZ. According to the *amalgamation view*, switching causes the agent's concept to broaden by applying it to H_2O and XYZ simultaneously. The switched agent's word 'water' ceases to be a natural kind term. His term 'water' is like our term 'jade', which applies to the two chemically distinct minerals jadeite and nephrite.

To see the problems with the conceptual addition view, let's examine each version of it, beginning with the ambiguity view. In the ambiguity view, switching causes 'water' to become ambiguous. For slow switching not to cause memory failure, a proponent of the ambiguity view has to assume that our mind is somehow equipped with a mechanism that selects the contextually appropriate meaning of the ambiguous term. This mechanism assures that the term 'water' employed by a switched agent means H_2O, when it is used in a memory claim, and XYZ otherwise. Without such a mechanism, slow switching would cause memory failure, for then the switched agent might use his *twater* concept to try to recount a past *water* thought. But it is far from clear how we should conceive of such a mechanism for filling in the appropriate meaning for ambiguous terms.

In response to this worry, Burge (1998) sets forth an account of memory that is modeled after his inclusion theory of self-knowledge (cf. p. 187). The inclusion theory of self-knowledge reconciles externalism with privileged self-knowledge by arguing that the content of a first-order thought is perforce contained in the content of the simultaneously entertained second-order thought and that the contents of both thoughts are determined by the same systematic relations to environmental conditions. Burge claims that there is a type of memory—he calls it *preservative memory*—that also rests on an automatic

---

6 The distinction between the two forms of the addition view goes back to Burge (1998: 352). Burge calls the ambiguity view the *disjoint type case*. This label is unfortunate since, given the amalgamation view, the post-switch concept expressed by 'water' also has a disjunctive reference: H_2O or XYZ.

containment process. When a victim of slow switching has the apparent memory of having thought that water is wet and when this is an expression of preservative memory, then the embedded content (*water is wet*) is identical with the content of the past thought it is memory-related to. Burge writes:

> The point of preservative memory is to fix the content in present mental acts or states *as the same as* the content of those past ones that are connected by causal-memory chains to the present ones. If the individual relies primarily upon preservative memory, and if the causal-memory chains are intact, the individual's self-attribution is a *reactivation* of the content of the past one, held in place by a causal memory chain linking present to past attributions.
>
> (1998: 359, my emphasis)

Through causal chains preservative memory revives past contents, without having to identify them. Memory is understood in analogy to pronominal back-reference. When using pronouns we don't need to be able to identify the referent of a pronoun in order to secure its reference. The reference is unfailingly secured by the chains inherent in the discourse. Similarly, the traces of preservative memory perforce connect later thoughts to earlier ones. Burge (ibid.) concludes that 'as long as the causal memory links are in place, preservative memory is authoritative in something like the way much immediate present-tense self-knowledge is'.

The first thing to notice about Burge's response to the memory argument is that it works only for what he calls *preservative memory*. When, instead of redeploying some preserved concept or reactivating some content, the subject *represents* some past content, event, or image, the past mental content isn't automatically contained in the present one. And when there is no causal-preservative link in place, slow switching may give rise to memory failures in the sense that the wrong kinds of concepts are used to represent past contents.

More importantly, however, Burge's conception of preservative memory commits us to the classical-computational approach to cognitive psychology. In this approach, mental states—including memory traces—are symbolic structures that have semantically evaluable constituents. The structure of a memory trace is said to correspond to the structure of the mental state it causally derives from and to the structure of the mental state it causally brings about (i.e. the state of remembering). This assertion is presupposed by the notion of preservative memory. For only if the symbolic and semantic structure of a memory trace is the same as that of propositional attitudes, does it make sense to claim that traces transmit concepts and contents that are automatically 'inserted' into memory states.

When memory traces are viewed connectionistically, however, there are no syntactically and semantically structured formulae in an internal code. Memory is not a storehouse for mental contents. Instead information is encoded in the weights (or strengths) of connections between the neurons. What is stored in memory is a set of changes in the instructions neurons send each other, affecting what pattern of activation can be constructed from a given input. Remembering occurs when an input 'travels' through an established activation pattern.[7]

To guard against misunderstanding I should stress that my complaint about the conception of preservative memory is *not* that it conflicts with connectionism. The debate between connectionism and computationalism about memory is still ongoing and it is conceivable that some day connectionism about memory will be disproven. Instead, my dispute with the notion of preservative memory is that it (implicitly) takes a side in the computationalism/connectionism debate. As long as the debate is undecided, it is prudent not to base the interpretation of slow switching scenarios on any one of the rival cognitive architectures.

Another point that speaks against the conceptual addition view is that it isn't able to account for Kripke's (1980) modal intuitions. To drive this point home, imagine someone who doesn't know that water is H_2O. The agent is unwittingly shuttled from Earth to Twin Earth and remains there for some time. Then he is confronted with this story: 'Suppose the substance designated by your word "water" is XYZ. Moreover, suppose somewhere in a nearby galaxy exists a planet which contains H_2O instead of XYZ. The inhabitants of this planet call H_2O "water". Do you think the substance they designate with "water" is really water?' According to Kripke's modal intuitions, the answer to this question has to be 'no'. Yet if we assume the amalgamation view and the ambiguity view, this answer is false. The proponent of the conceptual addition view owes us an explanation of why Kripke's modal intuitions are untrustworthy.

---

[7] Cf. pp. 135–7. Tye points out that the connectionist approach to memory takes away some of the perplexities of presentist externalism. 'Since it is now the case that the representations with such contents do not exist until the time of recollection, there are no contents that attach to the representations before they are retrieved, and hence there can be no question of the representations now having the contents they used to have in storage' (1998: 93).

In light of the problems surrounding the conceptual addition view, it would be welcomed if externalists were not compelled to adopt the conceptual addition view so as to be able to repudiate the memory argument. And in fact, externalists are not compelled to adopt the addition view. The anti-externalist conclusion of the memory argument can be repudiated even if we stick to the conceptional replacement view. This is what I will attempt to show in the subsequent sections.

Before I move on I would like to add one more comment regarding the conceptual addition view. What I have said so far about the interpretation of switching scenarios may give the impression that, granted the addition view, slow switching never causes memory failure. Yet things are not quite so simple. When combined with other premises, the addition view can indeed prevent a victim of switching from remembering his past thoughts.

So far we have assumed that the transfer from Earth to Twin Earth takes place without the subject's knowledge. Let us now, for a change, examine *knowledgeable* slow switching. At t_1, S lives on Earth and thinks a thought that he expresses by saying 'water is wet'. After having been switched to Twin Earth, at t_2, he acquires both the *water* concept and the *twater* concept. Then, at t_3, S is told that he has been switched but he is not told whether he is now on the same planet he used to be on at t_1. Shortly afterwards, S entertains a thought that he expresses by saying 'at t_1, I thought that water is wet'. Is this an accurate representation of S's original *water* thought? Does S's second-order thought at t_3 qualify as a memory of his thought at t_1?

Some philosophers maintain that S does remember his original thought involving the concept *water*. According to Kobes, for example, knowledgeable switching is not significantly different from unwitting switching. And since unwitting switching doesn't impair preservative memory, knowledgeable switching doesn't either. In both cases the switched agent possesses the very same concepts that he had before the switch. Kobes (1996: 88) concludes that S's belief at t_3, which he expresses by saying 'at t_1, I thought that water is wet', is indeed a 'bit of self-knowledge' and should be 'reckoned among his cognitive achievements'.

Gibbons is of a different opinion from Kobes. Combining externalism with functional role semantics, Gibbons holds that sameness of thought content is determined not only by sameness of relational properties but also by similarity of functional role. Granted that slow switching doesn't entail the loss of old concepts, at t_2 S possesses both a *water* concept and a *twater* concept. With respect to their relational properties and functional roles, S's *water* concept at t_1 is the same as his *water* concept at t_2. But, Gibbons maintains, the concept expressed by S's term 'water' at t_3—after he finds out that he has been switched—differs from the concept expressed by his term 'water' at t_1 and t_2. The reason is that, after S is informed of the switch, his thoughts about 'water' have a different functional role than before. For example, after he is informed, S doesn't take his beliefs involving *water* as evidence for or against his beliefs involving *twater*. Gibbons (1996: 309) concludes that because 'at t_3 [S] employ[s] concepts distinct from those [he] employ[s] at t_1, [he] cannot say or think what [he] was thinking then. But if [he] cannot think it, [he] cannot know it'. This is not the place to discuss Gibbons's position in detail. I only mention it to indicate that the conceptual addition view does not *guarantee* that remembering is compatible with slow switching. When externalism is combined with functional role semantics, knowledgeable switching brings about a conceptual shift that prevents us from accessing some of our past thoughts. The memory argument triumphs once again.

7.3 THE MEMORY ARGUMENT RECONSIDERED

The memory argument rests not only on the conceptual replacement view but also on the epistemic theory of memory, that is, the view that memory is a form of knowledge. To remember something is to know it, where this knowledge was previously acquired and preserved. The dependence of the memory argument on the epistemic theory of memory is particularly clear in the case of premiss (1), which states that if S forgets nothing, then what S knew at t_1, S can know at t_2. Unless remembering is a way of knowing, it might well be that S remembers that p without thereby knowing that p or having known that p. In Chapter 3 we saw that the epistemic theory of memory is mistaken in that what passes into memory may be merely a representation or belief, not knowledge. Knowledge supervenes on some but not all cases of remembering, for sometimes memory, though hitting the mark of truth, succeeds in an epistemically defective way.

Given the failure of the epistemic theory of memory, three of the four lines of the memory argument must be rephrased. Premiss (1) must be replaced by:

(1′) If S forgets nothing, then what S represented at t_1, S can represent at t_2.

Premiss (3) must be replaced by this condition:

(3′) S cannot represent at t_2 that p,

and conclusion (4) should read instead:

(4′) Therefore, S did not represent at t_1 that p.

We are now in a position to reformulate the memory argument. The *refined memory argument* looks like this:

(1′) If S forgets nothing, then what S represented at t_1, S can represent at t_2,
(2) S forgets nothing,
(3′) S cannot represent at t_2 that p,
(4′) Therefore, S did not represent at t_1 that p.

As in the case of the original memory argument, 'p' stands for a proposition involving a concept affected by a slow switch taking place between t_1 and t_2.

If an unwitting switch from Earth to Twin Earth causes S to lose his *water* concept (conceptual replacement view), he is unable to call to mind his past *water* thought (premiss (3′)). Given that S forgot nothing (premiss (2)), his inability to recount his past *water* thought indicates that he never entertained that *water* thought (premiss (1′)). Thus the moral of the refined memory argument is that, to have a thought right now, I need to be able to remember it later on. What one is currently thinking is determined by what one will be able to remember about one's present thoughts. What cannot be remembered wasn't thought. Future forgetting undoes the existence of past thoughts.

The conclusion of the original memory argument differs from that of the refined memory argument. Given the original memory argument, externalism about memory makes the *knowability* of one's present thought contents depend on whether one will be subjected to slow switching in the future. Given the refined memory argument, it is the *existence* of one's present thoughts that is affected by slow switching in the future. The latter conclusion is, of course, no less absurd than the former conclusion. So if the refined memory argument can be believed, this is reason enough to get rid of pastist externalism.[8]

7.4 TWO KINDS OF FORGETTING

Like memory, forgetting is not a unitary phenomenon.[9] Here I want to distinguish between two aspects of the commonsensical notion of forgetting that I will call the *wide* and the *narrow* notion of forgetting. The wide notion of forgetting refers to *any* kind of memory failure regardless of whether it is caused by the breach of an epistemic or moral duty or by an event beyond the subject's control. The narrow notion of forgetting, on the other hand, designates only those memory failures for which the subject is himself responsible, which would have been within his power to avoid. To illustrate the difference between these two notions of forgetting consider two offenders accused of the same kind of offense. One offender has suffered memory loss, albeit through no fault of his own, and cannot remember anything about the action he is accused of. In this case the forgetting may be used as evidence of incompetence to stand trial or in mitigation of criminal responsibility.

---

[8] Wittgenstein is sometimes taken to have advanced an anti-realist position regarding reports of one's own past mental states. On this interpretation, to put it crudely, it is one's present disposition to judge that one believed that p in the past that makes it true that one did. So the past belief has no existence independently of the report one subsequently makes or is disposed to make; it is simply a projection of the present report back into the past. This anti-realist position is a close cousin of the view proposed by the refined memory argument. Following Child (2006), I do not see that Wittgenstein has given us reason to think that a past belief may be constituted, not by anything that was true of oneself at the time, but by one's retrospective tendency to self-ascribe it.

[9] Psychologists distinguish four kinds of forgetting according to what causes the failure to retrieve the information recorded in the mind (cf. pp. 101–1, 121). One type of forgetting is a result of repression. Another type of forgetting is due to the decay of memory traces. Forgetting can also be brought about by interference with another memory; finally, forgetting can be due to the inability to find the right cue to jog the memory.
    The anthropologist Connerton (2008) distinguishes seven types of forgetting and highlights forgetting as an active rather than a passive process in both individual and larger cultural memory. What distinguishes the types of memory are the many and varied motivations for an individual, a generation, or a nation to forget particular events, details, or facts. The seven types of forgetting are: repressive erasure, prescriptive forgetting, forgetting that is constitutive in the formation of a new identity, structural amnesia, forgetting as annulment, forgetting as planned obsolescence, and forgetting as humiliated silence.

The other offender intentionally brought about the memory loss (say, by intoxicating himself) before committing the offense. The voluntary nature of his forgetting has the consequence that it doesn't mitigate his responsibility (cf. Birch 2000).

But does it even make sense to hold someone to account for having forgotten something? Common sense has it that although we can use all kinds of indirect methods of remembering and forgetting we cannot remember or forget on demand. Yet if memory and forgetting are not under our control, and if *ought* implies *can*, then it follows that it doesn't make sense to hold someone responsible for having forgotten something. Two responses result. First, it strikes me that the requirement of being able to do something on demand as a test for having it under control is an unreasonably high standard. Consider promise keeping, which is a paradigm subject for moral evaluation. To keep a promise I have to remember it. Forgetting a promise is an excuse but not a justification for not keeping it. Thus the duty to keep our promises includes the duty to remember them (Margalit 2002: 57). Second, the key feature of the narrow notion of forgetting is not that it is the proper subject for moral decrees; rather the key feature is that the effective cause for the memory failure lies within the subject not in the environment.

According to the wide notion, *forgetting* also includes memory failures due to slow switching. Given the narrow notion, memory failures caused by switching don't count as forgetting.[10] The refined memory argument is incoherent because it rests on a confusion of the two notions of forgetting. Premiss $(1')$ presupposes the wide notion of forgetting, whereas premiss (2) assumes the narrow notion. There is no single notion of forgetting that renders both premisses of the memory argument true. And since the notion of forgetting is the same in premiss $(1')$ as in premiss (1), this critique also applies to the original memory argument.

Let's start with premiss $(1')$: if S forgets nothing, then what S represented at t_1, S can represent at t_2. This premiss has the form of

---

[10] Keith Butler (1997: 791) declares that 'the ability to remember what one was thinking may not be infallible, but there is no reason (at least no reason independent of externalism) to suppose that its fallibility has anything at all to do with a change in environments'. Butler does not explain why he is reluctant to call memory failures due to environmental shifts 'forgetting'. Probably he tacitly assumes that forgetting implies that the factors causing the memory failure are within the agent's control. This at least is Kraay's reason for claiming that 'the memory failure brought about by conceptual shift [due to switching] is a paradigmatic instance of the kind of memory failure that does not constitute forgetting' (2002: 303–4).

an implication. For the consequent of the implication to be true, the antecedent has to rule out not only *some* but *all* memory failures. It has to exclude not only memory failures for which the subject is himself responsible but also memory failures for which he is not responsible. For any kind of forgetting between t_1 and t_2 has the consequence that S is unable to represent at t_2 what he represented at t_1—provided, of course, that he doesn't learn about it anew in the meantime. Therefore, the term 'forgetting' used in the antecedent of premiss (1') has to be understood in the wide sense. Premiss (1') may be rephrased thus: given the absence of *any* memory failures, what S represented at t_1, he can represent at t_2.

Next, consider premiss (2): S forgets nothing. Boghossian (2008: 158) motivates this premiss by claiming that 'in discussing the epistemology of relationally individuated content, we ought to be able to exclude memory failure by stipulation'. But is this really the case? Given the conceptual replacement view that Boghossian takes for granted, a conceptual shift due to unwitting slow switching *does* cause memory failure. And if we assume the wide notion of forgetting, it follows that switching causes forgetting.[11] Therefore the only way for Boghossian to reconcile the conceptual replacement view with the truth of (2) is to read this premiss as implying the narrow notion of forgetting. On the narrow reading, premiss (2) only makes sure that S does not forget owing to the violation of an epistemic duty. He may, however, forget because of other factors such as unwitting switching. In sum, the refined memory argument rests on an equivocation of the term 'forgetting'.[12]

We have seen that the memory argument fails at all events. Given the conceptual addition view, the memory argument simply dissolves.

---

[11] This point has been made before by Brueckner (1997: 6–7), Burge (1998: 368–9), and Tye (1998: 89).

[12] Nagasawa (2002) also criticizes the memory argument for equivocating on the notion of forgetting. Like myself, Nagasawa distinguishes between a 'narrow' and a 'wide' notion of forgetting. What distinguishes these two forms of forgetting according to him is that narrow forgetting is 'a kind of neurophysiological event' while wide forgetting 'is not a neurophysiological event in S's brain, but merely a shift of memory content caused by slow-switching' (ibid. 338). I find this way of drawing the distinction between the two notions of forgetting unfortunate. Since information is stored everywhere in the brain rather than anywhere in particular and since—quite independent of slow switching—a person's neurophysiological condition changes across time, none of S's post-switch brain states match any of his pre-switch brain states. But then any instance of Nagasawa's wide notion of forgetting is also an instance of his narrow notion of forgetting and the proposed distinction collapses.

Granted the conceptual replacement view, the memory argument is neither sound nor valid. The original memory argument is unsuccessful because it erroneously assumes that remembering is a form of knowing. Both the original and the refined memory argument fail because they rest on an equivocation of the term 'forgetting'. What are we to conclude from this? Is the critic of pastist externalism silenced forever? I think the debate with him is not played out yet. A critic could still worry about the compatibility of pastist externalism with our ordinary notion of memory. Pastist externalism has it that an environmental shift might rob us of the ability to access some of our past thoughts. More precisely, given the conceptual replacement view and the supervenience of memory content on past environmental affairs, slow switching makes us forget some of our past thought contents. But how is it possible, a critic of externalism might wonder, that environmental changes can affect our memory? Doesn't the ability to remember depend on our mental condition—on factors inside the head—rather than on the physical or social environment we live in? Pastist externalism seems to fail to countenance the autonomy of memory. This is the worry the memory argument comes down to, once it is freed of all the background noise.

A critic of externalism could try to come up with philosophical and psychological considerations in favor of the autonomy of memory and against the context dependency of memory. The goal of sections 7.5 and 7.6 is to show that neither of these lines of reasoning against pastist externalism is convincing. I will argue that doubts concerning the externalist thesis that unwitting switching can bring about memory failure don't have to be taken seriously, because there are no arguments to substantiate them.

7.5 CONTEXT-DEPENDENT MEMORY

Are there psychological reasons for rejecting the externalist thesis that an environmental shift can bring about memory failures? Quite the reverse. It has been known for a long time that remembering is highly dependent on the physical context. John Locke (1979: 399) cites a number of instances of the context dependency of memory, including the anecdote about a young man

who having learned to Dance, and that to great Perfection, there happened to stand an old Trunk in the Room where he learnt. The *Idea* of this remarkable piece of Household-stuff, had so mixed it self with the turns and steps of all his Dances, that though in that Chamber he could Dance excellently well, yet it was only whilst that Trunk was there, nor could he perform well in any other place, unless that, or some other such Trunk had its due position in the Room.

While this may be a somewhat extreme case, there is no doubt that physical features of the context serve as potent retrieval cues. David Goddon and Alan Baddeley (1975), for example, conducted an experiment in which scuba divers heard a list of thirty-six words in one of two different environments—under water and on land—and were later tested for recall in the same context in which the list had been studied and in another context. It did not greatly matter whether the divers were learning on land or under water. But if they learned in one context and recalled in the other, they remembered about 40 per cent less than if learning and recall occurred in the same environment. So recall is better if the environment at test is the same as the environment at study.

Smith, Glenberg, and Bjork (1978) performed another experiment demonstrating the importance of the physical context in memory. In this experiment, subjects had to study eighty common words in a distinctive basement room on the first day, and then attempt to recall them on a second day in either the same room, or in a fifth-floor room with quite different furnishings. Subjects who recalled in the original basement room tended to remember about eighteen words, significantly more than those who remembered in the different upstairs room, who recalled only about twelve words. Psychologists take these experiments to show that remembering requires cognitive resources normally used to represent the immediate environment.[13]

Given that cognitive psychologists emphasize the dependence of memory on the physical environment, one could try to turn the tables. Instead of worrying that externalism about memory conflicts with psychological findings, why not use psychological findings to establish externalism about memory? Unfortunately, this doesn't work.

---

[13] For a helpful survey of environmental context effects see Smith and Vela (2001). Some experiments indicate that the stability of contextual factors doesn't always have a positive effect on remembering. Thompson, Robertson, and Vogt (1982) found that eyewitnesses in court are excessively influenced by the clothing worn by the accused, leading to occasions on which misidentification occurs on this basis. On several occasions, when the defense lawyer arranged for someone other than the defendant to be wearing the clothes described by the witness, the witness mistook this person for the defendant.

The reason is that there is a crucial difference between psychological experiments and slow switching scenarios. In the above-mentioned psychological experiments, the subjects noticed whether and when they underwent an environmental shift. The whole point of unwitting switching, however, is that subjects don't notice the change of environments. For psychological data to back up the externalist account of memory, one would have to establish that environmental shifts can affect the ability to remember even when subjects are not aware that a shift took place. Unfortunately, there are no psychological studies examining the effects on memory of *unnoticed* changes in physical environmental contexts.

How would one go about setting up an experiment examining the effects on memory of unnoticed changes in environmental contexts? One possibility is to use two adjacent rooms on the same corridor of a building that look the same. After learning and before being tested the subjects could be returned to the same room or to the adjacent room. Another possibility is to change a background dimension very gradually, so that it is not noticeable. Such dimensions might include temperature, background noise or sound, lighting, odors, other people in the room, or visual displays.

Even though there are no experiments examining the effects on memory of unnoticed changes in physical context, there is one experiment that provides at least correlational data. Our memory is not only dependent on the physical environment but also on the *internal* environment, namely the pharmacological state. Psychologists call this kind of dependency *state dependency*. By and large, people show better memory if their pharmacological states match at study and test. A classical example for the state-dependency effect is that, when alcoholic subjects hide money and alcohol while drunk, they are often unable to find it when sober, but recall the hiding places when on their next binge (cf. Goodwin et al. 1969). Now Eric Eich and Isabel Birnbaum (1988) have shown that people don't necessarily have to become drunk to remember what they learned while they were drunk; people also exhibit state-dependent effects if they only think they are again drunk while in fact they are sober. Thus, for the state-dependency effect to work, it is sufficient that subjects believe they occupy the same pharmacological state they occupied at the time of learning.[14] As was said before, Eich

---

[14] Reconsider the above-mentioned room-experiment by Smith, Glenberg, and Bjork. In addition to the group of subjects who recalled the words in the same basement room where they

and Birnbaum's findings only provide correlational data for the point in question. It is one thing to misrepresent an environmental change and it is another to be completely oblivious of the fact that an environmental change took place.

Suppose psychologists could show that even unnoticed changes in the physical environment can affect memory. Would this result back up the externalist thesis that unwitting switching to Twin Earth can cause memory failure? No! The reason is that, in the case of unwitting switching, not only does the subject not notice the environmental change but he is also unaware of the fact that he forgot something. A victim of stealthy switching is convinced that he remembers everything and, what is more, it is fully rational for him to have this conviction. I see no way of setting up a real-life experiment where subjects are unaware of environmental changes *and* of their own memory failures. Thus it is unreasonable to count on psychology to back up externalism about memory. But it is equally unreasonable to worry that externalism about memory flies in the face of psychological data.

7.6 SLOW SWITCHING AND PERSONAL IDENTITY

After having shown that there are no *psychological* reasons for rejecting a slow-switching version of pastist externalism, we are left with the question of whether there are any *philosophical* reasons. The only philosophical reason that comes to my mind concerns the compatibility of the slow-switching version of pastist externalism with the psychological continuity account of personal identity.

As was explained in Chapter 2, the problem of personal identity is the problem of what makes a person at two different times one and the same person. The majority of philosophers believe in some version of a

had previously learned them and the group of subjects who recalled the words in a different upstairs room, there was a third group of subjects. These subjects learned the words in the basement room and were tested in the upstairs room. But they were instructed to try to recollect as much as possible of the original learning environment before starting to recall. Interestingly, they remembered about the same number of words (17.2) as those subjects who had physically returned to the learning environment (18). This suggests that for the context-dependency effect to work one doesn't have to physically return to the environment of information-encoding but that it is sufficient to mentally return to the original environment before trying to recall the encoded information. The negative impact on memory of an environmental change can be compensated for merely by thinking of the original environment.

psychological criterion of personal identity. In a nutshell, the idea is that person-stage X at t_1 belongs to the same person as person-stage Y at t_2 just in case X and Y are related by overlapping chains of psychological connections, and no other person-stage Z at t_2 exists who has equal or stronger psychological continuity with X. The paradigm case of a psychological connection is that between past experiences and present memories thereof.

By and large, advocates of the psychological criterion of personal identity don't concern themselves with the issue of mental content. Yet it is reasonable to assume that they hold that, for a state of recall to qualify as experiential memory, its content has to be the same as, or sufficiently similar to, the content of the original experience from which it causally derives. For how else should one draw the line between genuine memories and false ones? Given this reading of the psychological continuity account, personal identity depends in part on the continuity of memory, which in turn depends on the identity or similarity of mental contents across time.

Assuming that a past experience and a memory thereof must have the same, or sufficiently similar, contents, a critic of pastist externalism could come up with this argument: given pastist externalism and given the conceptual replacement view, slow switching causes forgetting. The forgetting brings about a psychological discontinuity that in turn undermines personal identity. After having been switched to Twin Earth, one isn't the same person one was before the switch occurred. Since this conclusion is thought to be unacceptable, the critic recommends that we get rid of pastist externalism.

The aim of this section is to examine the impact slow switching has on personal identity. While it is true that slow switching can undermine personal identity by causing psychological discontinuity, this shouldn't be used as an argument against pastist externalism. For insofar as one accepts the psychological continuity account one is not in a position to deny that an unnoticed change in the physical environment can undermine personal identity. It is an integral part of the psychological continuity account that someone's identity can be destroyed by events in the environment of which the agent is ignorant. This calls for some explanation.

As long as Earthian English and Twin Earthian English differ only with respect to a single notion—the notion *water*—the alteration of one's conceptual repertoire caused by slow switching probably isn't sufficiently extensive to undermine personal identity. But even when

Earthian English differs from Twin Earthian English with respect to many words, slow switching doesn't necessarily undermine personal identity. For the numerical identity of the switched subject is in jeopardy only if he tries to recount thoughts involving concepts that he lost as a result of the switching. But let's suppose the switched subject does attempt to recount thoughts involving notions he lost due to an environmental shift. Whenever he tries to recall events and thoughts from *before* the switch, he does so by using concepts he acquired *after* the switch. Is he numerically the same person he was before the switch? Is his personal identity undermined as a result of the environmental shift?

The answer to the question at hand crucially depends on whether Twin Earthian thoughts are sufficiently similar to their Earthian counterparts so as to meet the content condition for remembering. Are *water* thoughts and *twater* thoughts similar enough to stand in a memory-relation to one another? To answer this question I need to anticipate the results of section 8.3. Section 8.3 examines in what respect and to what extent two diachronic tokens of propositional content may differ from one another and the later one still be memory-related to the earlier one. My thesis is that two content tokens are memory-related if the later one is an entailment of the earlier one, where entailment is understood along the lines of relevance logic. In the case of non-inferential memory there is the further requirement that no additional premiss may be needed and used by the subject to derive the present content token (the implicans) from the past content token (the implicandum).

Proponents of the psychological criterion tend not to concern themselves with the issue of whether the kind of remembering essential to personal identity is inferential or non-inferential. As far as I can see, there is no good reason to suppose that only non-inferential memory relations can bring about the kind of psychological connectedness and continuity deemed essential for personal identity. I will therefore assume that the psychological criterion of personal identity is indifferent as to whether person-stages are connected by inferential or non-inferential memory.

Let's return to the issue of whether *water* thoughts and *twater* thoughts are similar enough to stand in a memory-relation to one another. Since a *water* thought, by itself, doesn't entail the corresponding *twater* thought, and *vice versa*, it is out of the question that there are non-inferential memory relations linking the two. Slow switching undermines non-inferential memory. But what about inferential memory? Can a *twater* thought and a *water* thought be related via inferential memory? Once again the answer is 'no'. First of all, given my account of content similarity, for a *twater* thought and a *water* thought to be related via inferential memory the agent must be able to derive the *twater* thought from the *water* thought in conjunction with additional premises regarding pastist externalism, slow switching, and the conceptual replacement view. Yet the additional information needed for the agent to deductively infer a *twater* thought from a *water* thought is not available to a victim of *unwitting* switching. For these additional premises state that the agent has recently been switched from Earth to Twin Earth and is currently undergoing a semantic changeover. Only in cases of knowledgeable switching a *water* thought and a *twater* thought can be related via inferential memory.

Second, to deductively derive a *twater* thought from a *water* thought one would have to be able—contra the conceptual replacement view—to simultaneously possess the *twater* concept and the *water* concept. Consider the following scenario: at t_1, while living on Earth, S comes to believe that water is wet. At t_2 he loses the *water* concept as a result of having been moved to Twin Earth. At t_3 S is told about his having been switched from Earth to Twin Earth and at t_4 he claims to remember from t_1 that twater is wet. Does S in fact remember what he claims to remember? Given my entailment account of content similarity, for S to inferentially remember his thought from t_1 he would need to deductively derive *twater is wet* from *water is wet* plus some additional premises. However, once the process of semantic changeover has been completed, S lacks the conceptual repertoire to entertain his past Earthian thoughts. At no point in time does he possess both the *water* concept and a *twater* concept.

Third, even if S could somehow hold on to the *water* concept while he already possesses the *twater* concept it is doubtful whether he could employ both concepts in the same reasoning process. For as was explained before (cf. p. 191), when an agent is engaged in reasoning, he intends throughout his reasoning to be using terms in a univocal way, where the meaning of the various tokens of a single word-form are determined in something like the way that the meaning of an anaphoric pronoun is determined.

The upshot of all this is that, since S is incapable of deductively reasoning his way from the *water* thought at t_1 to the *twater* thought at t_4, there cannot be an inferential memory-relation linking the two thoughts. Thus, there are neither inferential nor non-inferential memory-relations linking content tokens from before and after the semantic shift brought about by slow switching. Regardless of whether personal identity depends on inferential or non-inferential memory connections, slow switching undermines the diachronic numerical identity of the switched person.

So far we have only established that there are no *direct* memory connections between Twin Earthian thoughts and their Earthian counterparts. Yet it is commonly assumed that personal identity requires only *indirect* memory connections. For unless indirect memory connections are sufficient for personal identity, the psychological continuity account implies the contradictory position that someone could both be and not be identical to some past stage, an objection illustrated by the Thomas Reid's brave officer case (2002: 276). Suppose that a boy was flogged for stealing apples. This he remembers later while performing a brave deed as an officer. This brave deed he remembers even later, as a general. But the general has forgotten the flogging. If personal identity required direct memory connections, we would have to say that the brave officer is the boy, and that the general is the brave officer, but that the general is not the boy. Yet this contradicts the transitivity of identity.

The crucial question is whether, after the semantic changeover has been completed, one's seeming memories are *indirectly* continuous with one's thoughts from before the environmental shift. As was explained before (cf. pp. 169–70), content externalists suggest that Earth imparts some semantic impetus to one's mind, allowing it to withstand the absence of Earth itself, and permit one's words to continue to keep their old meaning, at least for a time. What we need to examine now is what happens *after* one arrives on Twin Earth and *before* one completely loses all Earthian concepts. Does the switched agent preserve his personal identity throughout the gradual changeover of concepts and contents that is triggered by an environmental shift and that culminates in the loss of the old concepts?[15]

---

[15] Baillie thinks that whenever switching takes place slowly it does not endanger the identity of the switched person. He declares: If we assume that it takes a slow rather than a quick switch to bring about a conceptual shift, then 'so long as the learning period

In section 7.2 we have seen that the conceptual addition view comes in two flavors: the ambiguity view and the amalgamation view. Either conception can be used to make sense of the gradual semantic transition that takes place after someone arrives on Twin Earth and before he completely loses his earthian concepts. Here I will focus on the ambiguity view: When S lives on Earth, at t_1, his word 'water' expresses the concept *water*. After he arrives on Twin Earth, at t_2, his word 'water' ceases to express the concept *water* and starts to express the disjunctive concept *water-or-twater*. Throughout the period of semantic changeover, S possesses this disjunctive concept. When the semantic transition is coming to an end, at t_3, his word 'water' no longer refers to either H_2O or XYZ but to XYZ only. In other words, S's word 'water' flip-flops back and forth from expressing a univocal concept to expressing an ambiguous one. What we need to consider now is whether the interpretation of the process of gradual changeover of concepts and contents along the lines of the ambiguity view preserves the personal identity of the switched agent. This question splits up into two. Are there memory connections linking, first, *twater* thoughts at t_3 to *water-or-twater* thoughts at t_2 and, second, *water-or-twater* thoughts at t_2 to *water* thoughts at t_1?

It requires little reflection to see that if there are any memory-relations connecting *twater* thoughts at t_3 to *water-or-twater* thoughts at t_2, and connecting *water-or-twater* thoughts at t_2 to *water* thoughts at t_1, they are relations of inferential memory. But it is more than doubtful that a *twater* thought can qualify as an inferential memory of a *water-or-twater* thought and that a *water-or-twater* thought can qualify as an inferential memory of a *water* thought. The reasons are the same as before. First, the additional information required to be able to deductively infer, for instance, *twater is wet* from *water-or-twater is wet* isn't available to a victim of *unwitting* switching. Second, to be able to deductively derive *twater is wet* from *water-or-twater is wet* the subject would have to simultaneously possess the *twater* concept and the *water-or-twater* concept. Similarly, to be able to deductively derive *water-or-twater is wet* from *water is wet* the subject would have to simultaneously possess the *water-or-twater* concept and the *water* concept. Yet the ambiguity view

governing the semantic changeover is gradual enough to ensure that psychological continuity is maintained . . . problems of personal identity would be averted' (1997: 327). Unfortunately, things are not quite that simple. The slowness of the switch, by itself, doesn't guarantee that switching preserves personal identity.

has it that someone undergoing slow switching has these concepts in succession rather than at the same time. Third, even if one could posses the *twater* concept and the *water-or-twater* concept simultaneously, it is doubtful that one could employ both concepts in one and the same inference.[16]

We have seen that there are neither direct nor indirect memory connections between Twin Earthian thoughts and their Earthian counterparts. Given pastist externalism, the conceptual replacement view, and the psychological continuity account of personal identity, unwitting slow switching can indeed undermine personal identity. Yet the fact that personal identity may not be preserved through slow switching shouldn't come as a surprise and, what is more, shouldn't be used as a *reductio* of pastist externalism. Let me explain.

Those who find it strange to suppose that slow switching can undermine personal identity might reason as follows: given that personal identity supervenes on psychological continuity and connectedness, only those environmental affairs can affect one's identity that have an impact on one's psychology. Unwitting slow switching, however, has no impact on one's psychology, for one doesn't even notice whether or when it happens. Therefore slow switching is not able to undermine one's identity. The problem with this reasoning is that it fails to appreciate the ramifications content externalism has for psychology. If the individuation conditions of mental content depend on environmental affairs, then slow switching does affect the agent's psychology, notwithstanding the fact that he cannot detect from the inside whether or when one is switched. In other words, there is more to psychology than meets the inner eye.

Quite irrespective of content externalism, the psychological continuity theory has the consequence that someone's identity can be undermined by environmental changes of which he is unaware. To see this reconsider fission scenarios discussed in section 2.1. Suppose someone's mind is stealthily downloaded while he is asleep, the information is uploaded into an 'empty' brain, and this brain is placed in a body that is qualitatively identical to the original person's body. Each of the emerging people—the fission-descendants—would then be psychologically identical to the original person whose mind was duplicated. On the psychological criterion of personal identity each of

---

[16] It should be obvious that essentially the same objections carry over to an interpretation of the semantic transition along the lines of the amalgamation view.

the fission-descendants would be the same person as the mind donor. But since the two fission-descendants are not the same person as each other, both of them cannot be the same person as the mind donor.

Those who analyze personal identity in terms of psychological continuity often impose a no-rival-candidate constraint (or a non-branching constraint) to avoid the problem of violating the transitivity of identity: S at t_1 is identical to S^* at t_2 just in case (1) S^* at t_2 is psychologically continuous with S at t_1 and (2) there is no rival candidate S^{**} at t_2 who has equal or stronger psychological continuity with S at t_1. Note that, on this view, personal identity depends, at least in part, on external factors of which the subject may be completely ignorant, namely the existence of a rival candidate. The psychological continuity theory of personal identity is 'externalist' as it is; adding content externalism merely amplifies the externalist nature. When the psychological continuity theory is combined with content externalism we simply add another externalist constraint to our account of personal identity, namely the non-switching constraint: S at t_1 is identical to S^* at t_2 just in case (1) S^* at t_2 is psychologically continuous with S at t_1, (2) there is no rival candidate S^{**} at t_2 who has equal or stronger psychological continuity with S at t_1, and (3) neither S nor S^* undergo slow switching between t_1 and t_2.

In conclusion, I have suggested reading a certain argument by Boghossian as a critique of pastist externalism about memory content. What I have labeled the *memory argument* states that, given pastist externalism, you can know your present thoughts only if you will not be subjected to slow switching in the future. One way to rebut the memory argument is to claim that slow switching causes an agent to adopt new concepts but not to lose old ones. Another way is to argue that the memory argument errs in assuming that memory is a form of knowledge. When the identification of memory with knowledge is given up, the memory argument takes on a new character. The *refined memory argument* states that to have a current thought you need to be able to remember it later. This argument fails because it rests on an equivocation of the term 'forgetting'. Then the critic of pastist externalism can—independently of the memory arguments—question the thesis that unwitting switching brings about memory failures. This worry, however, need not be taken seriously, for there are neither psychological nor philosophical arguments to substantiate it. Since nothing stands in the way of accepting pastist externalism and since its presentist and futurist rivals have problems that pastist externalism doesn't have (cf. sect. 6.3) I propose to interpret the content condition of memory along the lines of pastist externalism by replacing

(5) p is identical with, or sufficiently similar to, p*

with the condition:

(5′) p and p* supervene on the same environmental conditions at t_1 or p and p* are sufficiently similar.

8

The Authenticity of Memory

Throughout this study I have assumed that for a propositional attitude token at t_2 to stand in a memory-relation to a propositional attitude token at t_1, the contents of both tokens need not be type-identical but only sufficiently similar. And just as memory doesn't require that the (embedded) content of the propositional attitude token at t_2 be the same as the content of the propositional attitude token at t_1 it isn't necessary that, in the case of introversive memory, the psychological attitude ascribed at t_2 to one's former self be the same as the attitude one took at t_1 toward the proposition in question. Both attitudes need to be only sufficiently similar. This view flies in the face of the widespread identity theory of memory which demands type-identity of diachronic content tokens and attitude tokens. The goal of the present chapter is to try to determine to what extent two diachronic propositional attitude tokens may differ from one another and one of them still count as sufficiently similar to the other as to be memory-related to it.

Section 8.1 distinguishes two aspects of the veridicality constraint on memory: authenticity and truth. The truth of a memory report has to do with the memory content correctly representing objective reality. Authenticity, on the other hand, is an internal criterion concerning the accuracy of the reproduction of a past propositional attitude (true or false). Section 8.2 criticizes the identity theory of memory. Section 8.3 sets fourth the thesis that for two diachronic content tokens to be memory-related the later one must be entailed by the earlier one. One of the consequences of this thesis is that it is possible that the content of a memory state is entertained for the first time at the time of recollection. Section 8.4 compares and contrasts this position with Plato's theory of recollection whereby all learning is nothing but remembering. Section 8.5 addresses the question of when two diachronic attitude tokens are of the same kind and proposes a functionalist answer. Section 8.6 spells out the notion of attitude-similarity in terms of sameness of direction of fit and polarity.

8.1 TRUTH VS. AUTHENTICITY

'S remembers that p' entails that p is the case. If not-p, then S may think he remembers that p, but cannot actually remember that p. As was explained in the beginning (cf. pp. 38–9), a memory state must accord not only with objective reality but also with one's initial perception of reality. I can, for instance, remember that Brutus stabbed Caesar in 44 BC only if it is the case that Brutus stabbed Caesar in 44 BC *and* if I previously thought that Brutus stabbed Caesar in 44 BC. The direction of fit of memory is twofold: mind-to-world as well as mind-in-the-present-to-mind-in-the-past. Just as the faithful reproduction of a false proposition doesn't qualify as memory, neither does the inaccurate reproduction of a true proposition. For this reason there needs to be a content condition and past representation condition in addition to the truth-condition.

Memory reports can be false for a number of different reasons. The falsity of a memory report can be due to the malfunctioning of the memory process. If you inform me at t_1 that Brutus stabbed Caesar in 44 BC and if, when asked at t_2 'What year did Brutus stab Caesar?' I respond '43 BC' the mistake (presumably) lies in the memory process. Sometimes, however, a memory report is false despite the fact that the memory process functions properly. Consider the following example by G. E. M. Anscombe (1981*a*: 105–6). Someone mistakes a wax dummy for a person. Later on, he claims 'I remember that I saw a person'. This person's memory claim is false, but it is not his memory that is at fault, for it has no influence over whether the propositions fed into it are veridical.

Another source of blameless memory failures is slow switching. Suppose S has recently been switched from Earth to Putnam's imaginary planet Twin Earth and hasn't yet acquired the *twater* concept. He sees a glass on his kitchen table containing some clear liquid, wonders what liquid it might be, and then remembers having filled the glass with 'water'. S claims to remember that the glass contains water. The Earthian glass was indeed filled with H_2O but since, in the meantime, S has been whisked from Earth to Twin Earth, he is now facing the Twin Earthian counterpart of the Earthian water glass. The Twin Earthian glass contains XYZ. Thus S's memory claim to the effect that the glass in front of him contains water is false despite the memory process having worked flawlessly.

Granted that the memory process functions properly, if the proposition fed into it was true at t_1 and if there are no external circumstances changing the truth value of the proposition between t_1 and t_2, then, by and large, the proposition generated by the memory process at t_2 is true as well.[1] The memory process has no influence over whether the stored propositions are true or false;[2] but it does have some bearing upon whether the truth values change during storage. The memory process cannot make the stored contents true but it can help to preserve the truth of stored contents.

Truth preservation is not the primary function of memory. In the first instance, memory is meant to preserve content rather than truth. Yet by faithfully preserving contents the faculty of memory goes some way toward ensuring that the recalled contents are veridical, if the past contents were veridical. If there are no external circumstances changing the truth values of the retained contents and if the contents fed into the memory process are veridical, then truth preservation is a gratuitous by-product of content preservation.

The criterion for content preservation is the content condition. The content condition states that for a representation at t_2 that p, to be memory-related to a representation at t_1 that p*, p must be the same as, or similar to p*:

(1) p is identical with, or sufficiently similar to, p*.

(In the case of introversive memory it is the embedded content of the representation at t_2 that must match the content at t_1.) The content condition (1) has been revised in light of the pastist externalist account of memory set forth in section 6.3. The content condition now reads:

(1') p and p* supervene on the same environmental conditions at t_1 or p and p* are sufficiently similar.

---

[1] The proviso 'by and large' is meant to account for propositions whose verbal expression involves indexical referring expressions or tensed verbs. Frequently the truth value of such propositions changes while they are being retained in memory. Yet it is not clear that these changes in truth value are due only to 'external' factors rather than also to an 'internal' factor, namely the property of having context-relative truth-conditions.

[2] Two provisos: first, if what is stored in memory is the proposition *there is a proposition stored in memory*, then the memory process does make it the case that the stored proposition is true; second, in the case of introversive memory about factive attitudes there is a past truth-condition in addition to the present truth-condition. Not only does the content embedded in the memory content need to be true but so does the content of the past representation from which the memory state causally derives.

By ensuring that the content of the present representation and the content of the past representation are identical, or at least sufficiently similar, either version of the content condition increases the likelihood of the content tokens at t_1 and t_2 having the same truth value.

In the case of introversive memory it is not only the content component of a past propositional attitude that is retained but also its attitudinal component. The criterion for attitude preservation is the attitude condition which states:

> (2) The attitude that S represents at t_2 himself having taken (at t_1) toward p is the same as, or sufficiently similar to, the attitude that S took at t_1 toward p^*.

Since the term *content preservation* is too narrow to account for the preservative function of introversive memory I will drop this term and instead talk about *authenticity*. The way the term is used here, 'authenticity' denotes the property of a propositional attitude at t_2 to be related to a propositional attitude at t_1 in such a way that the content condition and the attitude condition are met. When a propositional attitude at t_2 meets both conditions, we may say it is an authentic reproduction (extroversive memory) or an authentic metarepresentation (introversive memory), respectively, of the propositional attitude at t_1.

Authenticity doesn't guarantee truth. Unless the content of the past representation from which the seeming memory state causally derives, p^*, was true at t_1 and remains true through t_2, the content of the seeming memory state at t_2 may be false. That is why memory is governed not only by the authenticity conditions $(1')$ and (2) but also by the truth-condition.

There is one kind of memory, however, that demands the (embedded) content to be only authentic not veridical: introversive memory about non-factive attitudes. In the case of introversive memory about non-factive attitudes the content embedded in the memory content, p, must be the same as, or sufficiently similar to, the content of the past representation, p^*, from which the memory states causally derives. Yet whether p or p^* are true is irrelevant to the truth of this type of remembering. For to remember having believed that p is to remember what attitude I had to p, not whether p is true.

Since introversive memory about factive attitudes requires truth *and* authenticity, it is more error-prone than introversive memory about non-factive attitudes which requires only authenticity. The following example adapted from Wolfgang von Leyden (1961: 60) illustrates the point: S witnesses a riot on the market square and thinks erroneously that it is a stage setting for a film. He takes himself to be seeing a setting for a film and later reports having seen a setting for a film at that time. Since there was no film setting, S cannot have seen a film setting and, consequently, cannot remember that he saw a film setting. The introversive memory claim 'I saw a setting for a film' is false. Yet it is not his memory but the original perception that is at fault; it is, as Leyden (Ibid.: 62) puts it, 'the inheritance of a mistake, not a mistake of inheritance'. S could rectify his memory claim by substituting a non-factual verb for 'to see' as in 'It seemed to me as if I saw a setting for a film' or 'I thought I saw a setting for a film'.

8.2 AGAINST THE IDENTITY THEORY OF MEMORY

Content condition (1′) and attitude condition (2) fly in the face of the standard view in philosophy whereupon our memory is nothing but a passive device for registering, storing, and reproducing information. As R. F. Harrod (1942: 49) once put it, 'the memory must be in some sense a copy of the thing remembered'. If I write 'Brutus stabbed Caesar' on a piece of paper and run it through a photocopier, I end up with two distinct inscription-tokens that have the same content. The conception according to which memory is like a photocopier producing duplicates of past propositional attitudes is committed to what I label the *identity theory of memory*, that is, the thesis that for a propositional attitude token at t_2 to stand in a memory-relation to a propositional attitude token at t_1, the contents of both tokens must be type-identical.[3]

An early advocate of the identity theory is Plato. In the *Theaetetus* Plato compares memory to a block of wax in which the perceptions are imprinted in the same way 'as we might stamp the impression of a seal ring. Whatever is rubbed out or has not succeeded in leaving an

---

[3] What I call the 'identity theory of memory' has been given various names: 'the copy theory of memory' (Brewer 1988: 26), 'the reappearance hypothesis' (Neisser 1967: 280–4), and 'passivism' (Casey 2000: 15). In my (2008: 144–6) I have called the identity theory the 'xerox model of memory'.

impression we have forgotten and so do not know' (191c8–e). The wax tablet metaphor is taken up by Aristotle in *De Memoria* (450a 28–32):

It is clear that one must think of the affection which is produced by means of perception in the soul and in that part of the body which contains the soul, as being like a sort of picture, the having of which we say is memory. For the change that occurs marks in a sort of imprint, as it were, of the sense-image, as people do who seal things with signet rings.[4]

Also Sigmund Freud (1961) was fascinated by the power of the wax tablet metaphor when he speculated on the 'mystic writing pad' as a model of the memory process. This child's toy allows writing to be erased by merely pulling free a covering sheet from another layer to which it adheres when pressed—the modern wax tablet.

Augustine (1991: 191) calls the memory the 'belly of the mind' and compares it to 'a large and boundless inner hall', a 'storehouse', and a 'vast cave' within which 'the images of things perceived' are laid away, to be 'brought forth when there is need for them'. Similarly, David Hume (2000a: 12) maintains that memory is about the re-experiencing of mental images that are copies of the original experience. He goes so far as to say that 'memory preserves the original form, in which its objects were presented, and that wherever we depart from it in recollecting any thing, it proceeds from some defect or imperfection in that faculty'. The conception of memory as a purely passive process of information storage is still very much with us today. It is a tacit assumption behind virtually all spatial analogies used to shed light on human memory.[5]

The identity theory of memory is at odds with what science tells us about the workings of memory. Neurobiologists have discovered that long-term memories are not etched in a wax-tablet-like stable form. Instead, long-term memories are sustained by a miniature molecular machine that must run constantly to maintain the memories; jamming this machine can erase long-term memories (cf. Shema, Sacktor, and

---

[4] I do not mean to suggest that Plato and Aristotle endorsed the identity theory of memory. The wax tablet metaphor is propounded to clarify the relationship between perceiving and knowing without implying that this is all that is involved in memorizing and recall. Nevertheless, the metaphor does illustrate the dangers of being captured by the attraction of a picture. Most classical and medieval writers seem to have been satisfied with the wax tablet as a metaphor for memory.

[5] Colville-Stewart (1975) and Rose (1992: 60–99) examine the history of the storehouse metaphor of memory. For a review of memory metaphors in cognitive psychology see Roediger (1980).

Dudai 2007). Moreover, cognitive psychology disproved the identity theory by showing that memory is not only a passive device for reproducing contents but also an active device for processing stored contents. The psychologist Susan Engel (1999: 6) explains:

Research has now shown that . . . retrieval is almost always more a process of construction than one of simple retrieval. One creates the memory at the moment one needs it, rather than merely pulling out an intact item, image, or story. This suggests that each time we say or imagine something from our past we are putting it together from bits and pieces that may have, until now, been stored separately. Herein lies the reason why it is the rule rather than the exception for people to change, add, and delete things from a remembered event.

And the psychologists Elizabeth Loftus and Katherine Ketcham (1991: 20) declare:

Memories don't just fade, as the old saying would have us believe; they also grow. What fades is the initial perception, the actual experience of the events. But every time we recall an event, we must reconstruct the memory, and with each recollection the memory may be changed—colored by succeeding events, other people's recollections or suggestions, increased understanding, or a new context.

To be sure, there is a difference between saying, as I do, that memory need not amount to the exact reproduction of some previously recorded content and saying, as Engel, Loftus, and Ketcham do, that, as a matter of principle, memory constructs rather then reproduces previously recorded contents. Engel and other proponents of constructivism about memory (such as Craig R. Barclay, William F. Brewer, and Ulric Neisser) seem to lose sight of the factivity and authenticity constraints on memory. By overemphasizing the reconstructive nature of memory the distinction between memory and confabulation becomes blurred. Yet constructivists are right to maintain that the fact that our memory not only stores but also processes the incoming information should not be regarded as an abnormal lapse of an otherwise reliable cognitive faculty, but as part of the very function of memory. As a result of such information processing, the content of a memory state may differ, to some degree, from the content of the original representation.

Though there has always been a minority view according to which memory involves the creative transformation of content rather than its reduplication, it has not been until recent times that full-fledged 'activist' models of memory have been developed. Ancestors of activist models are Freud's (1964) concept of interpretation and construction in psychoanalysis; Frederic Bartlett's (1964: 197–214) theory of the evolving character of memories as these are reconstructed by various memorial schemata; and Jean Piaget and Bärbel Inhelder's (1975: 1–26) proposal whereupon memories directly reflect changing schemes of accommodation to and assimilation of experience.

The content condition and the attitude condition reject the identity theory by allowing that a memory content is not type-identical with the relevant past content but only similar to it. Each condition gives rise to two questions. Taking the content condition first these questions are: what does it mean for two diachronic content tokens to be of the same type? Second, to what extent may two diachronic content tokens differ from one another and one of them still count as sufficiently similar to the other so as to be memory-related to it? The analogous questions regarding the attitude condition are: what does it mean for two diachronic attitude tokens to be of the same type? And what are the criteria for the similarity of psychological attitudes?

Of these four questions only the first one concerning identity conditions for content tokens has been addressed so far. Section 6.3 proposed a pastist externalist criterion for content identity: two content tokens are type-identical if they supervene on the same conditions in the subject's physical and social environment. The question concerning the identity of attitude tokens will be dealt with in section 8.5. The basic idea is that psychological attitudes are individuated by their functional roles and that attitude tokens are the same if their functional roles are the same.

The lion's share of this chapter is devoted to the question as to what extent two propositional attitude tokens may differ from one another—both with respect to their contents and their attitudinal components—and one of them still be memory-related to the other. Given that remembering doesn't require the duplication of past propositional attitudes, what is the permissible range of aberration between a propositional attitude and the memory thereof? What is the margin of error regarding content reproduction (extroversive memory) and content and attitude representation (introversive memory)? What are the bounds of authenticity with respect to remembering?

Saying that memory doesn't require identity, but only similarity, of past and present attitudes and contents isn't very informative since everything is similar to everything else. It is only within a context that claims concerning the similarity of things are meaningful. But even granting the relativity of similarity, it is not clear that the notion of similarity has explanatory value. There are three considerations that suggest that *similarity* is an idle notion. The first problem concerns the specification of the frame of reference. With a bit of imagination, for any two things, one can find a standard with respect to which they are alike. Any two things share *some* property (just as any two things are joint members of any number of sets). Second, assuming that *similarity* isn't an empty notion, it cannot be just any property that constitutes similarity. 'It must be,' as W. V. O. Quine (1969: 118) maintains, 'that properties are shared only by things that are significantly similar.' Following this proposal, the notion of similarity turns out to be circular: *similarity* presupposes the notion of a frame of reference which itself presupposes the notion of similarity. Third, once the frame of reference of a statement about similarity is specified, similarity has no role to play; the frame of reference does all the work. For example, if we say of two things that they are similar with respect to their shared property of, for instance, being green, what we say is nothing more than that they have the property of being green in common; the notion of similarity can be removed without loss. Statements of the form 'A is similar to B' in respect of C are reducible to statements of the form 'A and B share property C' (Goodman 1972: 444).

Because of these strictures on similarity, Quine (1969: 121) speaks of the 'dubious scientific standing' of this notion, and notes that 'it is a mark of maturity in a branch of science that the notion of similarity . . . finally dissolves, so far as it is relevant to that branch of science'. Goodman (1972: 437) uses even harsher terms. He declares that 'similarity . . . is a pretender, an imposter, a quack. It has, indeed, its place and its uses, but is more often found where it does not belong, professing powers it does not possess'. His conclusion is that while statements of similarity 'are still serviceable in the streets' they 'cannot be trusted in the philosopher's study' (ibid. 446).

The notion of similarity employed both in the content condition (1′) and the attitude condition (2) must be replaced by notions whose explanatory value is beyond dispute. In section 8.3 the notion of content similarity will be explicated in terms of the entailment relation. And in section 8.6 the notion of attitude-similarity will be defined in terms of sameness of direction of fit and polarity.

8.3 AUTHENTIC CONTENT REPRESENTATION

The issue at hand is to determine to what extent two diachronic tokens of propositional content may differ from one another and one of them still be memory-related to the other. My thesis is that two content tokens are memory-related if the later one is an entailment of the earlier one. For two diachronic content tokens to be suitably similar, in the sense of the content condition (1'), the present (embedded) content must be entailed by the past content. Entailment is the mark of authenticity. I shall label this thesis the *entailment thesis*:

> *Entailment Thesis*: A propositional attitude token at t_2 is memory-related to a propositional attitude token at t_1 only if the (embedded) content of the token at t_2 is entailed by the content of the token at t_1.

(The parenthetic addendum 'embedded' accounts for introversive memory. For in the case of introversive memory it is the content that is embedded in the memory content that must be an entailment of the past content.) To illustrate the entailment thesis consider this case. A while back, at t_1, you came to believe that Caesar was assassinated by Brutus. Today, at t_2, all you can remember is that Caesar died of unnatural causes—you have forgotten the circumstances of his death. Notwithstanding the fact that *Caesar was assassinated by Brutus* and *Caesar died of unnatural causes* are different propositions, it is natural to suppose that the latter belief is memory-related to the former one—provided, of course, the other memory conditions are met. The reason the discrepancy between the two content tokens doesn't and shouldn't prevent us from granting memory, I suggest, is that the proposition *Caesar died of unnatural causes* is entailed by the proposition *Caesar was assassinated by Brutus*.

Analyzing the notion of content similarity in terms of the entailment relation is perfectly compatible with the factivity constraint on memory. The reason is that the entailment relation preserves truth. If q is entailed by p, and if p is true, so is q. Thus if *Caesar was assassinated by Brutus* is true, so is *Caesar died of unnatural causes*. Provided that the contents fed into the memory process are veridical and that there are no external circumstances changing the truth values of the contents while they are in storage, the entailment thesis ensures that the retrieved contents are veridical as well. And since each proposition entails itself the entailment thesis also allows for cases where our memory works like a photocopier producing duplicates of past propositional attitudes.

As was explained before (cf. pp. 38–9, 74, 150–1), the authentic reproduction of a proposition that was false at the time it was initially entertained but which, in the meantime, has become true may qualify as memory. So there are cases of memory where the content of the propositional attitude token at t_1 is false but the entailed content of the propositional attitude token at t_2 is true. Consider this example. At t_1 you come to believe that the library's copy of Caesar's *Commentarii de Bello Gallico* has been checked out by S. The belief is false at the time. Unbeknownst to you, S checks out Caesar's *Commentarii* at t_2. At t_3 you seem to remember on the basis of your belief at t_1 that S has borrowed a book by a Roman statesman. Notwithstanding the fact that the propositional content of the representation at t_1 wasn't true, I see no reason to deny that you may genuinely remember what you seem to remember. Yet so as not to add unnecessary complications I will prescind from cases where the truth value of a proposition changes while it is retained in memory.

Before I continue to explain the entailment thesis and add some bells and whistles I need to consider an objection. A critic might agree that the belief at t_2 that Caesar died of unnatural causes can be memory-related to the belief at t_1 that Caesar was assassinated by Brutus while, at the same time, holding on to the identity theory of memory. The idea is that when you believed at t_1 that Caesar was assassinated by Brutus you also, though only implicitly or dispositionally, believed that Caesar died of unnatural causes. If you implicitly or dispositionally believe the entailments of the propositions you explicitly or occurrently believe, then one can insist that identity of contents is a necessary condition of memory and still accept that the content of a memory belief hasn't been entertained before the time of recollection. According to the revised identity theory, the content of a memory belief need not match the content of an explicit or occurrent past belief as long as it matches the content of an implicit or dispositional past belief.

In response to this objection I would like to make three points. First, the revised identity theory contradicts findings in cognitive psychology whereupon it is the function of memory to not only store but also process information. Second, the revised identity theory cannot explain the authenticity of *inferential* memory. When some of the information needed to infer the memory belief has been acquired only shortly before the act of remembering, then it is implausible to suppose that the agent implicitly or dispositionally believed all along what he now inferentially remembers. The entailment thesis, by contrast, affords an explanation of the authenticity constraint on both non-inferential and inferential memory. More on this below. Third, the revised identity theory cannot account for all instances of *non-inferential* memory. There are cases of non-inferential memory where there is no good reason for attributing to the agent a dispositional belief about p until he remembers p. A case in point is the kidnap example discussed before (cf. pp. 88–90). A proponent of the revised identity theory might try to explain cases like the kidnap example in terms of the agent having implicitly believed p. But since implicit beliefs are not actually present in the mind—since they are not tokenings in the belief box—they are doomed to be causally inert (cf. pp. 28–30). Implicit beliefs cannot give rise to memory traces. Thus the revised identity theory forces us to reject the trace theory of memory causation. Surely this is too high a price to pay.

Let's get back to the entailment thesis. Analyzing *entailment* in terms of the material implication gives rise to a number of well-known problems.[6] Since any conditional with a false antecedent is true (*ex falso quod libet*) and any conditional with a true consequent is true, the following formulas are true even though they strike common intuition as questionable or even downright wrong: (p → (q → p)), (p → (~p → q)), (~p → (p → q)), ((p ∧ ~p) → q), (p → (q ∨ ~q)). So '*The moon is made of green cheese* implies *Caesar was assassinated by Brutus*' is true and so is '*The moon is made of green cheese* implies *Caesar was not assassinated by Brutus.*' By extension, any contradiction implies anything (*ex contradictione quod libet*) and any tautology is implied by anything whatsoever. These problems are known as the *paradoxes of material implication*, though they don't elicit logical contradictions. Given these paradoxes, the notion of entailment employed in the entailment thesis should not be understood along the lines of the material implication. The material implication is too liberal to provide a plausible account of the authenticity of memory.

One could try to get around these paradoxes by interpreting the entailment thesis along the lines of C. I. Lewis's (1918) notion of *strict implication*: p strictly implies q if it is not possible that p is true and q is false. Possibility is invoked to clarify the notion of entailment. The statement '~◇(*The moon is made of green cheese* & ~(*Caesar was assassinated by Brutus*))' is false since one can easily imagine a world

---

[6] The terms 'to entail' and 'to imply' are used interchangably here.

where the moon is made of cheese and Caesar wasn't assassinated by Brutus. The notion of strict implication is more restrictive than that of material implication and seems to do a better job of expressing indicative conditionals. However, there are paradoxes of strict implication that are as vexing as those of material implication: '$\sim \Diamond$(*The moon is made of green cheese* & $\sim(2 + 2 = 4)$)', though counterintuitive, is true because $2 + 2 = 4$ holds in all possible worlds. One could try to avoid the paradoxes of strict implication by excluding necessary and impossible propositional contents from the scope of the entailment thesis. But this solution is at best ad hoc. For there are no independent reasons to suppose that the standard of similarity between necessary propositional contents is any different from the standard of similarity between contingent propositional contents.

What is unsettling about these paradoxes is that in each of them the antecedent is thematically irrelevant to the consequent. Since the entailment thesis allows for some far-fetched entailments of one's past thoughts to count as instances of memory it seems to go against the spirit of condition (1'). *The moon is made of green cheese* has nothing to do with *Caesar was assassinated by Brutus*. There is a lack of relevance. Consider another example. Given the physical conditions of Earth, the proposition that Caesar was assassinated implies the proposition that air molecules moved. Yet the thought that air molecules moved can hardly count as an authentic representation of one's thought that Caesar was assassinated. And so it seems that we need to impose a limit on how far removed a propositional content may be from its implicandum for it to qualify as an authentic representation of the implicandum.

To rule out cases in which the (embedded) content of the propositional attitude at t_2 is on a completely different topic than that of the content of propositional attitude at t_1 we seem to need a *relevant* notion of entailment along the lines of Alan Anderson and Nuel Belnap's (1975) relevance logic. According to Anderson and Belnap, p is relevant to q if and only if q can be inferred from (not just under) p; that is, if and only if p could be used in a deductive argument of q from p. For instance, they reject p $\rightarrow$ (q $\rightarrow$ q) because p may be irrelevant to (q $\rightarrow$ q) in the sense that p is not used in arriving to (q $\rightarrow$ q). In order to infer q from p it is necessary that p and q have some common meaning content. Since Anderson and Belnap think that in propositional logic commonality of meaning is carried by commonality of propositional variables, they conclude that p and q should share at least one propositional variable. The variable-sharing constraint forces the antecedent and the consequent to share some content, for then they are, in part, both about at least one or two or more propositions; they cannot be absolutely semantically irrelevant to one another.

Taking for granted that the antecedent and the consequent must have some common meaning content, it might be thought that the entailment thesis is still too liberal. *Caesar was assassinated in 44 BC* relevantly entails that *Calpurnia became a widow in 44 BC*. But, a critic might argue, the belief that Calpurnia became a widow can hardly count as an authentic representation of one's past belief to the effect that Caesar was assassinated.

The problem with this objection is that it fails to countenance memory based on inferential reasoning, or *inferential memory* (cf. p. 25). Inferential reasoning is (conscious or subconscious) reasoning that is based on additional premisses that are evidence for its conclusion, that entail its conclusion, or that make its conclusion plausible. While the belief that Calpurnia became a widow cannot qualify as *non-inferential* memory of the belief that Caesar was assassinated, it can meet the conditions for *inferential* memory. Provided you know about Caesar's third marriage, you are in a position to derive *Calpurnia became a widow in 44 BC* from *Caesar was assassinated in 44 BC*. By contrast, if you believe that Caesar was assassinated, you *eo ipso* believe that Caesar died of unnatural causes—no additional information is needed.

Other putative counterexamples to the entailment thesis are tautological implications such as these: $((p \rightarrow q) \land p) \rightarrow q$ [modus ponens], $((p \rightarrow q) \land \sim p) \rightarrow \sim q$ [modus tollens], $((p \lor q) \land \sim p) \rightarrow q$ [disjunctive syllogism], and $((p \rightarrow q) \land (q \rightarrow r)) \rightarrow (p \rightarrow r)$ [transitivity]. Consider modus ponens. At t_1 you came to believe that if p, then q and p. At the time you didn't realize that what you believe entails q. At t_2 you put two and two together and claim to have believed at t_1 that q. According to the entailment thesis, your second-order judgment at t_2 qualifies as an instance of introversive memory. Yet a critic might object that you cannot remember at t_2 that you believed at t_1 that q. The reason you cannot remember this is that it is not true. You did not believe q, though, of course, you could have believed it had you not failed to draw a deduction from what you in fact believed.

This objection, like the previous one, loses sight of the fact that the entailment thesis applies to both non-inferential and inferential memory. When you claim to remember at t_2 that you believed at t_1 that q and when, what you in fact believed at the time was $((p \rightarrow q) \land p)$, you are using the verb 'to remember' in an elliptical sense. When made aware of the facts, you would presumably agree to substitute for the statement 'I remember that I believed at t_1 q' something like the conjunctive statement 'I believed at t_1 that $((p \to q) \wedge p)$ and now (at t_2) I know that this entail q'. The statement 'I remember that I believed at t_1 q' is an ellipsis, the meaning of which is given by the conjunctive statement. The first conjunct expresses what you in fact believed, the second conjunct expresses the new information (cf. sect. 3.5). It is a strength of the entailment thesis, rather than a weakness, that it can account not only for non-inferential but also for inferential memory.

Notwithstanding the variable-sharing constraint, the entailment thesis licences conjunction elimination $((p \wedge q) \to p))$ and disjunction introduction $(p \to (p \vee q))$. There is no doubt that the move from conjunctions to conjuncts accords with our intuitions regarding the memorial authenticity. Suppose you believed at t_1 the proposition *Caesar was assassinated and Brutus was the culprit*. At t_2 you still remember having believed (at t_1) that Caesar was assassinated but you can't recall whom you took to be the culprit. I reckon we would all agree that your second-order judgment at t_2 to the effect that you believed (at t_1) that Caesar was assassinated counts as memory—provided, of course, the other memory conditions are met.

Things might seem less straightforward when a disjunction is deduced from one of its disjuncts. Suppose you believed at t_1 that Caesar was assassinated. At t_2 you are not quite sure what you took to be Caesar's cause of death. You claim having held at t_1 the belief that Caesar was assassinated or he died of unnatural causes. Does this second-order judgment meet the intuitive criterion for introversive memory? Certainly. For though the second-order judgment may not be sufficiently specific to be of much use it is nonetheless true and contains *some* information about your past belief. The move from disjuncts to disjunctions yields inferential memory since there is information added to the original belief content.

Finally consider the substitution of coreferential expressions. It is generally assumed that memory reports ought to be understood *de dicto* (cf. pp. 26–7). Now suppose that at t_1 you came to believe that Caesar was assassinated. At t_2 you claim to have believed at t_1 that the husband of Calpurnia and author of the *Commentarii de Bello Gallico* was assassinated. Given the entailment thesis, your second-order judgment qualifies as an instance of inferential introversive memory. (Note that it doesn't matter whether you have known all along that Caesar was the husband of Calpurnia and the author of the *Commentarii de Bello Gallico* or whether you have only learned this since t_1.)

When restricted to non-inferential memory, the entailment thesis looks something like this:

> *Entailment Thesis for Non-Inferential Memory*: A propositional attitude token at t_2 is memory-related to a propositional attitude token at t_1 only if (i) the (embedded) content of the token at t_2 is entailed by the content of the token at t_1 and (ii) no additional premiss is needed or used by the agent to derive the (embedded) content of the token at t_2 from the content of the token at t_1.

The phrase 'is needed or used' in clause (ii) takes care of cases where someone needlessly incorporates additional steps. Even though no additional premisses are needed to derive, for instance, *Caesar died of unnatural causes* from *Caesar was assassinated by Brutus*, someone may nevertheless make use of such premisses. Whenever additional premisses are involved it is not a case of non-inferential memory.

Let's take stock. I have rejected the claim whereby a propositional attitude token at t_2 cannot stand in a memory-relation to a propositional attitude token at t_1 unless the contents of both tokens are type-identical. Rather than demanding identity of content, memory demands only that the (embedded) content token at t_2 be an entailment of the content token at t_1. So I propose replacing the original content condition (1'):

(1') p and p* supervene on the same environmental conditions at t_1 or p and p* are sufficiently similar,

by the following revised content condition (1''):

(1'') p and p* supervene on the same environmental conditions at t_1 or p is entailed by p*,

where 'entailed' is understood along the lines of relevance logic. In the case of non-inferential memory there is the further requirement that no additional premiss is needed or used by the agent to derive p from p*.

In section 7.6 we have seen that there are no non-inferential memory relations linking Earthian beliefs with their Twin Earthian counterparts. The reason is that an Earthian belief, by itself, doesn't entail the corresponding Twin Earthian belief, and *vice versa*. And insofar as the subject is unaware of his being switched, there are also no inferential memory relations linking an Earthian belief with the corresponding Twin Earthian belief. Inferential memory relations are possible only if the subject is aware of his having undergone slow switching and if he is able to simultaneously possess Earthian and Twin Earthian concepts.

8.4 MENO'S PARADOX

Given the entailment theory, it is possible that the content of a memory state is entertained for the first time at the time of recollection. Yet this claim contradicts the intuition that to remember a proposition one must have represented it before and that this is what distinguishes remembering something from learning it for the first time. So there is a seeming tension between, on the one hand, the intuition that the content of a memory state must have been represented before and, on the other hand, the thesis that a memory content may differ (to some degree) from the content of the original representation. On the former thesis, learning afresh and remembering are incompatible while, on the latter thesis, they may coincide.

One way of resolving the tension it to reduce learning to remembering. This is the platonic strategy. In the *Meno* Plato suggests that 'every branch of knowledge' (85e5–6) is grounded in recollection (or *anamnesis*). The basic idea is that the acquisition of knowledge is the recovery of what was once known but forgotten. No one ever acquires knowledge that was previously unpossessed by him. What appears to be learning something new is really recollecting something already known. As Plato says, 'learning and research are wholly recollection' (ibid. 81d4–5).

Recollection, according to Plato, posits the immortality of the soul and claims that embodied souls have existed previously. In their reincarnations, these souls have learned everything there is to know; but in the process of embodiment, the souls forget this knowledge. Proper *elenctic* investigation, however, can access the forgotten information and restore knowledge. This is Plato's description of the doctrine of recollection:

Seeing then that the soul is immortal and has been born many times, and has beheld all things both in this world and in the nether realms, she has acquired knowledge of all and everything; so that it is no wonder that she should be able to recollect all that she knew before about virtue and other things. For as all nature is akin, and the soul has learned all things, there is no reason why she should not, by remembering but one single thing—an act which men call learning—discover everything else, if we have courage and faint not in the search; since, it would seem, research and learning are wholly recollection. (*ibid.* 81c5–d6)

In a nutshell, all learning is remembering because the soul is immortal and because it retains all the knowledge of its previous reincarnations.

In Socrates's examination of an uneducated slave boy in the *Meno* (82a7–86b4), Plato attempts to provide us with an example of recollection in action. The slave boy is presented with the problem of constructing a square that is double a given square. Socrates claims he is not imparting information but only asking questions. The slave boy is producing his own beliefs. At first, his beliefs are false; but, still by questions, he is led on to understand his mistakes and to form true beliefs and eventually knowledge. The aim of this story is to show that by a method of systematic questioning it is possible to elicit in the slave boy knowledge of certain geometrical propositions. The fact that, without any previous instruction in geometry, the slave boy is able to come to know propositions in geometry is said to imply that this knowledge was in the soul before it was incarnated in this body. Instead of learning new propositions, the slave's soul is prompted by Socrates's questions to remember things it has known all along. Plato reckons that what is true of the slave boy is true of all of us and what is true of geometry is true of 'every branch of knowledge' (ibid. 85e5–6).

In the *Meno* the doctrine of recollection is put forward to escape the problem that our knowledge in some way anticipates itself (80d6–e6): in order to learn what we do not know, we must already know it; otherwise we could not know that we need to learn, could not know how and where to learn or what to learn, and could not know at the end that we had found what we were seeking to learn. On the other hand, if we do have knowledge before we learn, learning is superfluous. Learning is thus either impossible or unnecessary. This paradox, called *Meno's Paradox* or the *Paradox of Inquiry,* assumes that the only choice is between complete knowledge and blank ignorance. The doctrine of recollection dissolves the paradox by distinguishing between implicit and explicit knowledge. Learning presupposes implicit knowledge and results in explicit knowledge.[7]

---

[7] There is considerable controversy about whether the doctrine of recollection is intended by Plato as a positive expression of his own views or whether it is a subtle refutation, in form of a *reductio,* of certain sophistic claims about the acquisition of knowledge (see e.g. Cobb 1973). The main reason to regard the doctrine of recollection with suspicion is that it does nothing to solve Meno's paradox. For even if it explains how the embodied soul learns in this

We saw that there is a tension between the intuition whereupon to remember a proposition one must have represented it before and the claim that the content of a memory state may differ (to some degree) from the content of the original representation. We also saw that this tension can be dissolved by following Plato in reducing learning to remembering. Yet it requires little reflection to see that the platonic doctrine of recollection is not compatible with the account of memory set forth in this study. First, the doctrine of recollection flies in the face of the naturalist interpretation of memory traces proposed in section 5.2. If memory traces are an essential component of memory causation and if traces are intracerebral occurrences, it follows that a disembodied mind (or soul) cannot retain the knowledge of its previous reincarnations. Second, though I concede that there are instances of learning that are instances of remembering I reject the view that 'learning [is] *wholly* remembering'. Not *all* learning is remembering. Learning and remembering coincide only when the memory content is entailed by something one has represented previously and when the memory state is suitably causally connected to the previous representation.

The view that one can remember a proposition one hasn't entertained before is a consequence of the rejection of the identity theory of memory. Thus we are faced with the choice between, on the one hand, endorsing the identity theory of memory and holding on to the idea that learning and remembering are incompatible or, on the other hand, rejecting the identity theory and maintaining that one can sometimes remember a proposition one hasn't entertained before. I choose the second alternative.

8.5 ATTITUDINAL IDENTITY

Inwardly remembering involves a twofold classification. Remembering that I believed that p involves remembering that the past state is about what I express by 'p' *and* remembering that the attitude I took toward p

life—what appears to be learning is nothing more than recollection of what the soul knew before it came into this life—Meno's paradox is posed in terms of the general possibility of learning. Thus the paradox immediately becomes applicable to the process by which the soul acquired knowledge prior to this life. If the doctrine of recollection were introduced to explain this learning process, we would fall into an infinite regress of recollections. So it seems that we need to posit an original learning which is not in terms of recollection.

was one of believing. The attitude condition for inwardly remembering reads:

(2) The attitude that S represents at t_2 himself having taken (at t_1) toward p is the same as, or sufficiently similar to, the attitude that S took at t_1 toward p^*.

After having examined to what extent two diachronic content tokens may differ from one another and one of them still count as sufficiently similar to the other so as to be memory-related to it we need to examine what it means for the representation of the attitudinal component to be authentic. When are two attitude tokens sufficiently similar in the relevant sense? But before we can attempt to come up with similarity conditions for psychological attitude tokens we need to address the question of when two diachronic attitude tokens are of the same kind.

Prima facie, one may say that the attitude a subject represents at t_2 himself having taken (at t_1) toward p is the same as the attitude he took at t_1 toward p^* only if the cognitive verb used at t_1 is the same as the cognitive verb used at t_2. If at t_1 S characterized his attitude toward p^* as 'to desire' and if he claims at t_2 having desired (at t_1) that p, then, and only then, S is accurately representing his past attitude. Given this proposal, the identity of diachronic attitude tokens supervenes on the sameness of the cognitive verb used by the agent to characterize these attitude tokens.

A little thought reveals that this account is not convincing. First, the proposed account of the identity of diachronic attitude tokens doesn't work for beliefs. The natural expression of the belief that p is simply 'p', not 'I believe that p'. For this reason S may speak the truth when he claims to remember at t_2 'I believed (at t_1) that p', even though at t_1 he did not use the cognitive verb 'to believe' to characterize his mode of presentation toward p^*. Second, we frequently misidentify our attitudes due to self-deception or lack of attention. Consider this example. At t_1 you are waiting in the lobby of a cinema. The film has already started but your friend has not yet arrived. Your friend is normally on time. You take yourself to be believing that you have a rendezvous at this cinema at this time and day. After ten minutes, at t_2, your belief dissolves into mere hope and while, for some time, you still think and sincerely say that you believe it, you are wrong about yourself. So as not to have to admit having made a mistake you deceive yourself by unconsciously misconstruing the attitude of your representation. Some time later, at t_3, you claim to remember having believed at t_2 that you had a rendezvous at this cinema at this time and day. Even though the same cognitive verb—'to believe'—is used at t_3 and t_2 to characterize the mode of presentation at t_2 it is questionable that we ought to grant you memory of your past attitude.

Another source of misidentification of attitudes, besides self-deception and lack of attention, is incomplete understanding of the cognitive verbs referring to attitudes. Content externalism has the consequence that one can have the concept F, or one can have beliefs to the effect that this is F, without knowing all, without knowing any, of the essential properties of Fs. As we have seen in section 6.1, Tyler Burge argues that one can have the concept *arthritis*, and believe that one has arthritis in one's thigh, without knowing what is essential to a disease being arthritis, without knowing that arthritis occurs only in joints.

Given that, as Burge (2007c: 106–7) claims, externalism applies to all concepts—maybe with the exception of some sensation concepts and certain logical concepts—attitude concepts too supervene on external factors of which the bearer of the concept may be ignorant. But if that is so one can imagine arthritis-like examples involving attitude concepts. Imagine an agent, S, who incompletely understands the term 'to believe'. S takes 'to believe', 'to suppose', 'to decide', and 'to consider' to be synonymous terms. In S's language community, however, 'to believe' means the mental act of placing trust or confidence in a person or thing, 'to suppose' means to assume something without reference to its being true or false, 'to consider' means to believe after deliberation, and 'to decide' means to pronounce a judgment. Despite S's confusion, content externalism seem committed to saying that the meaning of his word 'belief' need not differ from what the language community means by it. But then it is possible that S sincerely says at t_1 'I believe that p*', that he claims to remember at t_2 'I believed at t_1 that p', and that the memory claim is still false because the original identification of the attitude as a belief was incorrect.[8]

What this shows is that the identity of attitude tokens shouldn't be spelled out in terms of the sameness of the cognitive verbs used by the agent to characterize these attitudes. A more promising account of attitudes (going back to Aristotle) identifies them with functional roles. Functionalism has it that the defining feature of any type of

---

[8] In my (1996) I argue that, given content externalism, knowledge of one's occurrent contents is epistemically privileged while knowledge of one's occurrent attitudes is not. My argument is endorsed by Gibbons (2001).

attitude consists of its actual or potential causal relations to (1) distal (environmental) or proximal inputs, (2) other types of attitudes, and (3) behavioral outputs. Each attitude picks out a state with a distinctive collection of relations of types (1), (2), and or (3).[9] For example, the feeling of pain is a state that is often caused by damage to the body, it tends to produce a desire to get rid of that state, and tends to produce wincing, groaning, and so on. A belief, on the other hand, is a state normally resulting from perception or inference and giving rise to other beliefs or to behavior. Moreover, a belief state is a state that causally interacts with desires and actions in the way that state-of-the-art decision theory specifies, that causally interacts with memories and percepts in the way that state-of-the-art inductive logic specifies; and so on.

Alvin Goldman argues that functionalism about attitudes does not explain how a subject can determine which attitude he currently occupies. Knowing that one's attitude toward the proposition p is that of, say, believing is not a matter of knowing that it satisfies some complex causal and counterfactual condition that makes reference to many other of one's attitudes. 'There is a clear threat of combinatory explosion: Too many other internal states will have to be type-identified in order to identify the target state' (1993: 19). Goldman goes on to suggest that one identifies one's occurrent attitude as, say, a belief by noticing some qualitative property that all and only beliefs share. I am skeptical that there are any such qualitative properties. Fortunately, however, we need not concern ourselves with what is the basis on which we are able to tell whether a current state of ours is a desire rather than a belief, a hope rather a fear, etc.

According to functionalism about attitudes, the attitude a subject represents at t_2 himself having taken (at t_1) toward p is the same as the attitude he took at t_1 toward p^* only if the functional role of the attitude at t_1 is the same as the functional role of the attitude at t_2. The attitude condition (2) can be specified thus:

---

[9] This is a rather crude formulation of functionalism about attitudes. An important wrinkle in an adequate formulation of functionalism about attitudes is the counterfactual import of the relations among inputs, outputs, and other attitudes. Consider, for example, the functional role associated with desiring water. The kind of behavior the desire gives rise to depends, in part, on the kind of beliefs one holds. If one believes that there is a glass of water within arm's reach, the desire will cause one's arm to extend. Thus part of the functional role associated with the desire for water is the counterfactual property: if it were accompanied by this belief, the indicated behavior would occur.

(2′) The attitude that S represents at t_2 himself having taken (at t_1) toward p and the attitude that S took at t_1 toward p* are functionally identical or sufficiently similar.

Since, given content externalism, the correlation between attitudes and functional roles could be different in different environments, one can imagine slow switching scenarios with respect to attitude concepts. In order not to add unnecessary complications I will not explore this issue here.

8.6 AUTHENTIC ATTITUDE REPRESENTATION

Just as memory doesn't require that the present (embedded) content be the same as the past content it doesn't require that the psychological attitude ascribed to one's former self be the same as the attitude one took toward the proposition in question. Both attitudes need to be only sufficiently similar. This raises the question of which features diachronic attitude tokens must share to count as sufficiently similar. What is the permissible range of aberration between the attitude identified in a memory report and the original attitude? In preparation for an answer to this question we must identify the criteria which allow us to classify different attitudes toward a proposition—direction of fit, factivity, factorability, and polarity.[10]

Hume (2000*a*: 266) famously contrasted desires with beliefs by claiming that a desire does not contain 'any representative quality, which renders it a copy of any other existence or modification'. The modern version of Hume's claim is that desires have a different direction of fit than beliefs. Beliefs aim to track the world and have a thetic direction of fit, while desires aim to impose themselves on the world and have a telic direction of fit. The direction of fit analysis of beliefs and desires has been given a descriptive and a normative interpretation. According to the descriptive interpretation, beliefs and desires actually play different functional roles and can be distinguished descriptively. Alternatively, it might be thought that beliefs and desires ought to play different functional roles. Preferring the descriptive reading, I follow

---

[10] Note that many of the verbs referring to psychological attitudes that take that-clauses as complements also allow for non-propositional constructions. For instance, one can be aware that Caesar is wearing a laurel wreath and one can be aware of Caesar's laurel wreath.

Lloyd Humberstone (1992) in understanding the distinction between thetic and telic directions of fit in terms of different second-order background intentions. An attitude that p counts as thetic if it is subject to the second-order background intention of only being possessed when p is the case. An attitude that p counts as telic if it is subject to the background intention of p being the case given that the attitude is possessed. Examples of thetic attitudes other than believing are knowing, remembering, inferring, and seeing. Examples of telic attitudes other than desiring are preferring, intending, and attempting.

Among attitudes with a thetic direction of fit some imply truth while others aim at truth but do not imply truth. Knowledge, for example, is factive in the sense that an utterance of 'S knows that p' is true only if p is the case. If not-p, then S might think he knows that p, but cannot actually know that p. Other factive thetic attitudes are remembering, learning, and seeing. Among non-factive thetic attitudes are believing, suggesting, and considering.

Some attitudes are simple while others are composed of simple ones. An example of a complex thetic attitude is knowledge that has belief as one of its components (cf. sect. 3.4). Intending is an example of a complex telic attitude. Intending a certain state of affairs A by performing an action of type B is usually broken down to having a desire for A and believing that in performing B one can bring about A. Belief and desire are commonly thought to be the basic attitudes to which all other attitudes can be reduced. To see that the reduction thesis is untenable consider the attitude of fear. Fearing that p requires believing that it is possible that p and wanting it to be the case that not p. Yet it is not the case that whenever belief and desire are combined in this way they add up to fear. Even though there are many attitudes that cannot be reduced to beliefs and desires all attitudes seem to contain a belief and a desire component.[11]

---

[11] Cf. Searle 1983: 29–36. Some philosophers are convinced that there is a single ur-attitude that underlies all others—the determinable of which all other attitudes are determinates. According to Descartes (1984: 17), thought—the way it is used in the cogito argument—is this ur-attitude. Descartes defines thought as 'everything that is within us in such a way that we are immediately aware of it. Thus all the operations of the will, the intellect, the imagination, and the senses are thoughts' (ibid. 113). The role 'thought' plays for Descartes, Price attributes to 'entertaining'. Price (1969: 192) describes the attitude of entertaining in this way: 'The entertaining of propositions is the most familiar of all intellectual phenomena. It enters into every form of thinking and into many of our conative and emotional attitudes as well. Indeed, one might be inclined to say that it is the basic intellectual phenomenon; so

Propositional attitudes can be classified according to their polarity as positive or negative. One's attitude toward something is positive (a pro-attitude) if one favors the thing or is favorably disposed toward it, negative (a con-attitude) if one views it unfavorably. Examples of positive attitudes are believing, hoping, suggesting, and desiring. Examples of negative attitudes are to deny, to doubt, to be afraid, and to disclaim. It is worth noting that one can have a positive attitude toward a proposition that expresses a state of affairs one dislikes (e.g. I believe that I face a threat) and one can have a negative attitude toward a proposition that expresses a state of affairs one cherishes (e.g. I doubt that my lottery ticket will win).

In light of the criteria for classifying attitudes, we can return to the question of which features tokens of different attitudes need to share to count as sufficiently similar for the purpose of introversive memory. Since attitudes don't entail one another in the same way propositions do the entailment approach proposed in section 8.3 will not work here. But the idea guiding the entailment approach, namely that memory allows for the dilution of informational content *is* applicable to the issue of attitude similarity.

Let's start with direction of fit. For a second-order judgment to qualify as introversive memory it must represent the past propositional attitude as having the very direction of fit it did in fact have. Identity of direction of fit across levels of cognition is a necessary but not a sufficient condition for introversive memory. Suppose that S *hoped* at t_1 that p. At t_2, he reports having *preferred* at t_1 that p. (A common reason for reporting a past hope as a preference is that it became, or turned out to be, more probable than one took it to be at the time.) Though hoping and preferring are different attitudes, since they share the thetic direction of fit the second-order judgment S expresses by saying 'I preferred at t_1 that p' might qualify as introversive memory.

Next consider factivity. In the case of non-inferential introversive memory, factive attitudes may be represented as non-factive ones but non-factive attitudes may not be represented as factive ones. If S *saw* at t_1 that p, he might non-inferentially remember at t_2 it having *seemed* to him at t_1 that p. But if it only *seemed* at t_1 to him that p, then he cannot non-inferentially remember at t_2 having *seen* at t_1 that p. The reason a factive attitude may be represented as a non-factive one, but not

fundamental that it admits of no explanation or analysis, but on the contrary all other forms of thinking have to be explained in terms of it.'

vice versa, is that the requirements on factive attitudes are stricter than those on non-factive ones. Inferential memory, however, also allows for, say, a past non-factive attitude being reported as a factive attitude, provided the subject has subsequently learned that the content of the past non-factive attitude was true.

The authenticity constraint on factorability is analogous to that on factivity. In the case of non-inferential memory, a complex attitude may be represented as being one of the simple attitudes of which it is composed, but a simple attitude may not be represented as being one of the complex attitudes of which it may be a component. Suppose S *knew* at t_1 that p. At t_2, he claims to have *believed* at t_1 that p. Granted that knowledge implies belief, one cannot deny S non-inferential memory on the basis of his violating the factivity constraint.[12] Yet if S *believed* at t_1 that p and if, at t_2, he claims to have *known* at t_1 that p this second-order judgment qualifies, at best, as inferential memory.

To remember one's past propositional attitudes one must correctly identify their polarity. If one *doubted* at t_1 that p and if one takes oneself at t_2 to have *believed* at t_1 that p, one clearly fails to remember one's intentional state at t_1. Similarly, if one *wanted* at t_1 that p and if, later on, one claims to remember having *disliked* at t_1 that p, one makes a false claim and fails to remember. Polarity allows for degrees of strength. The polarity of the past attitude may be reported as being less intense than it in fact was. Memory allows representing, say, a state of *hatred* as one of *dislike*, a state of *deep love* as one of *affection*, and a *conviction* as a *belief*.

In light of the sketched analysis of attitude similarity, I propose replacing the attitude condition for introversive memory (2′):

> (2′) The attitude that S represents at t_2 himself having taken (at t_1) toward p and the attitude that S took at t_1 toward p* are functionally identical or sufficiently similar,

by the following revised attitude condition (2″):

> (2″) The attitude that S represents at t_2 himself having taken (at t_1) toward p and the attitude that S took at t_1 toward p* are functionally identical or the two attitudes share the direction of fit and polarity.

---

[12] Representing a complex attitude as one of the simple attitudes of which it is composed violates the authenticity constraint when the simple attitude is factive and the complex attitude is non-factive. Yet it is doubtful whether there are any non-factive attitudes that have factive attitudes as their components.

In the case of non-inferential introversive memory there are further requirements. In addition to the attitudes having to share the direction of fit and polarity the following conjunction must be met: (1) the polarity of the attitude at t_2 is not more intense than that of the attitude at t_1, (2) if the attitude at t_2 is factive so is the attitude at t_1, and (3) the attitude at t_1 is not a component of the attitude at t_2, nor *vice versa*.

9

Concluding Remarks

Though this study is primarily a philosophical work its relevance is not confined to the discipline of philosophy. I will terminate the study by saying a few words about its wider relevance.

It is a well-known fact that memory is fallible. People who attempt to remember the past may inadvertently and unknowingly misremember events. Notwithstanding the fallibility of memory, frequently we have no other way of acquiring knowledge about the past than to rely on apparent memories. That is why (eyewitness) memory reports are among the kinds of evidence admissible in the court room. Though in recent years there has been a fierce debate concerning the accuracy and admissibility of 'recovered' memories of child sexual abuse (cf. Brainerd and Reyna 2005), the widespread practice of basing verdicts on 'normal' everyday memory reports has not been questioned. Considering the crucial role (eyewitness) memories play in many trials it is surprising that, by and large, judges and jurors worry only about whether an alleged memory report corresponds to an external, target event, but not whether the report originates from memory. We have seen, however, that not every veridical report about what one has witnessed in the past qualifies as a piece of memory. Truth is a necessary but not a sufficient condition for remembering. Besides the truth-condition there are the past and present representation conditions, the content condition, and the connection condition. Someone may accurately report having seen X but not *remember* having seen X because, at the time, he falsely took himself to be seeing Y. Another reason for why one might not *remember* having seen X even though one correctly reports having seen X is that the causal process connecting the past witnessing of X with the current representation about the past witnessing is not of the right kind. Thus one of the lessons to be learned from the philosophy of memory is that an alleged memory report might fail to be a report of memory even if it corresponds to external reality.

It might be argued that judges and jurors should confine themselves to trying to unveil the truth and that it would be pointless for them to try to investigate whether a seeming memory conforms to the conditions for remembering, other than the truth-condition. However, this objection overlooks that frequently we have to devise proxies for truth because the past events have ceased to exist and hence are not available for the memory report to be checked against. Frequently we have to judge whether a memory report mirrors external reality in the absence of external reality. When there is no independent corroborative evidence to establish whether a memory report is veridical we have to use other criteria. Psychological research has revealed eight general criteria we use to assess the accuracy of our own and other people's memory reports: (1) attributes of the rememberer (age, expertise, confidence, personality, etc.), (2) conversational context (e.g. court room, job interview, hypnotic session), (3) vividness and richness of recollection, (4) memorability of recalled event, (5) logical consistency of recollection, (6) the recollection's consistency over time, (7) congruence with other knowledge and experience, and (8) consensus with other people's memories (Ross 1997: 57–67). These truth criteria have considerable face validity but, of course, offer no guarantee of success.

The commonsensical criteria we use to assess the accuracy of our own and other people's memory reports should be appraised in light of the philosophical analysis of memory. Consider, for example, the arguments in sections 3.2 and 3.3 to the effect that memory implies neither belief nor justification. Provided these arguments are sound and valid, we have no reason to expect a strong positive correlation between the confidence of an eyewitness and the accuracy of his report. A witness may be accurate and tentative, inaccurate and confident. Or consider the trace theory proposed in section 5.4 whereupon a person may genuinely remember an event even though he needs strict prompting to be able to report the event. If the trace theory is correct, it would be unreasonable to presume that free recollections are necessarily more trustworthy and accurate than prompted recollections.

It is a commonplace among psychologists that a memory report can be veridical even if it is not an exact copy of the target stimulus. This raises the question to what degree a memory report must correspond to the target stimulus to count as accurate. Surprisingly psychologists don't have a general test of validity; instead they define accuracy in bounded terms. It is common to explain to research participants at the time of encoding what would count as an accurate answer. If the participants' goal is to remember, say, a list of words, then their accuracy is typically determined by their recall of the words. Yet the problem with the bounded definition of accuracy is that recall of features of an event that seem insignificant at the time of encoding is an important aspect of some eyewitness testimony (ibid. 54). Therefore, it would be most useful to have a general criterion for the validity of memory. If the authenticity criterion developed in sections 8.3 and 8.6 can be believed, as I think it can, the philosophy of memory can make an important contribution to the science of memory.

One of the goals of this investigation has been to explain what it is that qualifies a person's mental state as a memory rather than some other mental state such as dispositional belief. Since memory is not the only kind of mental state whose function it is to store representations, the challenge is to identify the specific properties of memories. The investigation set off from a rough and preliminary analysis of extroversive and of introversive memory. Now, at the end of the investigation, the preliminary analyses can be replaced by the final product. Let's start with extroversive memory in the first-person mode. At t_2 S remembers that p, where 'p' stands for an extroversive proposition in the first-person mode only if:

(1) S represents at t_2 that p,
(2) S represented at t_1 that p^*,
(3) p is true at t_2,
(4) p and p^* supervene on the same environmental conditions at t_1 or p is entailed by p^* (where 'entailed' is understood along the lines of relevance logic),
(5) S's representation at t_2 that p is causally connected to S's representation at t_1 that p^* such that

    (5.i) S's representation at t_1 that p^* and S's representation at t_2 that p are connected by a persisting memory trace or a contiguous series of memory traces,

    (5.ii) the memory trace is at least an inus condition for S's representation at t_2 that p. If the memory trace is an independently sufficient condition, it is not preempted by another independently sufficient condition,

    (5.iii) if S hadn't represented at t_1 that p^* he wouldn't represent at t_2 that p.

The five conditions may be labeled, respectively, the *present representation condition* (1), the *past representation condition* (2), the *truth-condition*

(3), the *content condition* (4), and the *connection condition* (5). The connection condition consists of the *trace condition* (5.i), the *causal strength condition* (5.ii), and the *counterfactual condition* (5.iii).

This way of stating the conditions for remembering is slightly misleading since some of them, strictly speaking, don't qualify as necessary conditions. We have seen that memory presupposes personal identity only as a matter of contingent fact, not as a matter of logical or conceptual necessity. Moreover, it is an empirical hypothesis rather than a conceptual truth that memory causation involves intracerebral occurrences referred to as 'traces'.

As it stands, this is an analysis of *inferential* extroversive memory. In the case of non-inferential extroversive memory there is a further requirement on the content condition (4): not only must p be entailed by p* but also it must not be the case that additional premisses are needed or are used by S to derive p from p*.

When the memory content involves an indexical reference to the rememberer, the veridicality constraint on memory demands that the rememberer is numerically the same as the one who had the original experience/representation. Yet when the proposition remembered is 'anonymous', in the sense that it doesn't contain an indexical reference to the bearer of the past representation, remembering is consistent with the bearer of the present representation not being the same as the bearer of the past representation. In the case of extroversive memory in the third-person mode the past representation condition (2) becomes:

(2′) Someone represented at t_1 that p*.

The connection condition (5) becomes:

(5′) S's representation at t_2 that p is causally connected to someone's representation at t_1 that p*.

The causal strength condition (5.i) becomes:

(5.i′) Someone's representation at t_1 that p* and S's representation at t_2 that p are connected by a persisting memory trace or a contiguous series of memory traces.

And the counterfactual condition (5.iii) becomes:

(5.iii′) If someone hadn't represented at t_1 that p*, then S wouldn't represent at t_2 that p.

Turning now to introversive memory, the following analysis has arisen from the investigation: S remembers at t_2 that he represented (at t_1) that p, where 'represented' is a placeholder for a factive attitude only if:

(1′) S represents at t_2 that he represented (at t_1) that p,

(2) S represented at t_1 that p^*,

(3) p is true at t_2,

(6) p^* is true at t_1,

(4) p and p^* supervene on the same environmental conditions at t_1 or p is entailed by p^* (where 'entailed' is understood along the lines of relevance logic),

(7) the attitude that S represents at t_2 himself having taken (at t_1) toward p and the attitude that S took at t_1 toward p^* are functionally identical or the two attitudes share the direction of fit and polarity,

(5″) S's representation at t_2 that he represented (at t_1) that p is causally connected to S's representation at t_1 that p^* such that,

    (5.i″) S's representation at t_1 that p^* and S's representation at t_2 that he represented (at t_1) that p^* are connected by a persisting memory trace or a contiguous series of memory traces,

    (5.ii′) the memory trace is at least an inus condition for S's representation at t_2 that he represented (at t_1) that p. If the memory trace is an independently sufficient condition, it is not preempted by another independently sufficient condition,

    (5.iii″) if S hadn't represented at t_1 that p^* he wouldn't represent at t_2 that he represented (at t_1) that p.

The analysis of introversive memory about factive attitudes contains the same conditions as the analysis of extroversive memory in the first-person mode, though some of these conditions are worded slightly differently. The only substantial difference is the introduction of the *past truth-condition* (6) and the *attitude condition* (7).

In the case of introversive memory about non-factive attitudes the analysis looks just like the one of introversive memory about factive attitudes except that the present truth-condition (3) and the past truth-condition (6) are missing.

As it stands, this is an analysis of *inferential* introversive memory. In the case of non-inferential introversive memory further requirements must be added to the content condition (4) and the attitude condition (7). The content condition (4) then becomes:

(4') p and p* supervene on the same environmental conditions at t_1 or the following conjunction is met: (i) p is entailed by p* (where 'entailed' is understood along the lines of relevance logic) and (ii) no additional premisses are needed or used by S to derive p from p*.

And the attitude condition (7) becomes:

(7') The attitude that S represents at t_2 himself having taken (at t_1) toward p and the attitude that S took at t_1 toward p* are functionally identical or the following conjunction is met: (i) the two attitudes share the direction of fit and polarity, (ii) the polarity of the attitude at t_2 is not more intense than that of the attitude at t_1, (iii) if the attitude at t_2 is factive so is the attitude at t_1, and (iv) the attitude at t_1 is not a component of the attitude at t_2, nor vice versa.

At the end of the discussion of remembering in *The Analysis of Mind*, Bertrand Russell (1995: 187) laments that 'this analysis of memory is probably extremely faulty, but I do not know how to improve it'. Given the intricate nature of memory, I should probably say the same thing about my own analysis of memory.

Bibliography

Adams, F., and Aizawa, K. (2008). *The Bounds of Cognition*. Oxford: Blackwell.
——and Clarke, M. (2005). 'Resurrecting the Tracking Theories', *Australasian Journal of Philosophy* 83: 207–21.
Altmann, E. M., and Gray, W. D. (2002). 'Forgetting to Remember: The Functional Relationship of Decay and Interference', *Psychological Science* 13: 27–33.
Anderson, A. R., and Belnap, N. D. (1975). *Entailment: The Logic of Relevance and Necessity*, vol. 1 Princeton: Princeton University Press.
Annis, D. B. (1980). 'Memory and Justification', *Philosophy and Phenomenological Research* 40: 324–33.
Anscombe, G. E. M. (1981*a*). 'The Reality of the Past', in her *Collected Philosophical Papers*, ii. *Metaphysics and Philosophy of Mind*. Oxford: Blackwell, 103–19.
——(1981*b*). 'Memory, "Experience" and Causation', in her *Collected Philosophical Papers*, ii. *Metaphysics and Philosophy of Mind*. Oxford: Blackwell, 120–30.
Aristotle (1972). *De Memoria et Reminiscentia*, in R. Sorabji, *Aristotle on Memory*. Providence: Brown University Press, 47–60. (Written 350 BC)
Armstrong, D. M. (1970). 'Does Knowledge Entail Belief?', *Proceedings of the Aristotelian Society* 70: 21–36.
Audi, R. (1994). 'Dispositional Beliefs and Dispositions to Believe', *Noûs* 28: 419–34.
——(1995). 'Memorial Justification', *Philosophical Topics* 23: 31–45.
——(1997). 'The Place of Testimony in the Fabric of Knowledge and Justification', *American Philosophical Quarterly* 34: 405–22.
——(2003). *Epistemology: A Contemporary Introduction to the Theory of Knowledge*. 2nd edn. London: Routledge.
Augustine (1991). *Confessions*, ed. H. Chadwick. Oxford: Oxford University Press. (Written AD 397–8.)
Ayer, A. J. (1956). *The Problem of Knowledge*. Harmondsworth: Penguin.
Bach, K. (1988). 'Burge's New Thought Experiment Back to the Drawing Room', *Journal of Philosophy* 85: 88–97.
——(1997). 'Do Belief Reports Report Beliefs?', *Pacific Philosophical Quarterly* 78: 215–41.
Baillie, J. (1997). 'Personal Identity and Mental Content', *Philosophical Psychology* 10: 323–33.
Bartlett, F. C. (1964). *Remembering: A Study in Experimental and Social Psychology*. Cambridge: Cambridge University Press.

Beauchamp, T. L., and Rosenberg, A. (1981). *Hume and the Problem of Causation*. New York: Oxford University Press.

Bernecker, S. (1996). 'Externalism and the Attitudinal Component of Self-Knowledge', *Noûs* 30: 262–75.

—— (1998). 'Self-Knowledge and Closure', in P. Ludlow and N. Martin (eds.), *Externalism and Self-Knowledge*. Stanford, Calif.: CSLI, 333–49.

—— (2000). 'Knowing The World By Knowing One's Mind', *Synthese* 123: 1–34.

—— (2001). 'Impliziert Erinnerung Wissen?', in T. Grundmann (ed.), *Erkenntnistheorie*. Paderborn: Mentis, 145–64.

—— (2004). 'Believing That You Know and Knowing That You Believe', in R. Schantz (ed.), *The Externalist Challenge*. Berlin: de Gruyter, 369–76.

—— (2008). *The Metaphysics of Memory*. Dordrecht: Springer.

—— (forthcoming). 'Representationalism, First-Person Authority and Second-Order Knowledge', in A. Hatzimoysis (ed.), *Self-Knowledge*. Oxford: Oxford University Press.

Betts, G. H. (1909). *The Distribution and Function of Mental Imagery*. New York: Teachers College.

Birch, C. (2000). 'Memory and Punishment', *Criminal Justice Ethics* 19: 17–31.

Boghossian, P. A. (1992*a*). 'Externalism and Inference', *Philosophical Issues* 2: 11–37.

—— (1992*b*). 'Reply to Schiffer', *Philosophical Issues* 2: 39–42.

—— (2008). 'Content and Self-Knowledge', in his *Content and Justification: Philosophical Papers*. Oxford: Clarendon, 139–58.

Bonanno, G. A. (2006). 'The Illusion of Repressed Memory', *Behavioral and Brain Sciences* 29: 515–16.

Bower, G. H. (1981). 'Mood and Memory', *American Psychologist* 36: 129–48.

—— (2000). 'A Brief History of Memory Research', in E. Tulving and F. I. M. Craik (eds.), *The Oxford Handbook of Memory*. Oxford: Oxford University Press, 3–32.

Brainerd, C. J., and Reyna, V. F. (2005). *The Science of False Memory*. Oxford: Oxford University Press.

Brandt, R. (1955). 'The Epistemological Status of Memory Beliefs', *Philosophical Review* 64: 78–95.

Bratman, M. E. (1999). 'Practical Reasoning and Acceptance in a Context', in his *Faces of Intention: Selected Essays on Intention and Agency*. Cambridge: Cambridge University Press, 15–34.

Brewer, W. F. (1988). 'Memory for Randomly Sampled Autobiographical Events', in U. Neisser and E. Winograd (eds.), *Remembering Reconsidered: Ecological and Traditional Approaches to the Study of Memory*. Cambridge: Cambridge University Press, 21–90.

Broad, C. D. (1925). *The Mind and Its Place in Nature*. London: Kegan Paul, Trench, Trubner.

Brown, J. (2000). 'Against Temporal Externalism', *Analysis* 60: 178–88.

—— (2004). *Anti-Individualism and Knowledge*. Cambridge, Mass.: MIT.

Brueckner, A. (1997). 'Externalism and Memory', *Pacific Philosophical Quarterly* 78: 1–12.

—— (2002). 'Williamson on the Primeness of Knowing', *Analysis* 62: 197–202.

Burge, T. (1988). 'Individualism and Self-Knowledge', *Journal of Philosophy* 85: 649–63.

—— (1998). 'Memory and Self-Knowledge', in P. Ludlow and N. Martin (eds.), *Externalism and Self-Knowledge*. Stanford, Calif.: CSLI, 351–70.

—— (2003). 'Memory and Persons', *Philosophical Review* 112: 289–337.

—— (2007*a*). 'Introduction', in his *Foundations of Mind: Philosophical Essays*, ii. Oxford: Oxford University Press, 1–31.

—— (2007*b*). 'Other Bodies', in his *Foundations of Mind: Philosophical Essays*, ii. Oxford: Oxford University Press, 82–99.

—— (2007*c*). 'Individualism and the Mental', in his *Foundations of Mind: Philosophical Essays*, ii. Oxford: Oxford University Press, 100–50.

—— (2007*d*). 'Cartesian Error and the Objectivity of Perception', in his *Foundations of Mind: Philosophical Essays*, ii. Oxford: Oxford University Press, 192–207.

—— (2007*e*). 'Wherein is Language Social?', in his *Foundations of Mind: Philosophical Essays*, ii. Oxford: Oxford University Press, 275–90.

Butler, J. (1896). *The Analogy of Religion Natural and Revealed to the Constitution and Course of Nature*, in *The Works of Joseph Butler*, i., ed. W. E. Gladstone. Oxford: Clarendon (First pub. 1736).

Butler, K. (1997). 'Externalism, Internalism, and Knowledge of Content', *Philosophy and Phenomenological Research* 57: 773–800. (First pub. 1736)

Casey, E. S. (2000). *Remembering: A Phenomenological Study*. 2nd edn. Bloomington: Indiana University Press.

Child, W. (2006). 'Memory, Expression, and Past-Tense Self-Knowledge', *Philosophy and Phenomenological Research* 73: 54–76.

Clark, A. (2005). 'Intrinsic Content, Active Memory and the Extended Mind', *Analysis* 65: 1–11.

—— (2007). 'Curing Cognitive Hiccups: A Defense of the Extended Mind', *Journal of Philosophy* 104: 163–92.

—— and Chalmers, D. (1998). 'The Extended Mind', *Analysis* 58: 7–19.

Cobb, W. S. (1973). 'Anamnesis: Platonic Doctrine or Sophistic Absurdity?', *Dialogue* 12: 604–28.

Cohen, L. J. (1992). *An Essay on Belief and Acceptance*. Oxford: Oxford University Press.

Collins, A. F., and Hay, D. C. (1992). 'Connectionism and Memory', in P. Morris and M. Gruneberg (eds.), *Theoretical Aspects of Memory*. 2nd edn. London: Routledge, 196–237.

Collins, J. M. (2006). 'Temporal Externalism, Natural Kind Terms, and Scientifically Ignorant Communities', *Philosophical Papers* 35: 55–68.

Colville-Stewart, S. B. (1975). 'Physico-Chemical Models of the Memory Storage Process: The Historical Role of Argument from Analogy'. Dissertation, University of London.

Connerton, P. (2008). 'Seven Types of Forgetting', *Memory Studies* 1: 59–71.

Cusmariu, A. (1980). 'A Definition of Impure Memory', *Philosophical Studies* 38: 305–8.

Dancy, J. (1985). *An Introduction to Contemporary Epistemology*. Oxford: Blackwell.

Dartnall, T. H. (2004). 'We Have Always Been . . . Cyborgs', *Metascience* 13: 139–48.

Davidson, D. (1980*a*). 'Actions, Reasons, and Causes', in his *Essays on Actions and Events*. Oxford: Clarendon, 3–20.

—— (1980*b*). 'Psychology as Philosophy', in his *Essays on Actions and Events*. Oxford: Clarendon, 229–39.

—— (1989). 'The Conditions of Thought', *Grazer Philosophische Studien* 36: 193–200.

—— (2001*a*). 'Knowing One's Own Mind', in his *Subjective, Intersubjective, Objective*. Oxford: Clarendon, 15–38.

—— (2001*b*). 'What is Present to the Mind?', in his *Subjective, Intersubjective, Objective*. Oxford: Clarendon, 53–68.

Davies, M. (1995). 'Reply to Searle: Consciousness and the Varieties of Aboutness', in C. Macdonald and G. Macdonald (eds.), *Philosophy of Psychology: Debates on Psychological Explanation*, i. Oxford: Blackwell, 356–92.

Dennett, D. C. (1978). *Brainstorms: Philosophical Essays on Mind and Psychology*. Cambridge, Mass.: MIT.

—— (1996). *Kinds of Minds: Towards an Understanding of Consciousness*. New York: Basic Books.

Descartes, R. (1984). *Meditations on First Philosophy*, in *The Philosophical Writings of Descartes*, ii ed. J. Cottingham, R. Stoothott, and D. Murdoch. Cambridge: Cambridge University Press. (First pub. 1641)

De Sousa, R. (1971). 'How to Give a Piece of Your Mind', *Review of Metaphysics* 25: 52–79.

Deutscher, M. (1989). 'Remembering "Remembering" ', in J. Heil (ed.), *Cause, Mind, and Reality*. Dordrecht: Reidel, 53–72.

Dretske, F. (1981). *Knowledge and the Flow of Information*. Cambridge, Mass.: MIT.

—— (2000). 'Entitlement: Epistemic Rights Without Epistemic Duties?', *Philosophy and Phenomenological Research* 60: 591–606.

—— (2005). 'The Case Against Closure', in M. Steup and E. Sosa (eds.), *Contemporary Debates in Epistemology*. Oxford: Blackwell, 13–26.

—— and Yourgrau, P. (1983). 'Lost Knowledge', *Journal of Philosophy* 80: 356–67.

Dummett, M. (1993). 'Testimony and Memory', in his *Seas of Language*. Oxford: Oxford University Press, 411–28.

Ebbinghaus, H. (1913). *Memory: A Contribution to Experimental Psychology*, trans. H. A. Ruger and C. E. Bussenius. New York: Teachers College. (First pub. 1885).

Eich, E., and Birnbaum, I. (1988). 'On the Relationship between the Dissociative and Affective Properties of Drugs', in G. M. Davies and D. M. Thomson (eds.), *Memory in Context: Context in Memory*. Chichester: John Wiley, 81–93.

Engel, S. (1999). *Context is Everything: The Nature of Memory*. New York: W. H. Freeman.

Evans, G. (1982). *The Varieties of Reference*. Oxford: Clarendon.

Falvey, K. (2003). 'Memory and Knowledge of Content', in S. Nuccetelli (ed.), *New Essays on Semantic Externalism and Self-Knowledge*. Cambridge, Mass.: MIT, 21–40.

Fernandez, J. (2006). 'The Intentionality of Memory', *Australasian Journal of Philosophy* 84: 39–57.

Field, H. (1978). 'Mental Representation', *Erkenntnis* 13: 9–61.

Flage, D. E. (1985). 'Hume on Memory and Causation', *Hume Studies* 10, Suppl.: 168–88.

Fodor, J. A. (1982). 'Cognitive Science and the Twin Earth Problem', *Notre Dame Journal of Formal Logic* 23: 98–118.

——(1987). *Psychosemantics: The Problem of Meaning in the Philosophy of Mind*. Cambridge, Mass.: MIT.

——(1990). *A Theory of Content and Other Essays*. Cambridge, Mass.: MIT.

Freud, S. (1961). 'A Note upon the "Mystic Writing-Pad" ', in *The Standard Edition of the Complete Works of Sigmund Freud*, xix. ed. J. Strachey, London: Hogarth, 227–32. (First pub. 1924.)

——(1964). 'Constructions in Analysis', in *The Standard Edition of the Complete Works of Sigmund Freud*, xxiii. ed. J. Strachey London: Hogarth, 257–69. (First pub. 1937.)

Furlong, E. J. (1951). *A Study in Memory: A Philosophical Essay*. London: Thomas Nelson.

Galton, F. (1883). *Inquiries into Human Faculty and its Development*. London: Macmillan.

Gardiner, J. M., and Richardson-Klavehn, A. (2000). 'Remembering and Knowing', in E. Tulving and F. I. M. Craik (eds.), *Oxford Handbook of Memory*. Oxford: Oxford University Press, 229–44.

Gauker, C. (1991). 'Mental Content and the Division of Epistemic Labour', *Australasian Journal of Philosophy* 69: 302–18.

Gertler, B. (2001). 'Introspecting Phenomenal States', *Philosophy and Phenomenological Research* 63: 305–28.

Gibbons, J. (1996). 'Externalism and Knowledge of Content', *Philosophical Review* 105: 287–310.

——(2001). 'Externalism and Knowledge of the Attitudes', *Philosophical Quarterly* 51: 13–28.

Gibberman, D. (2009). 'Who they are and what de se: Burge on quasi-memory', *Philosophical Studies* 144: 297–311.

Gillett, G. (1991). 'Multiple Personality and Irrationality', *Philosophical Psychology* 4: 103–18.

Ginet, C. (1975). *Knowledge, Perception, and Memory*. Dordrecht: Reidel.

——(1988). 'Memory Knowledge', in G. H. R. Parkinson (ed.), *The Handbook of Western Philosophy*. New York: Macmillan, 159–78.

Glover, J. (1988). *The Philosophy and Psychology of Personal Identity*. Harmondsworth: Penguin.

Glucksberg, S., and King, L. J. (1967). 'Motivated Forgetting Mediated by Implicit Verbal Chaining', *Science* 158: 517–19.

Goddon, D., and Baddeley, A. D. (1975). 'Context-Dependent Memory in Two Natural Environments: On Land and Under Water', *British Journal of Psychology* 66: 325–31.

Goethe, von J. W. (2006). *Autobiography: The Truth and Fiction Relating to my Life*, trans. J. Oxenford, intro. T. Carlyle. Charleston, SC: Bibliobazaar. (First pub. 1811–13.)

Goldberg, B. (1968). 'The Correspondence Hypothesis', *Philosophical Review* 77: 438–54.

Goldberg, S. C. (2005). '(Nonstandard) Lessons of World-Switching Cases', *Philosophia* 32: 93–129.

——(2007). 'Semantic Externalism and Epistemic Illusions', in id. (ed.), *Internalism and Externalism in Semantics and Epistemology*. Oxford: Oxford University Press, 235–52.

Goldman, A. I. (1979). 'What is Justified Belief?', in G. Pappas (ed.), *Justification and Knowledge*. Dordrecht: Reidel, 1–23.

——(1993). 'The Psychology of Folk Psychology', *Behavioral and Brain Sciences* 16: 15–28.

Goodman, N. (1972). 'Seven Strictures on Similarity', in his *Problems and Projects*. Indianapolis: Bobb-Merrill: 437–46.

Goodwin, D. W., Powell, B., Bremer, D., Hoine, H., and Stern, J. (1969). 'Alcohol and Recall: State Dependent Effects in Man', *Science* 163: 1358.

Grice, H. P. (1941). 'Personal Identity', *Mind* 50: 330–50.

Hacking, I. (1995). *Rewriting the Soul: Multiple Personality and the Sciences of Memory*. Princeton: Princeton University Press.

Halbwachs, M. (1992). 'The Social Framework of Memory', in *On Collective Memory*, ed. and trans. L. A. Coser (Chicago: Chicago University Press, 37–189. (First pub. 1925.)

——(1980). *The Collective Memory*, trans. F. J. Ditter and V. Y. Ditter intro. M. Douglas. New York: Harper. (First pub. 1950.)

Hark, M. ter (1995). 'Electrical Brain Fields and Memory Traces: Wittgenstein and Gestalt Psychology', *Philosophical Investigations* 18: 113–37.

Harman, G. (1973). *Thought*. Princeton: Princeton University Press.

Harrod, R. F. (1942). 'Memory', *Mind* 51: 47–68.

Haugeland, J. (1998). *Having Thought: Essays in the Metaphysics of Mind*. Cambridge, Mass.: Harvard University Press.

Hayne, H., Garry, M., and Loftus, E. F. (2006). 'On the Continuing Lack of Scientific Evidence for Repression', *Behavioral and Brain Sciences* 29: 521–2.

Hazlett, A. (forthcoming). 'The Myth of Factive Verbs', *Philosophy and Phenomenological Research*.

Heal, J. (1998). 'Externalism and Memory', *Proceedings of the Aristotelian Society* 72 Suppl.: 95–109.

Heil, J. (1978). 'Traces of Things Past', *Philosophy of Science* 45: 60–72.

—— (1988). 'Privileged Access', *Mind* 47: 238–51.

Higginbotham, J. (1996). 'The Semantics of Questions', in S. Lappin (ed.), *The Handbook of Contemporary Semantic Theory*. Oxford: Blackwell, 361–83.

Hofmann, F. (1995). 'Externalism and Memory'. Manuscript, Department of Philosophy, University of Tübingen.

Holland, A. (1974). 'Retained Knowledge', *Mind* 83: 355–71.

Huemer, M. (1999). 'The Problem of Memory Knowledge', *Pacific Philosophical Quarterly* 80: 346–57.

Hughes, M. W. (1975). 'Personal Identity: A Defence of Locke', *Philosophy* 50: 169–87.

Humberstone, I. L. (1992). 'Direction of Fit', *Mind* 101: 59–83.

Hume, D. (2000*a*). *A Treatise of Human Nature*, ed. D. F. Norton and M. J. Norton. Oxford: Oxford University Press. (First pub. 1939.)

—— (2000*b*). *An Enquiring Concerning Human Understanding*: *A Critical Edition*, ed. T. L. Beaucham P. Oxford: Clarendon. (First pub. 1748.)

Hutchins, E. (1995). *Cognition in the Wild*. Cambridge, Mass.: MIT.

Jackman, H. (1999). 'We Live Forwards but Understand Backwards: Linguistic Practices and Future Behavior', *Pacific Philosophical Quarterly* 80: 157–77.

—— (2004). 'Temporal Externalism and Epistemic Theories of Vagueness', *Philosophical Studies* 117: 79–94.

—— (2005). 'Temporal Externalism, Deference, and Our Ordinary Linguistic Practice', *Pacific Philosophical Quarterly* 86: 365–80.

Jacoby, L. L., and Whitehouse, K. (1989). 'An Illusion of Memory: False Recognition Influenced by Unconscious Perception', *Journal of Experimental Psychology: General* 118: 126–35.

James, W. (1890). *The Principles of Psychology*. 2 vols. London: Macmillan.

Jenkins, J. G., and Dallenbach, K. M. (1924). 'Obliviscence during Sleep and Waking', *American Journal of Psychology* 35: 605–12.

Johnson, M. K. (1988). 'Reality Monitoring: An Experimental Phenomenological Approach', *Journal of Experimental Psychology: General* 117: 390–4.

Kallestrup, J. (2006). 'The Causal Exclusion Argument', *Philosophial Studies* 131: 459–85.

Kaplan, M. (2003). 'Who Cares What You Know', *Philosophical Quarterly* 53: 105–16.

Kihlstrom, J. F. (1997). 'Hypnosis, Memory and Amnesia', *Philosophical Transaction of the Royal Society of London: Series B: Biological Sciences* 352: 1727–32.

—— and Schacter D. L. (2000). 'Functional Amnesia', in F. Boller and J. Grafman (eds.), *Handbook of Neuropsychology*. ii. 2nd edn. Amsterdam: Elsevier, 409–27.

Kim, J. (1973). 'Causes and Counterfactuals', *Journal of Philosophy* 70: 570–2.

Kiparsky, P., and Kiparsky, C. (1970). 'Fact', in M. Bierwich and K. Heidolph (eds.), *Progress in Linguistics: A Collection of Papers*. The Hague: Mouton, 143–73.

Kneale, M. (1972). 'Our Knowledge of the Past and Future', *Proceedings of the Aristotelian Society* 72: 1–12.

Kobes, B. W. (1996). 'Mental Content and Hot Self-Knowledge', *Philosophical Topics* 24: 71–99.

Koriat, A., and Goldsmith, M. (1996). 'Memory Metaphors and the Real-Life/Laboratory Controversy: Correspondence versus Storehouse Conceptions of Memory', *Behavioral and Brain Sciences* 19: 167–228.

Kornblith, H. (2002). *Knowledge and its Place in Nature*. Oxford: Oxford University Press.

Kraay, K. J. (2002). 'Externalism, Memory, and Self-Knowledge', *Erkenntnis* 56: 297–317.

Kripke, S. A. (1980). *Naming and Necessity*. Cambridge, Mass.: Harvard University Press.

Lackey, J. (2005). 'Memory as a Generative Epistemic Source', *Philosophy and Phenomenological Research* 70: 636–58.

—— (2007). 'Why Memory Really is a Generative Epistemic Source: A Reply to Senor', *Philosophy and Phenomenological Research* 74: 209–19.

Landesman, C. (1961). 'Philosophical Problems of Memory', *Journal of Philosophy* 59: 57–65.

Laurence, J.-R., and Perry, C. (1983). 'Hypnotically Created Memory among Highly Hypnotizable Subjects', *Science* 222: 523–4.

—— Nadon, R., Nogrady, H., and Perry, C. (1986). 'Duality, Dissociation, and Memory Creation in Highly Hypnotizable Subjects', *International Journal of Clinical and Experimental Hypnosis* 34: 295–310.

Lehrer, K. (1965). 'Knowledge, Truth and Evidence', *Analysis* 25: 168–75.

—— (1970). 'Believing that One Knows', *Synthese* 21: 133–40.

—— (1990). *Theory of Knowledge*. Boulder: Westview.

—— and Richard, J. (1975). 'Remembering Without Knowing', *Grazer philosophische Studien* 1: 121–6.

Leite, A. (2005). 'On Williamson's Arguments that Knowledge is a Mental State', *Ratio* 17: 165–75.

Lewis, C. I. (1918). *Survey of Symbolic Logic*. Berkeley: University of California Press.

Lewis, David (1983). 'Survival and Identity', in his *Philosophical Papers I*. Oxford: Oxford University Press, 55–77.

Lewis, David (1986). 'Veridical Hallucination and Prosthetic Vision', in his *Philosophical Papers II*. Oxford: Oxford University Press, 273–86.

Lewis, Delmas (1983). 'Dualism and the Causal Theory of Memory', *Philosophy and Phenomenological Research* 44: 21–30.

Leyden, von W. (1961). *Remembering: A Philosophical Problem*. London: Duckworth.

Loar, B. (1988). 'Social Content and Psychological Content', in R. H. Grimm and D. D. Merrill (eds.), *Contents of Thoughts*. Tucson: University of Arizona Press, 99–110.

Locke, D. (1971). *Memory*. London: Macmillan.

Locke, J. (1979). *Essay Concerning Human Understanding*, ed. P. H Nidditch. 2nd edn. Oxford: Clarendon. (First pub. 1694.)

Loftus, E. F., and Ketcham, K. (1991). *Witness for the Defense: The Accused, the Eyewitness, and the Expert who Puts Memory on Trial*. New York: St Martin's Press.

Lowe, E. J. (2002). 'Review of T. Williamson's *Knowledge and Its Limits*', *International Journal of Philosophical Studies* 10: 483–503.

Ludlow, P. (1995*a*). 'Social Externalism, Self-Knowledge, and Memory', *Analysis* 55: 157–9.

—— (1995*b*). 'Social Externalism and Memory: A Problem?', *Acta Analytica* 14: 69–76.

—— (1999*a*). 'First Person Authority and Memory', in M. De Caro (ed.), *Interpretation and Causes: New Perspectives on Donald Davidson's Philosophy*. Dordrecht: Kluwer, 159–70.

—— (1999*b*). *Semantics, Tense, and Time: An Essay in the Metaphysics of Natural Language*. Cambridge, Mass.: MIT.

Lycan, W. G. (1988). *Judgement and Justification*. Cambridge: Cambridge University Press.

—— (1996). *Consciousness and Experience*. Cambridge, Mass.: MIT.

McClelland, J. L. (2000). 'Connectionist Models of Memory', in E. Tulving and F. J. M. Craik (eds.), *The Oxford Handbook of Memory*. Oxford: Oxford University Press, 583–96.

—— Rumelhart, D., and Hinton, G. (1986). 'The Appeal of Parallel Distributed Processing', in D. Rumelhart, J. McClelland, and PDP Research Group (eds.), *Parallel Distributed Processing: Explorations in the Microstructure of Cognition*. Cambridge, Mass.: MIT, 3–44.

Macdonald, C. (2007). 'Introspection and Authoritative Self-Knowledge', *Erkenntnis* 67: 35–72.

McDowell, J. (1997). 'Reductionism and the First Person', in J. Dancy (ed.), *Reading Parfit*. Oxford: Blackwell, 230–50.

—— (1998*a*). 'De Re Senses', in his *Meaning, Knowledge and Reality*. Cambridge, Mass.: Harvard University Press, 214–27.

—— (1998*b*). 'Singular Thought and the Extent of Inner Space', in his *Meaning, Knowledge and Reality*. Cambridge, Mass.: Harvard University Press, 228–59.

McGrath, M. (2007). 'Memory and Epistemic Conservatism', *Synthese* 157: 1–24.

Machery, E., Mallon, R., Nichols, S., and Stich, S. P. (2004). 'Semantics, Cross-Cultural Style', *Cognition* 92: B1–B12.

Mackie, J. (1965). 'Causes and Conditions', *American Philosophical Quarterly* 2/4: 245–55.

Magnus, P. D., and Cohen, J. (2003). 'Williamson on Knowledge and Psychological Explanation', *Philosophical Studies* 116: 37–52.

Malcolm, N. (1963). *Knowledge and Certainty*. Ithaca: Cornell University Press.

—— (1977). *Memory and Mind*. Ithaca: Cornell University Press.

Margalit, A. (2002). *The Ethics of Memory*. Cambridge, Mass.: Harvard University Press.

Margolis, J. (1977). 'Remembering', *Mind* 86: 186–205.

Martin, C. B., and Deutscher, M. (1966). 'Remembering', *Philosophical Review* 75: 161–96.

Martin, M. G. F. (1992). 'Perception, Concepts, and Memory', *Philosophical Review* 101: 745–63.

Meltzer, M. (1983). 'Poor Memory: A Case Report', *Journal of Clinical Psychology* 39: 3–10.

Menzies, P. (2003). 'The Causal Efficacy of Mental States', in S. Walter and H.-D. Heckmann (eds.), *Physicalism and Mental Causation: The Metaphysics of Mind and Action*. Exeter: Imprint Academic, 195–223.

Millikan, R. G. (1993). *White Queen Psychology and Other Essays for Alice*. Cambridge, Mass.: MIT.

Moore, G. E. (1959). 'Four Forms of Scepticism', in his *Philosophical Papers*. London: Muirhead Library, 196–226.

Moreland, R. L., and Argote, L. (2003). 'Transactive Memory in Dynamic Organizations', in R. Peterson and E. Mannix (eds.), *Leading and Managing People in the Dynamic Organization*. Mahwah: Erlbaum, 135–62.

Munsat, S. (1967). *The Concept of Memory*. New York: Random House.

Nagasawa, Y. (2000). ' "Very-Slow-Switching" and Memory: A Critical Note on Ludlow's Paper', *Acta Analytica* 15: 173–5.

—— (2002). 'Externalism and the Memory Argument', *Dialectica* 56: 335–46.

Naylor, A. (1971). 'B Remembers that P from Time T', *Journal of Philosophy* 68: 29–41.

—— (1983). 'Justification in Memory Knowledge', *Synthese* 55: 269–86.

—— (1985). 'In Defense of a Nontraditional Theory of Memory', *Monist* 68: 136–50.

Naylor, A. (1986). 'Remembering Without Knowing—Not Without Justification', *Philosophical Studies* 49: 295–311.

Neisser, U. (1967). *Cognitive Psychology*. New York: Meredith.

Nemiah, J. (1979). 'Dissociative Amnesia: A Clinical and Theoretical Reconsideration', in J. F. Kihlstrom and F. J. Evans (eds.), *Functional Disorder of Memory*. Hillsdale: Erlbaum, 303–24.

Newby, I. R., and Ross, M. (1996). 'Beyond the Correspondence Metaphor: When Accuracy Cannot be Assessed', *Behavioral and Brain Sciences* 19: 205–6.

Noonan, H. (2003). *Personal Identity*, 2nd edn. London: Routledge.

Northoff, G. (2000). 'Are "Q-Memories" Empirically Realistic? A Neurophilosophical Approach', *Philosophical Psychology* 13: 191–211.

Nozick, R. (1981). *Philosophical Examinations*. Cambridge, Mass.: Harvard University Press.

O'Brien, G. (1998). 'Being There: Putting Philosopher, Researcher and Student Together Again', *Metascience* 7: 78–83.

Odell, S. J. (1971). 'Malcolm on "Remembering That" ', *Mind* 80: 593.

Olick, J. K. (1999). 'Collective Memory: The Two Cultures', *Sociological Theory* 17: 333–48.

Owens, D. (2000). *Reason Without Freedom*. London: Routledge.

Pappas, G. S. (1980). 'Lost Justification', *Midwest Studies in Philosophy* 5: 127–34.

—— (1983). 'Ongoing Knowledge', *Synthese* 55: 253–67.

Parfit, D. (1984). *Reasons and Persons*. Oxford: Clarendon.

Parker, E. S., Cahill, L., and McGaugh, J. L. (2006). 'A Case of Unusual Autobiographical Remembering', *Neurocase* 12: 35–49.

Peacocke, C. (1996). 'Entitlement, Self-Knowledge and Conceptual Redeployment', *Proceedings of the Aristotelian Society* 96: 117–58.

Pears, D. (1975). 'Causation and Memory', *Philosophic Exchange* 2: 29–40.

Perner, J. (1991). *Understanding the Representational Mind*. Cambridge, Mass.: MIT.

Perry, J. (1993). 'Belief and Acceptance', in his *The Problem of the Essential Indexical and Other Essays*. New York: Oxford University Press, 53–67.

Piaget, J., and Inhelder, B. (1975). *Memory and Intelligence*. New York: Basic Books.

Pinker, S., and Prince, A. (1988). 'On Language and Connectionism: Analysis of a Parallel Distributed Processing Model of Language Acquisition', *Cognition* 23: 73–193.

Plantinga, A. (1993). *Warrant and Proper Function*. New York: Oxford University Press.

Plato (1921). *Theaetetus*, trans. H. N. Fowler, Loeb Classical Library. London: William Heineman, (Written *c.* 360 BC).

—— (1924). *Meno*, trans. W. R. M. Lamb, Loeb Classical Library. London: William Heinemann, (Written *c.* 380 BC).

Pollock, J. L. (1974). *Knowledge and Justification*. Princeton: Princeton University Press.

—— (1986). *Contemporary Theories of Knowledge*. Savage, Md.: Rowman & Littlefield.

Price, H. H. (1969). *Belief*. London: Allen & Unwin.

Price, J., and Davis, B. (2008). *The Woman Who Can't Forget: The Extraordinary Story of Living with the Most Remarkable Memory Known to Science*. New York: Free Press.

Pritchard, D. (2005). *Epistemic Luck*. Oxford: Oxford University Press.

Pryor, J. (1999). 'Immunity to Error Through Misidentification', *Philosophical Topics* 26: 271–304.

Putnam, H. (1975a). 'Explanation and Reference', in his *Philosophical Papers*, ii. *Mind, Language and Reality*. Cambridge: Cambridge University Press, 196–214.

—— (1975b). 'The Meaning of "Meaning" ', in his *Philosophical Papers*, ii. *Mind, Language and Reality*. Cambridge: Cambridge University Press, 215–71.

—— (1981). *Reason, Truth and History*. Cambridge: Cambridge University Press.

—— (1990). 'Is Water Necessarily H_2O?', in his *Realism with a Human Face*. Cambridge, Mass.: Harvard University Press, 54–79.

Quine, W. V. O. (1961). 'Two Dogmas of Empiricism', in his *From a Logical Point of View: Nine Logico-Philosophical Essays*. 2nd edn. Cambridge, Mass.: Harvard University Press, 20–46.

—— (1969). 'Natural Kinds', in his *Ontological Relativity and Other Essays*. New York: Columbia University Press, 114–38.

Radford, C. (1966). 'Knowledge—by Examples', *Analysis* 27: 1–11.

Reid, M. (1997). 'Narrative and Fission: A Review Essay of Marya Schechtman's *The Constitution of Selves*', *Philosophical Psychology* 10: 211–19.

Reid, T. (2002). *Essays on The Intellectual Powers of Man: A Critical Edition*, ed. D. R. Brookes. University Park, PA: Pennsylvania State University Press (First pub. 1785).

Roache, R. (2006). 'A Defence of Quasi-Memory', *Philosophy* 81: 323–55.

Roediger, H. L. (1980). 'Memory Metaphors in Cognitive Psychology', *Memory and Cognition* 8: 231–46.

Rose, S. (1992). *The Making of Memory*. London: Bantam.

Rosen, D. A. (1975). 'An Argument for the Logical Notion of a Memory Trace', *Philosophy of Science* 42: 1–10.

Ross, M. (1997). 'Validating Memories', in N. L. Stein, P. A. Ornstein, B. Tversky, and C. Brainerd (eds.), *Memory for Everyday and Emotional Events*. Nahwah: Erlbaum, 49–81.

Rowbottom, D. P. (2007). ' "In-Between Believing" and Degrees of Belief', *Teorema* 26: 131–7.

Rowlands, M. (1999). *The Body in Mind: Understanding Cognitive Processes*. Cambridge: Cambridge University Press.

Rupert, R. D. (2004). 'Challenges to the Hypothesis of Extended Cognition', *Journal of Philosophy* 101: 389–428.

Russell, B. (1995). *The Analysis of Mind*, intro. T. Baldwin. London: Routledge. (First pub. 1921.)

Ryle, G. (1949). *The Concept of Mind*. London: Hutchinson.

Salmon, N. (1979). 'How Not to Derive Essentialism from the Theory of Reference', *Journal of Philosophy* 76: 703–25.

Saunders, J. T. (1965a). 'Professor Malcolm's Definition of "Factual Memory" ', *Theoria* 31: 282–8.

—— (1965b). 'Does all Memory Imply Factual Memory?', *Analysis* 25: 109–15.

Sawyer, S. (2002). 'In Defence of Burge's Thesis', *Philosophical Studies* 107: 109–28.

Schacter, D. L. (1987). 'Implicit Memory: History and Current Status', *Journal of Experimental Psychology: Learning, Memory, and Cognition* 13: 501–18.

Schaffer, J. (2006). 'Contrastive Knowledge', in T. S. Gendler and J. Hawthorne (eds.), *Oxford Studies in Epistemology*, i. Oxford: Clarendon, 235–72.

Schechtman, M. (1990). 'Personhood and Personal Identity', *Journal of Philosophy* 87: 71–92.

—— (1996). *The Constitution of Selves*. Ithaca: Cornell University Press.

Schiffer, S. (1992). 'Boghossian on Externalism and Inference', *Philosophical Issues* 2: 29–37.

Schnider, A., Gutbrod, K., Hess, C. W., and Schroth, G. (1996). 'Memory without Context: Amnesia with Confabulations after Infarction of the Right Capsual Genu', *Journal of Neurology, Neurosurgery, and Psychiatry* 61: 186–93.

Schumacher, J. A. (1976). 'Memory Unchained Again', *Analysis* 36: 101–4.

Schwitzgebel, E. (2001). 'In-Between Believing', *Philosophical Quarterly* 51: 76–82.

—— (2002). 'How Well Do We Know Our Own Conscious Experiences? The Case of Visual Imagery', *Journal of Consciousness Studies* 9: 35–53.

Searle, J. R. (1983). *Intentionality: An Essay in the Philosophy of Mind*. Cambridge: Cambridge University Press.

—— (1990). 'Consciousness, Explanatory Inversion and Cognitive Science', *Behavioral and Brain Sciences* 13: 585–96.

Sellars, W. (1974). 'Language as Thought and as Communication', in his *Essays in Philosophy and History*. Dordrecht: Reidel, 93–117.

Senor, T. D. (1993). 'Internalistic Foundationalism and the Justification of Memory Belief', *Synthese* 94: 453–76.

—— (2007). 'Preserving Preservationism: A Reply to Lackey', *Philosophy and Phenomenological Research* 74: 199–208.

Shema, R., Sacktor, T. C., and Dudai, Y. (2007). 'Rapid Erasure of Long-Term Memory Associations in the Cortex by an Inhibitor of PKMζ', *Science* 317: 951–3.

Sherouse, M. A. (1979). 'Memory and Knowledge: An Examination of the Epistemic Theory of Memory'. Dissertation, Ohio State University.

Shoemaker, S. (1967). 'Memory', in P. Edwards (ed.), *The Encyclopedia of Philosophy*, v. New York: Macmillan, 265–74.

—— (2003*a*). 'Self-Reference and Self-Awareness', in his *Identity, Cause, and Mind*. Oxford: Clarendon, 6–18.

—— (2003*b*). 'Persons and Their Pasts', in his *Identity, Cause, and Mind*. Oxford: Clarendon, 19–48.

Shope, R. (1973). 'Remembering, Knowledge, and Memory Traces', *Philosophy and Phenomenological Research* 33: 303–22.

Siebel, M. (2000). *Erinnerung, Wahrnehmung, Wissen*. Paderborn: Mentis.

Slors, M. (2001). 'Personal Identity, Memory, and Circularity: An Alternative for Q-Memory', *Journal of Philosophy* 98: 186–214.

Smith, S. M., and Vela, E. (2001). 'Environmental Context-Dependent Memory: A Review and Meta-Analysis', *Psychonomic Bulletin and Review* 8: 203–20.

—— Glenberg, A., and Bjork, R. A. (1978). 'Environmental Context and Human Memory', *Memory and Cognition* 6: 324–53.

Spiegel, D. (1995). 'Hypnosis and Suggestion', in D. L. Schacter (ed.), *Memory Distortions: How Minds, Brains, and Societies Reconstruct the Past*. Cambridge, Mass.: Harvard University Press, 129–49.

Squire, L. R., and Kandel, E. (1999). *Memory: From Mind to Molecules*. New York: Scientific American Library.

Squires, R. (1969). 'Memory Unchained', *Philosophical Review* 78: 178–96.

Stalnaker, R. (1984). *Inquiry*. Cambridge, Mass.: MIT.

Stanley, J., and Williamson, T. (2001). 'Knowing How', *Journal of Philosophy* 98: 411–44.

Stein, D. G., and Glasier, M. M. (1995). 'Some Practical and Theoretical Issues Concerning Fetal Brain Tissue Grafts as Therapy for Brain Dysfunctions', *Behavioral and Brain Sciences* 18: 36–45.

Sterelny, K. (2004). 'Externalism, Epistemic Artefacts and the Extended Mind', in R. Schantz (ed.), *The Externalist Challenge*. Berlin: de Gruyter, 239–54.

Stern, D. G. (1991). 'Models of Memory: Wittgenstein and Cognitive Science', *Philosophical Psychology* 4: 203–18.

Steup, M. (1996). *An Introduction to Contemporary Epistemology*. Upper Saddle River: Prentice Hall.

Stiffler, E. (1980). 'Malcolm on Impure Memory', *Philosophical Studies* 38: 299–304.

Stoneham, T. (2003). 'Temporal Externalism', *Philosophical Papers* 32: 97–107.

Stroud, B. (1977). *Hume*. London: Routledge.

Sutton, J. (1998). *Philosophy and Memory Traces: Descartes to Connectionism*. Cambridge: Cambridge University Press.

—— (2004). 'Memory', in E. N. Zalta (ed.), *The Stanford Encyclopedia of Philosophy*, summer 2004 edn. <http://plato.stanford.edu/archives/sum2004/entries/memory/>, accessed 2 June 2009.

Sutton, J. (2006). 'Memory', in D. M. Borchert (ed.), *Encyclopedia of Philosophy*, vi. 2nd edn. New York: Thomson Gale, 122–8.

—— (forthcoming). 'Exograms and Interdisciplinarity: History, the Extended Mind, and the Civilizing Process', in R. Menary (ed.), *The Extended Mind*. Cambridge, Mass.: MIT.

Taschek, W. (1995). 'On Belief Content and That-Clauses', *Mind and Language* 10: 274–98.

Thompson, D. M., Robertson, S. L., and Vogt, R. (1982). 'Person Recognition: The Effects of Context', *Human Learning* 1: 137–54.

Tollefsen, D. (2006). 'From Extended Mind to Collective Mind', *Cognitive Systems Research* 7: 140–50.

Traiger, S. (1978). 'Some Remarks on Lehrer and Richard's "Remembering Without Knowing" ', *Grazer philosophische Studien* 6: 107–11.

Tulving, E. (1972). 'Episodic and Semantic Memory', in E. Tulving and W. Donaldson (eds.), *Organization of Memory*. New York: Academic Press, 381–403.

—— (1985). 'Memory and Consciousness', *Canadian Psychology* 26: 1–12.

Tye, M. (1998). 'Externalism and Memory', *Proceedings of the Aristotelian Society* 72 Suppl.: 77–94.

Unger, P. (1972). 'Propositional Verbs and Knowledge', *Journal of Philosophy* 69: 301–12.

Vendler, Z. (1972). *Res Cogitans: An Essay in Rational Psychology*. Ithaca: Cornell University Press.

—— (1980). 'Telling the Facts', in J. R. Searle, F. Kiefer, and M. Bierwich (eds.), *Speech Act Theory and Pragmatics*. Dordrecht: Reidel, 273–90.

Wegner, D. M. (1986). 'Transactive Memory: A Contemporary Analysis of the Group Mind', in B. Mullen and G. R. Goethals (eds.), *Theories of Group Behavior*. New York: Springer, 185–208.

—— (1995). 'A Computer Network Model of Human Transactive Memory', *Social Cognition* 13: 1–21.

Weinberg, J. M., Nichols, S., and Stich, S. P. (2001). 'Normativity and Epistemic Intuitions', *Philosophical Topics* 29: 429–60.

Wessel, I., and Moulds, M. L. (2008). 'Collective Memory: A Perspective from (Experimental) Clinical Psychology', *Memory* 16: 288–304.

Wiggins, D. (1967). *Identity and Spatio-Temporal Continuity*. Oxford: Blackwell.

Wikforss, A. (2008). 'Semantic Externalism and Psychological Externalism', *Philosophy Compass* 3: 158–81.

Williams, B. (1973). 'Deciding to Believe', in his *Problems of the Self: Philosophical Papers 1956–1972*. Cambridge: Cambridge University Press, 136–51.

Williamson, T. (2000). *Knowledge and its Limits*. Oxford: Oxford University Press.

—— (2007). 'On Being Justified in One's Head', in M. Timmons, J. Greco, and A. R. Mele (eds.), *Rationality and the Good: Critical Essays on the*

Ethics and Epistemology of Robert Audi. Oxford: Oxford University Press, 106–22.

Wittgenstein, L. (1958). *Philosophical Investigations*, trans. G. E. M. Anscombe. 3rd edn. New York: Macmillan.

—— (1960). *The Blue and the Brown Books*, ed. R. Rhees. 2nd edn. New York: Harper & Row.

—— (1969). *On Certainty*, ed. G. E. M. Anscombe and G. H. von Wright. New York: Harper & Row.

Wollheim, R. (1979). 'Memory, Experiential Memory, and Personal Identity', in G. F. MacDonald (ed.), *Perception and Identity: Essays Presented to A. J. Ayer with his Replies to Them*. London: Macmillan, 186–234.

—— (1984). *The Thread of Life*. Cambridge, Mass.: Harvard University Press.

Zemach, E. (1968). 'A Definition of Memory', *Mind* 77: 526–36.

Index